GRANTS

*How to Find Out About Them
and What to Do Next*

GRANTS

*How to Find Out About Them
and What to Do Next*

BY VIRGINIA P. WHITE

Graduate School and University Center, CUNY

PLENUM PRESS • NEW YORK AND LONDON

Library of Congress Cataloging in Publication Data

White, Virginia P
   Grants: how to find out about them and what to do next.
   Includes bibliographical references and index.
   1. Research—United States—Finance. 2. Research grants—United States.
I. Title.
Q180.U5W47   001.4′4   75-15831
ISBN 0-306-30842-8

First Printing — September 1975
Second Printing — February 1976
Third Printing — April 1976
Fourth Printing — June 1976

© 1975 Plenum Press, New York
A Division of Plenum Publishing Corporation
227 West 17th Street, New York, N.Y. 10011

Printed in the United States of America

To Henrietta and Alexander Hollaender

Preface

Almost half a million institutions in the United States are supported wholly or in part by grant-making organizations. And the number of students and scholars who receive education and training subsidies by individual grants in one form or another is much greater. But the grant-making boom of the 1950s and 1960s has passed. Those days when grants, like rain, fell upon the just and the unjust have taken their place in the archives of nostalgia.

While it lasted, however, there seems to have been no activity so esoteric, so unusual, or so trivial that it would fail to find support. The neophyte applicant finds it both cheering and dismaying to learn that grants have been awarded to train Good Humor peddlers, to study the goat in the Croatian landscape and the biological rhythms of the catfish in India, to determine why children fall off tricycles, to learn all about the frisbee, and to delve into the mating calls of Central American toads.

These subjects or others of similar significance will continue to be funded from time to time, but it just isn't as easy as it used to be. Grant funds in both the public and private sector are decreasing and the number of scholars and researchers applying for them has grown. Grant seekers today must be prepared to meet powerful competition. Not only must they be well trained and competent in their fields of specialization, but they must be skilled in identifying the most likely sources of funding and able to make presentations that stand out among the vast and increasing tide of applications now flooding all grant-making organizations.

Systems for winning in the grants game abound and are passed on from mentor to disciple with the same confidence and authority that characterized the delivery of the Ten Commandments. Some say the idea is all that matters; others insist that it all depends upon the proposal—the presentation of the idea. Still others scorn the entire application procedure. Forget all that, they advise, and get on the phone to your friend who worked in the last presidential campaign—on the winning side, of course. And they may all be right, because in grant getting, as in love, horse racing, and losing weight, there is no system that hasn't worked somewhere, sometime, for somebody.

But whatever system is employed or whatever philosophy is adopted, every candidate for a grant must decide which organizations to approach and must present those organizations with an application in some form. In order to identify the most likely sources of funds for a particular activity, all grant-making sectors must be researched—government, private foundations and similar organizations, and business and industry.

Governmental sources are the most difficult to research because the information is so voluminous that sifting the useful from the total mass can be a tough job. Foundations are beginning to understand the advantages of making information about their programs available and the search of the grant seeker, although not easy, is much less arduous than it used to be. The industrial sector, unfortunately, still has no central source of information about grant programs and interests, except through company foundations, and does not yet see the need for it. Identifying corporations that may sponsor an activity or a piece of research requires initiative, energy, imagination, and persistence. The guidelines contained here were gleaned mainly from conversations with corporation executives who for the most part see the problem only from their point of view and do not yet fully understand the relationship between industry and the grant applicant, especially if the proposal is for basic research that appears to have no immediate applicability to a product.

There are a number of good publications on the market—many of them mentioned here—that summarize the interests of various foundations based on their past grant-making record. There are a few good guides to the preparation of grant proposals, also referred to. And there is an abundance—almost an overabundance—of material available from the federal government describing specific grant programs. But grant programs are subject to changing trends and modes not unlike those that affect the fashion and automobile trades. Last year's best seller may be this year's white elephant, and the forces dictating the changes are often mysterious and nearly always unforeseen. Therefore, every grant seeker must learn to identify the organization most likely to be interested in his proposal at the time it is written—not yesterday or last year. Also, the scholar or researcher who starts out without knowing whether his proposal might be more acceptable to a government agency, a foundation, or a corporation needs a basic guide—a kind of road map that tells where to start when you don't know exactly where you are going.

The purpose of this book is to provide that kind of guide, and to suggest a format for approaching and applying to potential funders once they have been identified. General sources of information for all grant-making sectors are described, and following that, each sector is dealt with in detail. The material is arranged in order of grant-making volume: Government sources, by far the most abundant, lead off, followed by foundations and business and industry in that order. The application process is described in a separate section.

In the preparation and writing of this book, I have been assisted by many people who gave advice, provided information and materials, and offered criticism, encouragement, and moral support. It would be impossible for me to list all of them, but I would like to name a few to whom I am deeply indebted for their generous help and advice.

The following people read all or portions of the manuscript and made constructive comments and suggestions that resulted in significant improvements: Marianna O. Lewis, The Foundation Center; Professors David Caplovitz and Lindsey Churchill, Graduate School of the City University of New York; Drs. Ann E. Kaplan, Marcia D. Litwack, and Thomas P. Cameron, National Cancer Institute, NIH; Melvin Weinstock, Institute for Scientific Information; and Edward Thompson, Council on Foundations, Inc.

Information and/or assistance in research were contributed by the following: Professor Claire Bowie, Graduate School Library, City University of New York; Norman Latker, Department of Health, Education, and Welfare; Robert Mayer, New York Community Trust; R. S. Baldwin and Dr. Willard Marcy, Research Corporation; Joseph Elliott Slater, Aspen Institute for Humanistic Studies; Benjamin Read,

The German Marshall Fund of the United States; Rowan A. Wakefield, Center for Government-Education Relations; Paul Feinberg, The Ford Foundation; Lynn Slavitt, Research for Social Change, Inc.; Dr. Herbert I. Fusfeld, Kennecott Copper Corporation and the Industrial Research Institute; Professor Feliks Gross, Graduate School of the City University of New York; Dr. Allen H. Heim, National Cancer Institute, NIH; Dr. Harold M. Davidson, Division of Research Grants, NIH; Dr. Harold Cannon, National Endowment for the Humanities; Fanny Taylor, National Endowment for the Arts; Brooke Harris, Initial Teaching Alphabet Foundation; Prof. Mary Esther Gaulden, The University of Texas Southwest Medical School; Prof. John Jagger, The University of Texas at Dallas; Prof. Marcia Guttentag, Harvard University; Dr. Julius J. Marke, Law Librarian, New York University; Dr. Wilton S. Dillon, The Smithsonian Institution; Lawrence N. Gold, City University of New York; Carol Katzki, City University of New York.

Guidance, encouragement, and assistance in a variety of forms was given by these people: Jeanette and Vernon Akins, Charles Cohen, Elizabeth Farley, Robert McFarland, Diana Rosenblatt, Adelaide Schlanger, and Charles White.

I want to mention especially my deep appreciation to Patrick Tarantino for advice and assistance in many forms but predominantly for help in determining the kinds of material to be included.

The resources of the following libraries were made available to me and I want to thank the staff of each for their courtesy and helpful assistance: Library of the Graduate School and University Center, City University of New York; the New York Public Library; The Foundation Center Library, New York; and the Library of the Association of the Bar, New York.

In the final preparation of the manuscript, I was assisted by Charlotte Fisher.

Virginia P. White

New York
July, 1975

Contents

What Is a Grant?

Grant giving is almost as old as charity and may even be *as* old. Four thousand years ago the Chinese set aside properties to support religious observances, and wealthy Egyptians of that same period established funds to maintain the pyramids of assorted pharaohs. The *Egyptian Book of the Dead*, which recorded the deeds of good men in order to assure them of a proper reception in the next world, contains an entry for one deceased philanthropist which may be regarded as the first record of, or at least the forerunner of, the bricks and mortar grant. It noted that the man in his lifetime "gave bread to the hungry, water to the thirsty, raiment to the naked; he gave a boat to a man who had none." Feeding the hungry and clothing the poor are charitable acts. Giving a man a boat provides him with the means to carry on his work and thus qualifies as a very early example of grant making.

Unlike charitable gifts, where need is the overriding determinant, grants and endowments have, since their beginning, expressed the concerns and interests of the donors.

In ancient Greece *philanthropia* described man's love and concern for his fellow man and included any action befitting a civilized and cultured being. However, philanthropy in the Greek world before Christ was limited for the most part to friends, relatives, and allies. It depended mainly upon the disposition of the rulers and was confined largely to the civilized Hellenes. Demosthenes counseled that philanthropy should govern the relations between citizens but enemies deserved wrath and hatred.

Roman emperors used the term *beneficium* to describe portions of land given to their soldiers and friends as a reward for past service and a retainer for future service. The Church copied this practice, using as a model the five-year leases granted by the Roman exchequer. The Church called these gifts, which served both as reward to followers and inducement to proselytes, *precariae*, and many were extended from the original five years to become lifetime grants.

Similar rewards were used by the Church to promote the building and endowment of parochial churches. Those who contributed to their erection by a donation of land, by building, or by endowment became entitled to nominate a clerk of their choice to the bishop, who was technically empowered to veto the appointment if he considered the candidate's qualifications insufficient, but that seldom occurred. After the Norman conquest, it became quite usual for patrons to appoint clerks not only without the consent but even against the will of the bishops.

The rights and privileges enjoyed by such clerks, on condition of discharging the services prescribed by canon law, were called *benefices*. Beneficed clerks were restricted by the Lateran Council of 1215 from holding more than one "benefice with cure of souls" at a time, but this was later relaxed (by the Pluralities Acts 1885 Amendment) to permit the holding of two benefices if the churches were within four miles of each other and the annual value of one of them did not exceed 200 pounds.

(Modern grants may carry an exclusivity provision forbidding the recipient to hold another grant or fellowship simultaneously with them. And the restrictions against "overload"—when a grantee's total commitments add up to more than 100 percent of full time—are standard. The principle underlying these stipulations probably goes back to this decree of the Lateran Council in 1215 limiting the number of "benefices with cure of souls" to be held by a clerk.)

Byzantine philanthropy was rooted in both Greek and Christian thought, but the idea of selfless love was somewhat bewildering in the early years. The emperor Julian late in the fourth century complained that the Christians were extending their philanthropies to his people, writing to Arsacios, the high priest of Galatia, "It is disgraceful that . . . the impious Galilaeans support not only their own poor but ours as well." Julian later changed his mind and in a letter to a pagan priest exhorted him to exercise "philanthropia" which included the concept of both love and mercy for mankind. It is to Byzantium that we are indebted for the term "eleemosynary." The Byzantines saw their God as both loving and merciful—a *philanthropos* or *eleemon Theos*, and *Eleemon* was the model or ideal men were expected to imitate. Those who came closest were given the surname *Eleemon* or *Eleemosynary*. John, the famous Patriarch of Alexandria, was called John the Eleemosynary. And Philaretos, a wealthy resident of Pontos, who moved to Constantinople when his granddaughter married the emperor Constantine VI, received the surname Eleemosynary because of his legendary humanitarian works.[1]

The "concession," which has been known for centuries in widely separated parts of the globe and first appeared in Europe during the Middle Ages, is a type of franchise, contract, charter, or license which, in England, is usually called a grant. The concession was made by a prince or a king—in royal phrase *concessimus* or *damus et concedimus*—and was confined largely to gifts of land. Later it was extended to the endowment of chartered companies such as the East India Company, the London Company, the Massachusetts and Hudson Bay Companies, and came to include in addition to land a measure of sovereign power awarded to citizen adventurers in return for which they were expected to develop the territory for the good of the mother country.

Many of the concepts embodied in these mechanisms for rewarding past services and for encouraging or directing future activities are present in the modern grant.

The word "grant" itself carries in its ancestry the implications of faith (the Latin *credere*, to believe) and obligation (Late Latin verb, *creantare*, to promise). And every grant agreement, no matter how casual or formal the negotiations that preceded it or the terms of the final conveyance, carries with it the understanding that the recipient, the grantee, has a commitment to perform some activity and thus fulfill some expectation of the benefactor, the grantor.

In this, the individual benefactor is not so different from

[1] Demetrios J. Constantelos, *Byzantine Philanthropy and Social Welfare* (New Brunswick: Rutgers University Press, 1968), p. 16.

governments and the Church; he uses gifts, bequests, endowments to express his personal desires and fulfill his own hopes and dreams, and records exist of many highly imaginative, even eccentric individual endowments.

In England, in 1344, a Nottingham laundress named Margery Doubleday left her entire estate to endow a morning bell to awaken her fellow washerwomen and thus prevent them from losing money through oversleeping.

One early Christian philanthropist established a fund to make sure the Church always had on hand plenty of "faggots for the burning of heretics."

And there is no doubt about the prepossessions of those benefactors whose bequests provide scholarship aid to Harvard students today for "some poor scholar (tho' to no dunce nor rake)," or for those "whose fathers are deceased and whose mothers have not remarried," or to "scholars not necessarily brilliant in their studies."

The United States institution that has become the world's largest museum complex was conceived and endowed by an amateur natural historian who had never been in this country, an Englishman named James B. Smithson. When the United States Congress was presented with the bequest in 1835 to "found at Washington, under the name of the Smithsonian Institution, an establishment for the increase and diffusion of knowledge among men," it would have been difficult to find a more unlikely body to carry out its provision.

The Congress of that period is described by L. H. Butterfield, editor-in-chief of *The Adams Papers*, this way: "While on the one hand the American people in the age of Andrew Jackson were committed to and advancing toward universal education and were producing some of the seminal ideas and books of modern times, an opposite and thoroughly anti-intellectual point of view pervaded national politics. It is perhaps not too much to say that most Congressmen of the 1820's and 1830's would as soon have been caught in adultery as in writing a book."[2]

[2] "The Great Design." Two lectures on the Smithson Bequest of John Quincy Adams, delivered at Quincy and Boston in November, 1839, first published together from contemporary printed and manuscript texts in Washington, D.C. in 1965 by the Smithsonian Institution, edited and with an introduction by Wilcomb E. Washburn.

Intellectual diffusion and growth were about the last things on the legislative agenda and, but for the persistence of John Quincy Adams, the bequest of half a million dollars not much today but worth a great deal more then, might have been, in Adams's words, "squandered on cormorants or wasted in electioneering bribery." (Indeed, it came close to being lost when, after two years of discussion, Congress invested most of it in Arkansas state bonds—which promptly defaulted.) But thanks to the persistence of Adams, who, according to Professor Butterfield, saw the bequest as "an electrifying challenge . . . the finger of Providence, compassing great events by incomprehensible means," the Smithsonian Institution was established in 1846 (by strange providence, the same week the planet Neptune was discovered). It has become the largest single center for visitors in the United States today, more than twice as popular as Disneyland, with a staff of over 3,100, an annual operating budget of $76 million, and a collection of 75 million items that grows at the rate of 1 million a year.

The "incomprehensibility" of the bequest led to much speculation, rumor, gossip, and the usual suspicions that are aroused by unexpected and unexplained generosity. It was suggested by some that Smithson was insane. Also, it was widely assumed that he was the "antenuptial" son of the first Duke and Duchess of Northumberland. The two theories very likely led to Mr. Smithson's being dubbed with an epithet that has since become an almost universal appellation for those with the power to make endowments or bestow grants.

The great philanthropic trusts were not formed until early in this century. Cecil Rhodes founded the Rhodes Trust in 1902 to provide scholarships to Oxford University for students from all parts of the British Empire, the United States, and Germany. This was just about the time that individuals in the United States began to amass personal fortunes so large that the "millionaire's problem" began to be of concern: what to do with all that money.

The puritan and capitalistic ethics were so intertwined in the American conscience of that period that if Andrew Carnegie (as he is reported to have done) did say to W. E. Gladstone, "It is disgraceful to die a rich man," he probably meant it. (The extent to which this spirit in our society has disappeared is well illustrated by a *New York Times* report on February 6, 1974 of an interview with the currently richest man in the world, J. Paul Getty. In response to questions on his eighty-first birthday about the future disposition of his fortune, Mr. Getty said he had no intention of setting up a foundation; his money will continue in his companies. "It always works against the grain to see these foundations so opposed to what I know was the philosophy of the founder," he is quoted as saying. "You can't tell me that 90 percent of what the Ford Foundation is doing would have been approved by Henry Ford.")

Private philanthropy in the United States, out of which the foundations developed, generally followed the English pattern of the eighteenth and nineteenth centuries, which was wide ranging and vigorous, inspired by religion, patriotism, and the needs brought about by the industrial revolution. Both in England and in the United States, it was individual philanthropists who assumed the role of advocacy for social welfare legislation, waging lengthy and powerful campaigns to persuade officials and legislators to deal with social issues.

In England in 1787, William Wilberforce began his long campaign to outlaw slave trade and to free existing slaves, which led to parliamentary action in 1833 to free all slaves in the British dominions. Anthony A. Cooper, seventh earl of Shaftesbury, devoted his career to a long struggle against the many abuses of the nineteenth-century industrial system and did much to improve public health and housing and to introduce badly needed reforms in mental institutions, or "lunatic asylums" as they were then called.

In the United States, enactment of many welfare laws such as the first juvenile court law, the first workmen's compensation laws, and other legislation to assist the poor and protect the unskilled worker came about through the efforts of Jane Addams and her colleagues working out of their commune in the old Hull mansion on Chicago's west side during the late nineteenth and early twentieth centuries.

Once the federal government began to recognize its social responsibilities, it did much to encourage foundations and corporations to accept a share of the burden. The encouragement to foundations was direct, by tax exemptions for charitable and philanthropic gifts and expenditures. Encouragement to corporations was, for the most part, indirect, by the imposition of excess profits taxes and by legislative actions such as those requiring equal employment opportunities, which forced the industrial sector to become concerned about such things as education and community development.

Thus the progression of the grant-making concept may be said to have been from the individual philanthropist to governments and foundations, and finally to business and industry. The federal government of the United States is today the richest source of grant funds in the world. The two other major sources in this country are private philanthropic organizations such as foundations, community trusts, etc., and business and industrial corporations.

Governmental support of foundations in the form of immunity from taxation encouraged their proliferation, and some think their influence, especially following World War II. Investigations in the 1960s into the financial behavior of foundations exposed incidents of abuse of the tax-exempt privilege, and the 1969 Tax Reform Act outlawed interlocking directorates with corporations as well as "self-dealing" activities, and imposed upon private foundations a pay-out requirement and a tax on investment income.

In general, the record of the larger foundations—the approximately one thousand that hold 90 percent of all foundation assets—is one in which they can take pride. Their independence to select programs and activities and to administer them free from the restraints imposed by the constant surveillance of a voting constituency has enabled foundations to respond to new ideas and new needs more rapidly than it is possible for governmental agencies to do. Foundations have been ahead of the government in recognition of social problems and support of new technology. They have pioneered in areas such as legal aid and defense for the poor, rocketry experiments, and studies on pollution and on population control.

Corporations are not very comfortable with the idea of philanthropy. It conflicts with their deep inner sense that there is something fundamentally wrong about giving money away—money is to be invested in enterprises that promise a fair return.

The roots of business and industrial philanthropy go back to the times when there were few if any fringe benefits for employees to protect them in times of illness, death, unemployment, and so forth. Educating an occasional child of a favorite employee and passing out the Christmas goose or turkey accompanied by or in place of a gold piece—the annual bonus—were early forms of industrial "philanthropy." After the passage of welfare and social legislation to protect the workingman more adequately, such considerations as the corporate image and pressure of the excess profits tax were the chief motivations prompting corporate support of activities for the general welfare.

In the past thirty years, however, the owners and managers of business and industrial organizations have begun to develop an understanding of the interdependence between a healthy economy and a healthy nation, between the corporation and the campus, and between the mental health of a population and its gross national product.

Corporate philanthropy is often dispensed through company foundations, which permits complete separation between the business interests of an organization and the social objectives it supports and encourages. Since the enactment of the 1969 Tax Reform Act, company foundations have become less attractive. The previous advantage of using the company foundation to provide reserves during good profit years for continued company contributions in the "lean years" when profits were lower but community social needs continued has been modified by new government requirements and by new restrictions on tax deductions, and many companies are tending to favor direct company grants.

Industrial corporations also assign the performance of research to individuals and institutions outside of their own laboratories, through the research contract, in order to make use of the specialized knowledge and facilities of other institutions.

Corporate philanthropy on the whole has become much more directed and considerably more sophisticated than it was in the early part of the century when John D. Rockefeller, Sr. passed out dimes to everyone he met in the course of his daily activities.

The history of the federal grant in the United States is somewhat unclear; governmental support of many activities was at first disguised in the annual appropriations bills—a practice that has not entirely disappeared from the scene. The federal government sponsored the Lewis and Clark Expedition in 1803, but the first record of a specific congressional grant-making action appears to have been the award to Samuel F. B. Morse, in the amount of $30,000 appropriated on March 3, 1842 by the Twenty-seventh Congress. (This was four years after the Smithson bequest, 105 bags of gold sovereigns plus eight shillings seven pence, had arrived in New York by packet boat. In 1842 it was still, as John Quincy Adams wrote in his diary, "in the fangs of the state of Arkansas," while Congress agonized over what to do about it.) The Morse grant provided funds for testing the feasibility for public use of the electromagnetic telegraph system, on which Professor Morse had already done the basic work. (Or, perhaps Joseph Henry, the first head of the Smithsonian Institution was, as he claimed, the first inventor of the electromagnetic telegraph, but that is another story.) The bill was very brief, 18 lines in the Congressional Record, and gave the grantee almost total freedom in the use of the funds. It stated that he could pay "such sums of money as he may deem to be fair compensation for the services of the said Samuel F. B. Morse and the persons employed under him. . . ."

The mechanisms utilized by the federal government for support of research and other activities have grown considerably more complicated since 1842 and the provisions under which funds are made available considerably more restrictive.

As the government has increasingly assumed responsibility for public services previously in the domain of the states or private institutions, the original idea of the grant or concession has reappeared. That is to say, the elements of favor, privilege, grace, or gift, predominant in private philanthropy, have been replaced by a form of contract in which the chief elements are bargain, exchange, and open competition. Just as the recipients of concessions, benefices, *precariae*, or charters were expected to perform or continue to perform services for the sovereign or the Church, awards of governmental grants are made with an eye to their potential for contributing in some way to the well-being or improvement of the society.

The instrument used for the conveyance of funds from grantor to grantee takes many forms. Foundation agreements tend to be less legalistic than those of corporations or government agencies, but the terminology is essentially the same. A "grant" has come to mean anything from a contract to build an urban transportation system to a stipend for a nursing trainee. It may describe any form of sponsorship whether for education, research, community improvement, or construction of a housing development. Strictly speaking, this is not always accurate. The mechanisms most commonly used for assistance or sponsorship awards by funding organizations or individual benefactors are: grants, contracts, fellowships, and scholarships.

Grants

Foundations and corporations both make use of the grant instrument; the federal government uses it in relations with governmental subdivisions and with educational, charitable, and other nonprofit institutions, and sometimes to individuals. (For agreements between the government and commercial organizations, the *contract* must be used.)

Grants are made for conferences, travel, education, research, or training; for health, welfare, performing and creative arts projects. They may provide funds for construction, acquisition of equipment, or to supplement operating costs. Grants are supportive in character and often entail ideas originated and designed by the applicant.

Predictability of outcome is a key factor in the determination of the award instrument, the grant being preferred when there is no expectation of a specific service or end product as a *quid pro quo* for the award. Basic research is, by its very nature, exploration into the unknown and the end result cannot be anticipated. Therefore, although it is not completely accurate to say that grants are used for basic research and contracts for applied research, it can be stated that, in general, grants are the preferred instrument for basic research projects and applied research may be supported by either contracts or grants.

Another important criterion for selection of the grant mechanism concerns the amount of direction or control the awarding agency expects to exercise over the manner of performance or timing of the work. Grantees expect to be given extensive freedom in carrying out the activities supported by the grant.

Review and selection procedures vary widely but in most cases grant applications are evaluated on the basis of originality and significance of the idea, and on the applicant's ability, including competence and access to necessary facilities, to carry it out—always assuming that the proposed activity falls within the program guidelines and the monetary limitations.

The policies of the grantor and the specific guidelines issued for a program may and often do require compliance with regulations on civil rights, protection of human subjects, acquisition and disposition of property, patents and copyrights, and care of laboratory animals.

Expenditure reports and final progress reports are always required of grant holders, but the reporting requirements for some foundations are minimal. Governmental agencies require detailed expenditure reports and all records of governmental grants are subject to audit by the comptroller general's office. Narrative progress reports are expected to accompany all applications for renewal or continuation of grants.

Within the grant category, there are a number of subdivisions or subspecies. Those most commonly used by the federal government—and that is where the greatest variety really flourishes—are listed in Appendix I.

Contracts

One federal agency that is mainly concerned with research explains the difference between research grants and contracts this way: A grant is an agreement to support research, whereas a contract is an instrument to procure research.

A fundamental point is that grants entail ideas originated and defined by the applicant. Contracts contain work requirements specified by the funding agency, which are offered competitively (usually) to organizations or individuals who present "bids" or "proposals" based on the specifications.

The contract is the preferred instrument of corporations in support of research or development outside of their own laboratories or factories. It is used by the federal government for all agreements with commercial, profitmaking organizations, and sometimes in dealing with nonprofit organizations.

Two types of contract frequently used are the *fixed-price* contract and the *cost-reimbursement* contract.

Fixed-price contracts are used when reasonably definite design or performance requirements can be specified and the total cost can be estimated with reasonable accuracy.

Cost-reimbursement (CR) contracts provide for payment to the contractor of allowable costs incurred in the performance of the contract.

The version of the CR type of contract used most often for research at educational and other nonprofit institutions is referred to as a *straight cost-reimbursement* contract, and just as the term implies, the contractor is reimbursed only for the costs incurred.

In negotiations with commercial, profitmaking organizations, the federal government frequently uses another version of the CR contract, and that is the *cost-plus-fixed-fee* (CPFF) contract. This type provides for reimbursement of costs incurred plus payment of a fixed fee that does not vary with actual cost but may be adjusted if the contract requirements are changed.

A type of governmental contract that may be used for either profitmaking or nonprofit institutions is the *cost-sharing* (CS) contract, under which the contractor receives no fee and is reimbursed for only a portion of the costs. This arrangement is employed when the benefits of the work to be performed accrue to both parties to the contract.

Contract terms and conditions are embodied in two separate groups of clauses: *general* provisions and *special* provisions. General provisions (the "boilerplate") consist of clauses required for all contracts; special provisions constitute the elements of the agreement which apply to each particular contract, such as the scope of the work, price, delivery date, and other matters related to the requirements of each specific project.

Government contracts include provisions dealing with matters such as: rights in patents and inventions; rights in technical data; and publication of results. There is no uniform federal policy on these matters and the entire national patent structure may soon change pending the outcome of current litigation. A challenge to the right of federal agencies to grant exclusive licenses on patents already owned by the government has won one court round, and another suit is attacking the policy permitting federal agencies to grant principal rights in inventions to performing organizations at the time of award as is being done by some agencies under institutional agreements. Both parties to the contract must have a clear prior understanding on invention rights if the project is likely to produce patentable results.

Industrial corporations are keenly aware of the necessity for unambiguous documentation on all proprietary matters, and provisions on this point will be meticulously dealt with in contracts they negotiate.

Federal government policies on some matters are fairly consistent throughout all federal agencies, such as those covering purchase of equipment with government funds, compliance with civil rights laws and with regulations concerning the protection of human subjects and care of laboratory research animals. Many educational and nonprofit institutions have adopted the federal policies on these matters and apply them to all work carried on at the institution regardless of the source of funds.

Reporting requirements are also quite consistent. At the completion of a contract, a comprehensive report must be submitted, and the contractor may be required to submit interim progress reports, depending upon the nature of the project and the length of the contract.

Visits to the project site by representatives of the funding agency or organization for consultation or an up-to-date review of the progress being made are not unusual during performance of a contract.

Some academic researchers react negatively to the very word "contract"; its implications suggest "control," a threat to the freedom of inquiry to which they are unalterably dedicated. Contracting officers who negotiate and manage large numbers of federal *research contracts* say the *research contract* need not be any more restrictive than the *research grant* and usually is not. Some contracting officers will even point to advantages of the contract over the grant mechanism—for example, contracts may be "incrementally funded." That means the total effort is described for a multiple-year period, and funds are allotted from time to time to cover increments of performance. This allows contractors to plan on long-range utilization of their manpower resources and they are relieved of the burden of negotiating a series of individual yearly extensions to complete the entire project. In some cases, contracts may be awarded for an initial period of eighteen or twenty months, instead of the usual grant period of one year; the contractor can complete start-up procedures and get underway before it is time to write an application for extension or continuation of the project and prepare a "progress report" before any real progress has been made.

Under certain circumstances, some federal agencies can award contracts on a noncompetitive basis—for example, if the offeror possesses exclusive or preeminent qualifications or has access to unique, necessary facilities, or is the sole source for meeting the requirements. Such an award may result from the submission of an unsolicited proposal embodying an original idea or concept that the agency finds acceptable. The originator, in that situation, has preeminent qualifications—the idea is his, and he is the sole source capable of carrying out the project.

Review and processing of contract awards used to flow through the administrative channels faster than grants but recent reports indicate that the time between submission and notification is very nearly the same for both mechanisms.

Legislation has been introduced in Congress calling for the establishment of uniform government-wide standards for selection of appropriate legal instruments, in order to distinguish federal assistance relationships from federal procurement relationships. One current bill proposes the use of three instruments: grants, contracts, and cooperative agreements to acquire property and services from or give assistance to state and local governments and other recipients, including charitable and educational institutions.

Under the terms of the bill, *contracts* would be used for the acquisition by purchase, lease, or barter of property or services for the direct benefit or use of the federal government; or to acquire property or services intended for ultimate public use.

Grants would be the method of transferring property, money, services, or anything of value to a recipient in order to accomplish a public purpose authorized by statute (and not the acquisition by purchase, lease, or barter of property or services for the direct benefit or use of the federal government), when *no substantial involvement of the federal agency in the performance of the activity is anticipated.*

Cooperative agreements would be used to transfer property, money, services, or anything of value to a recipient in order to accomplish a public purpose authorized by federal statute (and not the acquisition by purchase, lease, or barter of property or services for the direct benefit or use of the federal government), whenever *substantial involvement between the recipient and the federal government in the performance of the contemplated activity is anticipated.*

This bill, which may or may not be enacted, is an attempt to clear up the confusion created by imprecise labeling of federally financed activities, and the sometimes arbitrary choice by funding agencies of one instrument over another in making an award.

Fellowships

Fellowships are awards made to support advanced or continued education of scholars or researchers. There are several categories of fellowships grouped according to the level of training involved. Eligibility depends mainly upon academic credentials and need, but other factors may be considered. For certain programs, the field of specialization, age, sex, or ethnic affiliation may influence the decision.

Fellowships have been established for many purposes and from a variety of motivations; those established by individuals are especially likely to represent the interests, biases, or preferences of the benefactor. The ones offered by foundations, professional societies, and governmental agencies are likely to have field of study, or academic excellence or promise as the main criterion. In the past few years, many have been set up primarily to offer opportunities and assistance to certain groups, such as ethnic minorities or women, that have been at a disadvantage in past competition for educational assistance.

Some fellowships set age limits which vary with the field or discipline, but this is beginning to change as funding organizations become more aware that scholarly abilities do not cease on a given birthday anniversary. The change is not occurring as rapidly as it should in order to meet the needs of the growing numbers of people who wish to expand their professional knowledge or move into new careers in midlife. Leniency in respect of age requirements has special significance for women who return to their professional fields after several years of fulltime motherhood and homemaking.

Postdoctoral fellowships are available to scholars who have recently received a doctoral degree. Their purpose is to support advanced training in a specialized field. They are usually one-year awards, sometimes renewable for a second year but rarely extended beyond two years. Governmental agencies are the major sources of these awards.

There are also *senior postdoctoral fellowships* for scholars or researchers with five years or more of research or teaching experience. The federal government is the major source of such awards.

Many postdoctoral fellowships, regular and senior, offer support for visits to other institutions, at home or abroad, to permit collaborative work between or among scholars in the same fields.

Predoctoral fellowships are given to graduate degree candidates. The only commitment on the part of the fellow is to continue his education. Awards are for annual periods, often renewable up to the limit of a reasonable time for completion of study for the advanced degree.

Doctoral candidates who have completed all course work and selected a dissertation topic may apply for *dissertation fellowships*. The awarding organization's interest in the dissertation topic is often a determining factor. Foundations support dissertation research in some subjects; professional societies may support doctoral research in their particular fields. Industrial corporations often use this mechanism to support research relevant to their products. A number of federal agencies offer dissertation fellowships, preferring usually to make the award to a faculty advisor on behalf of the graduate student. The responsibility for fulfillment of the fellowship provisions is thus shared by the professor and the student. Some dissertation fellowships cover only research costs and do not include stipends for the student. The fellowship amount may be established by the terms of the program or may be based on a budget similar to that required for grant applications, with all categories of cost itemized.

Candidates for dissertation fellowships must fully understand the provisions accompanying any award for which they apply. If patentable or publishable results are anticipated, it is imperative that the recipient and the donor fully understand their respective obligations and rights in the matter. All organizations making such awards expect recognition of their support in some form if the dissertation is published, and sponsors should always be given copies. Assignment of patent rights must be determined and unambiguously stated for any sponsored activity expected to produce an invention or other patentable product. The provisions of some fellowships stipulate that the recipient agrees to some form of service obligation following the completion of his training, or repayment of the support funds.

Scholarships

A scholarship is the undergraduate equivalent of the fellowship and may be made to a student at any level below graduation from college.

Most awards made for scholarship purposes are based on academic credentials and the need for assistance. Applications may require extensive documentation attesting to the level of need and delving into the family income in detail in order to confirm the inability of the family to support the student.

Organizations that support scholarship programs usually include information about them in the same publications, brochures, and literature concerning other awards. Therefore, many reference materials on grant sources will yield information on available scholarships, but there are also special reference sources that deal only with scholarships.

And so, the term "grant" cannot be taken too literally. It may mean any form of financial assistance or support to carry on a wide range of activities. But no matter what names they are called or how long they have been around or what sources provide them, there is one generalization that can be made: Everybody wants one. This was the message in a cartoon that appeared in a late 1973 issue of *The Chronicle of Higher Education.* In the academic world's desirability scale, a grant comes in ahead of tenure, and the *Chronicle* itself runs a poor third.[3]

[3] Reprinted with permission of *The Chronicle of Higher Education.*

How to Find Out About Grants and Who Gives Them

The three main sources of grant funds in the United States are: governmental agencies, predominantly the federal government; foundations and community trusts; and business and industrial organizations.

Program interests and emphases are changing all the time and the applicant most likely to be successful is one who directs his application to the agency that has a definite interest in his area of study or activity. It is impossible to research every grant-making agency, but it is relatively easy to identify those whose program interests include the field of a proposed project.

Government sources provide an overwhelmingly major portion of assistance to research, education, and social welfare programs. Current federal spending for activities in the general category of "human services" now approaches $100 billion annually, and expenditures for civilian (nonmilitary) research alone exceed $7.5 billion. Some of the research is performed in government laboratories and some by private industry, but a great deal of it is done in the laboratories of colleges, universities and nonprofit or not-for-profit institutions under research grants or contracts.

Foundations now distribute about $2.4 billion annually. Compared with government outlays this seems quite small, but foundations can be more flexible in administering their programs—they don't have to answer to a voting constituency—and can respond more readily to changing priorities.

19

Business and industrial corporations make some of their grants through company foundations, and those figures show up in foundation totals. It is, therefore, difficult to make a realistic estimate of corporate grant making. Figures on corporate philanthropy are given as about $1 billion annually but this does not take into account research grants and contracts that are assigned as part of the research and development programs of the industrial sector.

The channels of information concerning grant-making programs and activities of private funding organizations and especially of the federal government are forbiddingly abundant. The novice, particularly, hardly knows where to start. There are guide books, advisory specialists, and information services, both commercial and nonprofit, that specialize in assisting grant seekers. There are professional proposal writers, grants specialists, reference volumes, and a number of periodical publications that print both general and specific information on the subject.

All the various information sources will be discussed here in four sections, beginning with basic sources of information, followed by government sources, foundations, and business and industry. Only that information which is known to be reliable has been included, and any channels suggested are those that have proven to be effective. The only exceptions are those publications and services too recently established or issued to be evaluated, in which case they are identified as such.

How to Find Out About Grants and Who Gives Them

BASIC SOURCES OF INFORMATION

It is clear from the nature of some proposed activities that the search should begin with governmental, foundation, or other potential funding organizations. But in many cases, grant seekers wish to explore the possibilities that exist within the broadest possible range of funding sources and thus must consult publications and services for guidance in focusing their exploratory efforts.

The main sources of information on the whole range of grant-making organizations are libraries; institutional grants offices; subscriber information services; workshops and institutes; and all the news media—newspapers, radio, television—and word-of-mouth.

LIBRARIES

General information on grant-making organizations can be found in college, university, and public libraries and most special libraries. Standard reference volumes, periodical literature, and daily newspapers containing helpful information are available in all libraries with a reference collection.

Reference Volumes

Among the reference works commonly found on library shelves are: *The Foundation Directory,* which specializes in foundations; the *Catalog of Federal Domestic Assistance,* which lists governmental funding programs; and the *Annual Register of Grant Support,* which tries to list everything.

The *Annual Register of Grant Support* is a directory of fellowship and grant support programs of government agencies, foundations, and business, professional, and other organizations. It is the only annually revised directory of sources of financial assistance.

The *Register* is organized by disciplines: humanities, social sciences, sciences, health and medical sciences, area studies, and environmental studies. The material is indexed according to subject, geographic locations, organizations, and personnel. Each entry includes the address of the grant-making organization and the contact address and telephone number; dates of its founding and of the establishment of the program; total amount granted by the organization in the most recent year of record and amount given for each award, or the average; names of trustees, directors, and other officers of the organization.

One unusual and very helpful item is the information given on total number of applications received and number of awards made in any one year. This is an indicator of the statistical possibility of an applicant's success.

The *Register* is the only compact volume that attempts to cover both public and private granting sources and while it has some shortcomings, it is the best publication available for the grant candidate who does not know where to start. One of its drawbacks is that there is a great deal of duplication which could be eliminated with a cross-indexing system. It is impossible to include every public and private grants program in one volume, but a good cross-indexing system would allow for many more entries in the same number of pages and greatly enhance the value of the publication. It purports to be a "comprehensive directory" and although it is far from that, it does cover a broad span with listings that include labor unions, fraternal orders, business and professional organizations, and competitions, in addition to foundations and governmental agencies.

The *Annual Register of Grant Support* is published by Marquis Who's Who, 4300 West 62nd Street, Indianapolis, Indiana 46206. The price of the 1974–75 edition is $47.50.

A sample page from the current *Register* with notations on the function of each entry is found on pages 24 and 25.

Periodical Literature

Professional and society journals cover one field or profession, e.g., science, the arts, education, etc. Some organizations publish informational brochures or newsletters that contain information on grant programs directed toward one discipline or one group.

Specialized journals that will be found in many library reading rooms are: *Science*, publication of the American Association for the Advancement of Science (AAAS); the *Commerce Business Daily* of the U.S. Department of Commerce; and *Science and Government Report—the independent bulletin of science policy*. These publications contain useful information on federal funding sources, and are discussed in the section on governmental sources.

Science is based in Washington and is an excellent source of information on governmental programs but also contains articles and items of general interest.

The *Chronicle of Higher Education*, also published in Washington, covers both foundation and federal grant news of interest to colleges and universities. A weekly (forty-two issues per year) publication, its listing of significant awards made by foundations and federal agencies in support of higher education is a regular feature. It also publishes application deadline dates for grant programs in the education field. There is a section headed "Status of Legislation," updated weekly, that shows the exact status of pertinent congressional legisla-

(1) **S. S. HUEBNER FOUNDATION FOR INSURANCE EDUCATION**   [591]
W-133 Dietrich Hall
3620 Locust Walk
Philadelphia, Pennsylvania 19174
(215) 594-7620

(2)

(3) FOUNDED: 1940

(4) TYPE: Doctoral fellowships for graduate study in risk and insurance leading toward a Ph.D. degree in business and applied economics.

(5) YEAR PROGRAM STARTED: 1941

(6) PURPOSE: To provide support for students interested in becoming teachers of insurance in colleges or universities and to publish materials in this area.

(7) ELIGIBILITY: Persons with high academic records and a bachelor's degree from an accredited United States or Canadian institution are eligible to apply.

(8) FINANCIAL DATA: Fellowships include expenses for tuition and fees plus $350 per month for single Fellows and $400 per month for married Fellows with children.
AMOUNT OF SUPPORT PER AWARD: Approximately $6500.
TOTAL AMOUNT OF SUPPORT: $97,277 for the year 1972.

(9) NUMBER OF APPLICANTS MOST RECENT YEAR: Approx. 25.

(10) NUMBER OF AWARDS: 13 for the year 1972.

(11) APPLICATION INFORMATION: Official application materials are available upon request to the Foundation at the address below.

(12) DURATION: Fellowships are granted for one year with the possibility of renewal for up to three years of support.

(13) DEADLINE: Applications must be received by February 1.

(14) TRUSTEES:
Change each year.

(15) OFFICERS:
Dan m. McGill, Executive Director and Chairman of the Administrative Board
Mildred A., Brill, Administrative Assistant

(16) ADDRESS INQUIRIES TO:
S. S. Huebner Foundation for Insurance Education
W-133 Dietrich Hall
3620 Locust Walk
Philadelphia, Pennsylvania 19174

(17) *SPECIAL STIPULATIONS: Fellows must certify their intention of becoming college teachers of risk and insurance upon completion of the fellowship program.

THE CALVIN K. KAZANJIAN ECONOMICS FOUNDATION, INC.   [592]
P.O. Box 452
Wilton, Connecticut 06897
(203) 762-7488

FOUNDED: 1947

TYPE: Grants for research and study projects in the general field of economic education, including the strengthening of teaching on all levels and the improvement of adult understanding of economics. Emphasis is on new and effective educational techniques or approaches.

PURPOSE: To promote and support research and study in the field of economics and related areas of the social sciences.

ELIGIBILITY: Qualified individuals with appropriate interests are eligible for support. Applicants are usually functioning in cooperation with a college or university or other accredited institution.

FINANCIAL DATA: Grants are normally between $500 and $1,500 in size. A few larger grants are awarded, however, in amounts ranging from $2,500 to $5,000.
AMOUNT OF SUPPORT PER AWARD: $500-$5,000.
TOTAL AMOUNT OF SUPPORT: $28,709.15 for the year 1971.

NUMBER OF AWARDS: 8 for the year 1971.

APPLICATION INFORMATION: Prospective applicants should submit a letter describing the essential purposes of the proposed project, the means to achieve these purposes, duration, a detailed budget, expected outcomes, and the amount of grant support desired. A copy of Internal Revenue Service Form 4653 should be submitted when available.
DEADLINE: Applications must be received on or before May 1 and December 1 of each year.

TRUSTEES:
Mrs. Lloyd W. Elston, President
William A. Forbes, Vice President
Guerin B. Carmody, Secretary
Lloyd W. W.Elston, Treasurer
John C. Schramm, Managing Director

OFFICERS:
John C. Schramm, Managing Director

ADDRESS INQUIRIES TO:
Managing Director
The Calvin K. Kazanjian Economics Foundation, Inc.
P. O. Box 452
Wilton, Connecticut 06897

*Please note that all funds have been committed for the next three (3) years.

(1) NAME, ADDRESS, AND TELEPHONE NUMBER OF THE ORGANIZATION
May or may *not* be the place to send for information. See item **(16)**.

(2) ENTRY NUMBER
Indexes refer to this number, *not* to the page number.

(3) FOUNDED
Date the organization was established.

(4) TYPE
Type of support; i.e., fellowship, grants, etc. Must be combined with items **(6)** and **(7)** to fully determine applicant eligibility.

(5) YEAR PROGRAM STARTED
Tells how long the program has been in effect.

(6) THE PURPOSE OF THE PROGRAM
Very important in determining appropriateness of the proposed activity. Also, it may indicate a commitment on the part of the recipient extending beyond the grant period.

(7) ELIGIBILITY
Specific eligibility requirements; e.g., educational level, citizenship, ethnic background, sex, etc. Some programs are set up to deal with problems of specific groups; e.g., women, ethnic minorities, etc., and may be restricted to members of the group concerned. Many governmental grants have U. S. citizenship requirement.

(8) FINANCIAL DATA
Amount of support for each grant, and information as to whether stipends are paid. Total amount awarded by organization for all grants during year of record; a good indicator of the "odds."

(10) NUMBER OF APPLICANTS MOST RECENT YEAR and NUMBER OF AWARDS
These two items are the best "odds" indicators. They tell whether the organization is seriously in the grant-making business or just barely complying with the law. If an insignificant number of grants is being made, and the total amount shown in **(8)** for annual support is very low—forget it.

(11) APPLICATION INFORMATION
Tells how to apply or how to obtain application materials.

(12) DURATION
Most grants are for one-year period; renewal information also given here—very important for activities that cannot be completed in one year, especially fellowships.

(13) DEADLINE
When applications must be submitted; may be a postmark date or arrival date.

(14) TRUSTEES
Organizations with a paid staff may leave decision up to staff; trustees rarely meddle in the operational procedures. When board or council makes final award decisions, they usually accept staff recommendations. In small family foundations the trustees decide on the awards, but seldom give them to "strangers". This listing is helpful to denote any special biases that might exist in the grant-making policies. If a trustee is known to be active in a certain field or has a reputation for endorsement of a particular cause, it may give a clue to the organization's special interests.

(15) OFFICERS
Officers are the organizational personnel the applicant is most likely to meet in negotiating for a grant, and the individuals to whom communications should be directed.

(16) ADDRESS INQUIRIES TO
Tells where to send for information on programs, application forms, etc.

(17) SPECIAL STIPULATIONS
There is no heading for "special restrictions" but the *Register* usually adds them at the end of each entry marked by an asterisk.

tion. A section titled "Washington Notes" contains brief background items on federal actions of interest to education. Each issue also carries more lengthy articles on current issues affecting or likely to affect educational institutions or the academic community.

Foundation News, journal of the Council on Foundations, Inc., publishes articles, reading lists, and commentary by leaders in the foundation world. The "Foundation Grants Index," found in the centerfold of each issue, is assembled by The Foundation Center and is the best current guide to foundation grant-making activity.

Foundation Center Information Quarterly updates information in *The Foundation Directory*, 1971 edition, reflecting changes in *Directory* data. The 1975 edition contains fewer foundations than the 1971 edition which, with updated information contained in the quarterlies, is still a useful volume.

American Education, journal of the Education Division of the U.S. Department of Health, Education, and Welfare, prints information of interest to education and on federally funded grant programs.

A new periodical, launched in 1974 for the purpose of providing information and guidance for seeking grant support from both government and private sources, is *The Grantsmanship Center News*, published by The Grantsmanship Center, 1015 West Olympic Boulevard, Los Angeles, Cal. 90015. Plans are to publish eight issues each year—during the first year only four or five came out, but they were full of up-to-date, accurate, well-written material. If it continues at the same level, it will be one of the best sources of information for individuals as well as institutional grants offices. A few libraries subscribed immediately and it is likely that more of them will be ordering it in the future.

The Grantsmanship Center also operates training programs covering all aspects of grant seeking, which are described under Workshops and Institutes.

Far Horizons is a State Department publication on research funding, research conferences, new research centers for U.S. government-supported and private research dealing with foreign areas, international relations, and foreign policy.

Intercultural Studies Information Service, published by the Foreign Area Materials Center, contains information on foreign area studies and intercultural and international education.

Newspapers

An excellent source of information on foundation activities and interests is the daily newspapers; they are also the most convenient source of information on the progress of federal or other governmental legislation that may lead to grant programs. Two daily newspapers that give useful and accurate information on the status of current bills in Congress are the *Washington Post* and the *New York Times*; both of them are found in many libraries, and the *Times* in nearly all libraries.

The *New York Times* publishes a chart of "Major Bills in Congress" every Monday when Congress is in session, which sets out the status of bills under the following headings: Vetoed; Enacted; Awaiting Action by the President; Awaiting Agreement Between Two Houses; Passed by One House; Awaiting Action in Both Houses; and Constitutional Amendments.

Other Library Materials

Some libraries receive foundation annual reports. If preliminary research indicates a foundation possibility—and the foundation is one that issues a separately published annual report—program interests of the foundations can be confirmed through the most recent report of its grant-making activities. Most annual reports also include a statement concerning future plans.

For random articles on a particular topic or about a particular organization, the *Reader's Guide to Periodical Literature* may be checked for references. Weekly magazines and magazine sections of newspapers often carry articles that give "inside" or in-depth descriptions of the activities of a public or private grant-making organization.

INSTITUTIONAL GRANTS OFFICES

In recognition of the importance of grants for support of research and education programs, many academic and other nonprofit institutions provide their staff and faculty with professional assistance in seeking grant support. Offices that are established for that purpose may be called grants offices, or research administration departments, offices of sponsored research, or other names, but their functions include some or all of the following: identification of granting sources; liaison with potential project sponsors up through the preliminary inquiry stage; assistance in proposal preparation; and grants administration. The quality and level of the service depends a great deal upon the qualifications and size of the staff and the resources at its command. The best offices will have a good library of standard reference volumes on all funding sources, including those previously mentioned under Libraries as well as an extensive collection of brochures, program guides, informational literature on governmental and private granting organizations, and application forms.

The grant seeker who is affiliated with an institution should look for such an office before doing anything else. If there is a good library and a competent, helpful staff, the initial exploration for potential support sources can be considerably shortened and refined.

Subscription Information Services

The need for and effectiveness of a professional information service is very much an individual matter. What will serve one institution superbly may be totally inadequate for another. It is, therefore, impossible to evaluate them in terms of comprehensive criteria. It can be stated, however, that no one should subscribe to a service without examining the materials thoroughly and determining that the cost is justified in terms of the function it will serve the subscribing organization. The small institution that is geographically isolated from a large metropolitan center and is without access to a good reference library or the regional federal offices, regional foundation libraries, etc., may find a service worth the cost. Most of the information accumulated and disseminated by all funding information services is derived from channels available to everyone, such as the *Federal Register,* current legislative actions, daily press, The Foundation Center publications, and periodical literature on government and foundation activities and programs. Some organizations view subscription to information services as an economical way to keep abreast of current trends in grant making on the assumption that it reduces research staff requirements. But it should be borne in mind that a constant flow of information into an office is useful only if it is thoroughly screened for items of specific interest to the subscriber, and it will best serve those who have the personnel to peruse, evaluate, and follow up on the ideas or leads that result from it.

Very few information services try to cover the whole field of grant support, but three recently established organizations are offering to provide information on a wide range of funding programs, including private as well as governmental sources. They are the *ORYX Press Grant Information System*, *Funding Sources Clearing House, Inc.* and *Educational Resource Systems, Inc.*

The *ORYX Press Grant Information System* offers to provide information on United States government agencies, state government research organizations, private foundations, associations, and United States corporations. The system, designed primarily for colleges and universities, is the creation of William K. Wilson, Coordinator of Sponsored Research at the State University of New York, College of Fredonia. It was tested at Fredonia from 1970 to 1974 and reports are that it worked well.

Subscribers receive an annual loose-leaf reference volume, which lists grant programs organized by discipline and application deadline date. It is indexed by grant name, sponsoring organization (name and type), and subject. There is also a section on "Preparing Your Grant Proposal."

The annual volume is updated quarterly with new information on grant offerings, and significant changes in status of the listings.

Monthly bulletins are issued in six general subject categories: Creative and Performing Arts; Education; Health; Humanities; Physical and Life Sciences; Social Sciences. The current cost of the service is $375 annually.

Complete information is available from:

> The ORYX Press
> 7632 East Edgemont Avenue
> Scottsdale, Arizona 85257

Funding Sources Clearinghouse, Inc., (FSC) is a nonprofit, tax-exempt membership organization which offers to match grant seekers with grant makers. For an annual membership fee of $250, subscribers receive a monthly news digest of current grant activities; bulletins from time to time calling attention to grant opportunities in specific program areas; a practical guide to successful proposal development; unlimited use of the data bank of funding sources; and the privilege of directing specific funding questions to FSC by telephone, in writing, or in person. Data bank searches to identify a member's best funding prospects cost $25.00 per search (the first search is included in the membership) and members may order biographical profiles on foundation decision-makers at $1.00 per profile.

FSC claims to have essential data on every U.S. foundation, *all* federal grant-making agencies, and thousands of corporations and associations that make grants, giving their data bank holding as "50,000 public and private funding sources," and stating that they have information not available through standard directories or commercial services. On that basis, the organization should be very useful for certain institutions.

Detailed information on FSC can be obtained by writing to:

> Funding Sources Clearinghouse, Inc.
> 2600 Bancroft Way
> Berkeley, California 94704

Educational Resource Systems, Inc. is designed primarily for colleges interested in program and institutional support. It publishes the *Educational Resources Newsletter* ten times yearly to call attention to the latest federal and foundation programs. The *Newsletter* includes reviews of upcoming programs with descriptions of purpose, eligibility, funding levels, deadlines, and high priority areas. Subscription cost is $45.00 per year. Additional subscriptions to the same college are $7.50 each. For full information write to:

> Educational Resource Systems, Inc.
> 1200 Pennsylvania Avenue, N.W.
> Box 6180
> Washington, D.C. 20044

Workshops and Institutes

Colleges and universities frequently hold workshops that concentrate on technicalities of proposal writing, institutional and sponsoring agency requirements, and methods of exploring potential grant sponsorship. These sessions are primarily for the faculty and/or staff of the institutions where they are held.

Grants training institutes, workshops, or seminars offered on a national basis have a dual purpose: to inform on current trends in grant making and to educate professionals in the grants field in techniques of locating granting sources and procedures for following up on them.

The two described here have some similarities and a great many differences. They are both open to registrants on a national basis; they both cover a broad range of subjects; the tuition costs are comparable. One of them, the National Graduate University, is quite well known—some of its seminars are in their tenth year—and concentrates on current trends in grant programs and information on funding sources. The Grantsmanship Training Program is younger and emphasizes the workshop aspect, providing individual assistance and guidance to participants in the conception and preparation of written proposals.

National Graduate University

Courses offered by National Graduate University are designed for representatives of organizations and institutions. They are helpful to the individual but are primarily for the professional in the sponsored research or grants field. Some are organized around the interests of state and local government representatives; others focus on the interests of colleges, universities, hospitals, and other nonprofit organizations.

The emphasis is on trends in federal government funding and current major federal agency programs and subjects. Recently, sessions on private foundations and on affirmative action administration have been included. The institutes are convened in Washington, D.C.

and in major cities selected on the basis of subject matter and interest; courses have been offered in New Orleans, Dallas, Chicago, Boston, and San Francisco.

Tuition costs vary, ranging from $140 to $242 for the two- or three-day meeting. When travel expense is added, this can be expensive, but the courses are well planned and well run. Registration is not limited and sessions are too large for many individual questions or discussions. There is no wasted time; well-informed speakers from government or private organizations are scheduled at approximately half-hour intervals. They are usually explicit in their presentations, whether it concerns future programs of the agencies they represent, anticipated effects of new legislation, or explanation of unfamiliar administrative procedures. The tuition costs include lunch, during which an outstanding or keynote speaker is scheduled.

Announcements and schedules of future courses may be requested from:

> National Graduate University
> 3408 Wisconsin Avenue, N.W.
> Washington, D.C. 20016

Grantsmanship Training Program

Organized by The Grantsmanship Center in Los Angeles, California, this is an intensive one-week, small group workshop, which covers all aspects of grant seeking: resource materials; private foundations; the federal government; program planning; and proposal writing for federal agencies and private foundations.

The workshops are held at various locations where a host organization provides space, a local arrangements representative, and local publicity. Sessions have been hosted in Seattle, San Francisco, Los Angeles, Honolulu, Salt Lake City, Dallas/Fort Worth, Chicago, Kansas City, Boston, New York City, Philadelphia, Cleveland/Columbus/Cincinnati, Providence, Washington, D.C., Detroit, and Atlanta.

Students are encouraged to bring to the workshops proposals, program ideas, details of the structure of the organizations they represent and its financial needs, and descriptive literature. During the workshop, the entire class, which is limited to eighteen participants, focuses on the needs and current efforts of the organization of each student. Thus the examples used are practical, not theoretical.

This program is relatively young but reports from participants are enthusiastic. It provides a very useful training course for personnel responsible for grants activities at academic and/or nonprofit institutions.

Tuition as of May 1975 is $275 for the one-week course. For information on the workshops or on becoming a host organization for a session, write:

> The Grantsmanship Center
> 1015 West Olympic
> Los Angeles, California 90015

News Media and Word-of-Mouth

Stories of large or unusual grants made by foundations, launching of new programs, and of large governmental appropriations appear in the press and are broadcast on the air. They have relevance for the grant seeker insofar as they indicate changing trends or new opportunities for support in a particular field of interest. The implications of some announcements can be very far reaching and they are always worth noting.

The significance of following the progress of governmental legislation through the daily press has already been mentioned, and the alert reader soon develops a sense of the impact of specific legislation on programs in his field of activity.

One of the best-of-all and worst-of-all sources of information comes from colleagues in the same field. Those who have been through the mill—who have researched the potential for support, made application, received awards, and conducted the project through to the final reports—are the most reliable informants of all. If they are willing to share their knowledge, those who are known to be reliable reporters can give advice, guidance, and detailed counsel that is available nowhere else. Even "negative" information from a colleague can be useful—if a proposal was recently rejected by a funding source because of some specific reason, that too is helpful information for the potential applicant.

General information sources of grant support serve one purpose: to narrow down the field. The searcher is then ready to move to specific informational materials and sources.

How to Find Out About Grants and Who Gives Them

GOVERNMENT GRANTS

The largest single source of grant funds in the world is the federal government of the United States. The current issue of the *Catalog of Federal Domestic Assistance*, a compendium of programs that "provide assistance or benefits to the American people," lists more than 1,000 programs that are administered by sixty different federal departments, agencies, commissions, or councils. Approximately 650 of them provide support to state and local governments and related organizations—it is estimated that grants in this category alone total $40 billion annually. About 290 of the programs listed provide aid to individuals (such as student aids) or to nongovernmental agencies and organizations through various types of grant programs.

Total expenditures for research and development in the United States exceed $30 billion annually, and the federal government accounts for more than 50 percent of it. Governmental research is conducted in federal laboratories and at colleges, universities, and other institutions through grants and contracts. Most of the nation's

35

basic research—three-fifths in 1973—takes place in colleges and universities, where 78 percent of externally supported R & D is funded by the federal government.[1]

In the 1974 academic year, more than 3 million college students received some $6.4 billion in financial assistance, an increase of more than 6,000 percent over 20 years before.

Governmental grant making on today's scale is a recent phenomenon, dating back only to the late 1950s. The federal government has become such a usual source of support for all kinds of activities that it is hard to believe that before the middle of this century, responsibility for social, charitable, educational, and other human needs in this country was borne chiefly by private philanthropic institutions and by the state and local governments. Individual philanthropists and social welfare organizations began to awaken the conscience of the federal government to a certain extent around the turn of the century. In 1909 the first White House conference was held to discuss ways of dealing with the problem of neglected, dependent, and handicapped children, and labor leaders were beginning to agitate for better working conditions and social benefits for the unskilled worker. It was not until the depression of the 1930s, however, that major responsibility began to be shifted from private, community, and state shoulders to those of the federal government for welfare, health, education, and other social needs.

The Roosevelt administration ushered in a period of frantic legislation authorizing the establishment of federal assistance programs, largely in the general category of welfare. The most far-reaching legislation of that era was the Social Security Act of 1935, which included unemployment compensation, retirement insurance, and income security for workers' families. Even in that radical (for the time) atmosphere, programs to ensure open employment and educational opportunities for the disadvantaged and ethnic minorities, or for education of the mentally retarded and physically handicapped, would have been considered wildly visionary and were at least a quarter of a century in coming. Support for the advancement of

---

[1] National Science Foundation, NSF 74-306. Science Resources Studies Highlights, May 8, 1974.

knowledge through the basic sciences received little attention from federal funding sources. The scientist, especially the physicist, had a public image as a kind of "queer duck" and depended mainly on private philanthropy for research support, even after the quantum physics breakthroughs around 1930. That situation improved dramatically following World War II, but during the fifteen years between 1945 and the late 1950s only about thirty major new grant programs were inaugurated by the United States Congress.[2] Support of scientific research improved, but slowly.

When the Soviet Union in 1957 successfully launched its space capsule, *Sputnik*, it simultaneously launched a new era in support of science and technology in the United States. In that year, the federal budget for research and development was $12 billion; by 1967 it had doubled to $24 billion.

The National Aeronautics and Space Administration (NASA) was established in 1958 for the exploration of space with manned and unmanned vehicles and reached its pinnacle of achievement in July, 1969 when an American astronaut was the first earthling to set foot on the moon. NASA's budgetary pinnacle was reached in 1966 when its obligations for research and development totaled $5 billion. It has gone downhill ever since; NASA spending for R & D for 1974 was under $3 billion, and the American public has forgotten, if indeed it ever noticed, that the bill for that trip to the moon came to $26 billion!

In 1958 the National Defense Education Act (NDEA) was approved, providing for expanded and improved teaching in science, mathematics, and foreign languages, and vocational training centers, teacher training, guidance counseling and testing, research in educational uses of television and other media, and loans to needy college students. It was followed during the next few years by the Higher Education Facilities Act, the Vocational Education Act, the Elementary and Secondary Education Act, and the Higher Education Act.

The National Science Foundation Act was passed in 1950 to "promote the progress of science; to advance the national health, prosperity, and welfare; to secure the national defense; and for other purposes." By 1952, the total congressional appropriation to the

[2] Tax Foundation, Inc., Research Publication No. 29.

National Science Foundation (NSF) had reached $3.5 million, and in 1958 stood at a little over $51 million. In one year it more than doubled (to $136.5 million, the 1959 budget) and by 1962 it had doubled again. In 1968 the NSF appropriation stood at $495 million, almost ten times the 1958 figure; the current NSF budget is close to $800 million.

Beginning in 1958, vast amounts of money went into large expensive aerospace systems demanding costly facilities and hardware, and into the training of scientists, particularly in the hard sciences, and engineers. Basic research was supported at heretofore unimagined levels.

Then in the 1960s something else happened. Social problems in the form of urban riots, campus unrest, increased crime, and mounting violence exploded across the nation, focusing attention on housing, health and nutritional needs, education, transportation, and the special problems of the ethnic minorities and other disadvantaged groups.

It became apparent that advances in technology, landings on the moon, and the most sophisticated weaponry could not solve all problems; that the strength and prestige of the nation rested not only on powerful defense programs and impressive achievements in space exploration, but also on the physical and mental health of its citizens.

Under President Lyndon Baines Johnson's bivalent banner—"War on Poverty" and "The Great Society"—an unprecedented wave of legislation rolled out of the Congress, aimed at improving the human condition of every individual in the United States. Rufus E. Miles, Jr., for many years a career official in the Department of Health, Education, and Welfare, and author of *The Department of H.E.W.*, wrote: "The Eighty-Ninth Congress, which came into office in January, 1965, was undoubtedly the most liberal Congress on domestic issues in the history of the country."[3]

Bills appeared to have been written overnight and sped through the normally cumbrous and torpid legislative process with amazing swiftness. Expenditures were authorized for education; health care and research; minority business enterprise; drug research and treat-

[3] Rufus E. Miles, Jr. *The Department of H.E.W.* New York: Praeger Publishers, Inc., 1974. 326 p.

ment programs; day care centers; community mental health facilities; preschool, youth, and aging programs; hospital construction; and activities related to the implementation of the 1964 Civil Rights Act.

In 1969 hearings before the House Government Operations Subcommittee on Intergovernmental Relations, the committee chairman, Congressman L. H. Fountain of North Carolina, referred to "well over 420" existing grant authorizations and noted that at least two-thirds of them had been enacted since 1963.[4]

The advent of the Nixon administration brought an end to that era. The Congress continued to make appropriations in support of previously authorized programs and to introduce new bills, but many fell under one or the other edges of the presidential axe: the veto or impoundment.

Establishment of new grant programs has slowed in the 1970s, and some existing ones have been curtailed or abolished.

Other changes of a different kind are also taking place, changes in both form and substance of federal spending that will affect grant making during the remainder of this decade, and perhaps for longer.

The change in *form* is embodied in the so-called New Federalism—a philosophy expounded by ex-President Nixon and endorsed by President Ford—which favors strengthening the role of state and local governments in decision making and administration of federally appropriated funds.

The *substance* will be affected by the energy crisis, which might turn out to be the *Sputnik* of the seventies.

The New Federalism

There is a theory that national trends progress for about half a century and then reverse themselves. The present-day "federalism" would seem to support that. It was just a little over forty years ago that individuals and communities began to look to Washington for solutions to their social and welfare problems. Since that time, the increasing size of the nation's population, the complexity of its insti-

---

[4] U. S. Congress, House Committee on Government Operations, Subcommittee on Intergovernment Relations, *Grant Consolidation and Intergovernmental Relations*, June, 1969.

tutions, and the extremely wide divergence in problems and needs experienced by urban and rural areas as well as the fast-growing, trouble-ridden "exurbia" centers have made decentralization of responsibility to the lower governmental subdivisions to some extent inevitable. Federal grants to states and localities doubled in the four years between 1969 and 1973 and were disbursed through literally hundreds of separate programs. Funds were distributed in the form of "block" (or "bloc") grants to the states—a mechanism under which allocations are made according to some formula such as population, unemployment figures, or other socio-economic factors, and which allow the grantee great flexibility in use of the funds as long as they are applied to the overall purposes for which they were appropriated. Another mechanism used in grants to states and other governmental subdivisions is the "categorical" grant, which is like a block grant in that it is distributed according to an established formula but allows the grantee less flexibility for spending—the "categories" are spelled out. In some categorical programs, the state may serve as a "pass through" and merely administer the funds under the supervision and guidelines of the national agency. Manpower, law enforcement and criminal justice, and rural development programs are delegated to the states under the block grant mechanism, and institutions or individuals apply for grants under those programs through the appropriate state office or agency. The presidential message to the Congress for 1975 proposed extending the decentralization principle to include federal assistance for health, education, community development, and transportation.

Block grants are not the same as revenue sharing, which was legislated in 1972 to return federal funds directly to lower levels of government with few or no strings attached. The 38,000 governmental jurisdictions eligible to receive funds under this program—from states to very small municipalities—pounced upon the first year's allotment and gobbled it up for maintenance purposes in education, public safety, public transportation, and environmental protection, to limit tax increases, or just to make ends meet. Almost none of the 1972 distribution of the five-year, $30.2 billion program went for "new spending," which may be partly accounted for by the time limitation—the act was passed in October 1972 and made retroactive to January, 1972—but the pattern seems to have continued. It is conceivable and to be hoped that in the future some Revenue Sharing funds will provide seed money to launch new community programs or be used for research, planning, and demonstration projects to be conducted by institutions and individuals through competitive grant programs.

In September, 1974, the National Science Foundation announced that it was making a number of awards available for research related to the Revenue Sharing law and for studies to evaluate existing and alternative allocation formulas for distribution of funds under the Revenue Sharing Program. (For information on Revenue Sharing, write to National Clearinghouse on Revenue Sharing, Suite 201, 1785 Massachusetts Avenue, N.W., Washington, D.C. 20036.)

The influential Advisory Commission on Intergovernmental Relations has proposed the creation of "umbrella" type local government units, under the name of Umbrella Multi-Jurisdictional Organization (UMJO), to handle multicounty area-wide developments and serve as the regional clearinghouse for federal assistance matters. If the concept of UMJO is accepted by the federal, state, and local governments, it would produce significant changes in the structure of federal assistance. Among the functions envisioned for the UMJOs would be to review and comment on applications for federal grants in each area and act as the implementing instrumentality for all federally encouraged districting programs under state legislation. UMJO functions would reach into every aspect of state and local government and in effect create a third level of government between Washington and the people. All activities that look to the federal government for support would be especially affected since both the application for and functioning of such programs would be handled through UMJO.

A certain amount of decentralization has already occurred as more and more federal programs are being administered through the federal regional offices.

There are ten regional areas; every department and many of the specialized agencies have regional offices that represent the national office or agency in that region. They provide liaison, information, and assistance to individuals and institutions or local government agencies located in the region, and in some cases grant applications to federal agencies must have the approval of the regional director. The actual amount of decision-making authority exercised by the regional directors in dealing with funding requests varies from region to region and from agency to agency, but the spirit of the New Federalism with its implications for greater regional autonomy is very evident in this trend.

The decentralization of programs formerly administered at the national level poses problems but may also provide opportunities for the grant applicant. The first difficulty is that it necessitates becoming acquainted with an entirely new bureaucratic layer. State and local agencies have established organizations that are counterparts of the national agencies and of each other, resulting in overlap of state, county, municipal, and federal units. The staffs in the subnational and especially substate level units are neither as experienced nor as professionally objective as their counterparts at the national level, whose view of proposed activities encompasses a much broader range. Local reviewers will inevitably take local problems and needs into account, thus placing the basic researcher whose subject has universal significance at a disadvantage, but favoring the problem-solving, locally focused, action-oriented program.

State and local agencies are also more sensitive to the way research or program activities may be perceived by local political office holders or influential leaders. The researcher at a publicly supported institution, such as a state university, for example, is particularly vulnerable to being caught in the crossfire between competing political factions. Academic freedom, which must be zealously guarded at those institutions under the best of circumstances, is particularly vulnerable when programs are reviewed and funds distributed by local representatives who may have their own axes to grind.

On the practical level, many local governmental officials do not fully comprehend the cost principles established by the federal government for funding research and other programs at educational and other nonprofit institutions. The point was made by Spriestersbach, Hoppin, and McCrone in *Science*, that ". . . they typically have difficulty in accepting the legitimacy of reimbursing indirect costs. . . . It ought to be a matter of public concern that many state agencies are not asking the federal government to support the agencies' indirect cost expenses, because they assume that these charges reduce the funds available for direct support of the program's mission. However, by not collecting these actual administrative expenses, they shift this portion of the program's support unwittingly to the taxpayers of their state."[5]

The grant applicant, especially the academic researcher, must be alert to the special conditions that pertain in local administration of federal programs that are nonexistent in dealing on the national level. While he can expect the staff to understand more immediately the proposed activity that has relevance to the community where it will take place, there is the ever-present risk that a project will become "politicized" or co-opted by groups seeking data to support a favored thesis or to discredit the claims of an opponent. It also places a heavy burden on state and municipal administrators to maintain objectivity in the selection process—to be responsive to local needs without being conscripted into any one of the local "camps."

Energy

The national effort to achieve energy self-sufficiency by 1985, affirmed and christened "Project Independence" by ex-President Nixon and since reaffirmed by President Ford, is going to skew the federal budget in the direction of fuel resources programs for the next decade and perhaps for the remainder of this century. Analyzing the 1975 presidential budget, *Science* commented, "Not since the early, halcyon days of the space program has an administration seen fit to inject so much money so rapidly into a single major sector of civilian research as the Nixon administration proposes to pump into energy R & D next year: an 81 percent, $816 million increase over the billion dollars obligated in fiscal 1974. Some, like Senator Henry Jackson (D–Wash.), believe the government could justifiably spend even more on energy R & D but the infusion of funds proposed for fiscal 1975 is nonetheless massive."[6]

It appears that Senator Jackson and others have prevailed—the Congress seems inclined to raise the energy appropriations higher

---

[5] *Science*, Vol. 186, 25 October 1974. D. C. Spriestersbach, Margery E. Hoppin, John McCrone, "University Research and the New Federalism." pp.324–327.
[6] *Science*, Vol. 183, 15 February 1974.

and has moved to concentrate all the main energy research and development programs under one unified agency, the new Energy Research and Development Administration (ERDA).

The most dramatic increases in the 1975 presidential budget are in previously neglected areas of solar energy, geothermal power, and conservation research and development, although the actual sums for those purposes are still less than for the major fossil fuel and nuclear efforts. Nuclear programs account for about 50 percent of the total energy R & D budget, most of which is for nuclear safety, uranium enrichment, and reactor development. A large part of that research will be done in the national laboratories and very little will be assigned by grants or contracts to academic and nonprofit institutions. About 23 percent of the energy budget is for coal research, with emphasis on coal gasification and liquefaction, oil and gas recovery techniques, and research and testing on modifying existing technologies in fossil fuel gasification and liquefaction. It is anticipated that a good part of this research may be carried on in college and university laboratories.

The establishment of the new administration, ERDA, brought to a head the conflict that had been brewing among the federal agencies concerned and among congressman and senators over the commitment of the nation to nuclear power relative to alternate energy sources. In the formulation of the organizational structure of ERDA, the Atomic Energy Commission (AEC)—nuclear oriented by its very nature—was abolished and its research programs parceled out to several other agencies. This is probably one effect of the efforts exerted in the Senate to modify the legislation setting up ERDA so as to prevent its domination by the Atomic Energy Commission, and to ensure that federal funding and organizing is neutral among competing technologies. A Nuclear Regulatory Commission was given responsibility for the safety of nuclear energy sources.

The appointment of Interior Secretary Rogers C. B. Morton to chair the Energy Resources Council, the nation's top energy policy group, seems to signify emphasis on research and development of fossil fuel resources. Interior's Office of Coal Research and Bureau of Mines received large portions of the increased energy funds and most of their activity was placed under ERDA. At the same time, the solar and geothermal research and development programs within the National Science Foundation (NSF) also received increased support, and were subsequently transferred to ERDA. The Environmental Protection Agency has not been entirely trampled underfoot in the rush to expand energy resources, but it appears that ERDA will assume responsibility for some former EPA activities, particularly those pertaining to research and development to improve protective technologies and policies, and will monitor their implementation.

Until details of the organization and goals of the new energy agencies are worked out, it is impossible to estimate the amount of federal spending to be allocated for specific areas, but current estimates are that the energy programs will be funded at about $12 billion during the next five years—more than $20 billion during the next ten years. This includes, in addition to scientific and technological research, environmental and health effects research, basic research, and manpower development. It is reasonable to assume that academic and other nonprofit institutions will be assigned a portion of the research and the manpower development programs through grants and contracts.

Given the complexity of the federal government, it is exceedingly difficult to identify the department or agency to approach on any matter, grants included, but it is not impossible.

The first step is to learn the language. The language of the federal government is the acronym, and learning it is a continuous process because the vocabulary grows and changes daily. Acronyms appear to emerge spontaneously from the name of a governmental office or department, but it is sometimes hard to believe there isn't a staff of civil service specialists with responsibility for creating names that will result in salutary acronyms. There is no doubt that the acronym influences the choice of an organizational title, and precisely descriptive departmental names have been shelved because the acronym would be unfortunate, ludicrous, or even lewd. When it was set up in 1953, the department we know as Health, Education, and Welfare was slated to be called Health, Education, and Social Security until it was observed that the resulting acronym would spell HESS, the name of Hitler's deputy to whom *Mein Kampf* was dedicated. And in 1974, President Nixon called his executive reorganization plan the New American Revolution, until it began to be referred to by Nelson A. Rockefeller's initials.

It is customary in writing about a governmental unit to spell out the full name the first time it is used, followed by the acronym in parentheses, and to refer to it thereafter by the acronym. Since this is not always followed, the Acronym List given in Appendix II is a guide to the governmental agencies, offices, and departments most often referred to in print or by the news media in connection with grant programs.

After acquiring a working knowledge of "governmentese," the next step is to determine which sectors of the federal organization are concerned with grant making and learn how to identify within those sectors the programs relevant to the immediate need.

Federal funds are appropriated by the legislative branch and turned over to the executive branch which dispenses and administers them. The executive branch comprises the executive office of the president, the cabinet-level departments, and a number of independent offices and agencies.

The federal government makes grants for just about every conceivable activity that isn't illegal or immoral, and it has been questioned whether those lines are sometimes crossed. In general, however, governmental awards fall into the categories of health; physical, life, and social sciences; science technology; education; welfare; the arts; and the humanities.

Most departments and many of the independent or specialized agencies have programs through which grants are made to states and other governmental subdivisions, to educational, nonprofit, and not-for-profit institutions, and to individuals. The departments of Agriculture, Commerce, Housing and Urban Development, Interior, Labor, and Transportation all have substantial grant programs, but by far the largest grant-making department—one that accounts for one-third of the entire federal budget—is the Department of Health, Education, and Welfare.

DEPARTMENT OF HEALTH, EDUCATION, AND WELFARE (HEW)

Since 1972, HEW has surpassed every other department of the federal government in expenditures, including the Department of Defense. The HEW budget exceeds the total national budget of any nation outside the United States, except possibly the Soviet Union. The federal government spends forty or fifty times as much as private foundations in this country for programs in the category of "human services," and most of that is expended through HEW-administered programs. When the fiscal 1974 figures are totaled up, they are expected to show that HEW spent more than $100 billion; the request for 1975 was $113.7 billion. Even though more than two-thirds of that goes to Social Security for assigned purposes, the chance of getting a grant from HEW is statistically greater than that of getting one from all other grant sources combined.

HEW employs the full range of grant mechanisms in dispensing funds under its multifarious programs, or, to put it another way, it spends money any way it can. Block grants are made to state health authorities to assist states in attacking those health problems they consider of most immediate importance. Project grants are awarded to public and nonprofit agencies for health-related programs, with particular emphasis on urban poverty neighborhoods and remote rural areas. Categorical grants are made to states for educational activities. Formula grants are made to states for constructive social and welfare services on a matching fund basis. Capitation grants (based on enrolment) are made to institutions to support training in certain fields. Research grants and contracts are assigned to colleges, universities, and other nonprofit and not-for-profit institutions and sometimes to individuals to conduct basic and applied research relevant to the objectives of the department. Special funds are earmarked for health care to migrant agricultural workers and their families and dispensed through various mechanisms. Educational assistance in the form of fellowships, loans, and grants is given to individuals and, in the form of training grants, to institutions.

The National Research Act of 1974 repealed existing HEW training programs in NIH and ADAMHA and consolidated all research training authorities of those agencies into a single National Research Service Awards authority. Training grants in existence when the act was passed are being honored until their completion. Future training assistance will be in the form of institutional or individual research fellowships and will be limited after July 1, 1975 to subject areas in which a need for personnel has been determined. Predoctoral support will be given only through institutional grants and the institution will be responsible for the choice of trainees. National Research Service Awards are limited to three years in the aggregate and recipients are subject to a service obligation or must repay the government for the cost of their training. The service obligation has been set at: (1) twelve months of health research or teaching for each year of support; or (2) if the trainee is a physician, nurse, dentist, or other professional trained to provide health care directly to patients, twelve months' service with the National Health Service Corps for each year of support; or (3) alternate form of service as determined by the HEW secretary if there are no suitable health research or teaching positions available to the individual.

The diversity of programs assigned to HEW and the continuous growth, expansion, and incorporation of activities under its aegis have created an admittedly unmanageable administrative monster. Numerous recommendations have been put forth for breaking it up into two, three, or more departments but so far all were rejected for what seemed like good reasons. The latest proposal calls for the creation of a superdepartment, the Department of Human Resources, that would absorb everything HEW now has plus the manpower and unemployment insurance functions of the Department of Labor, as well as some functions now assigned to the Departments of Agriculture, Housing and Urban Development, and a few others. This new superagency would be organized into three major administrations, with a much enlarged staff, operating under new delegations of power. There would be a Health Administration, a Human Development Administration, and an Income Security Administration. This proposal was part of ex-President Nixon's Departmental Reorganization Plan and was aimed at greater centralization of the executive functions within the White House. With the advent of a new president in August, 1974 and a new mood in the Congress concerning the power of the presidency, the future of this plan is doubtful.

Other proposals have focused on reducing the department; one suggestion was that the National Cancer Institute (NCI) be set up as a NASA-like independent agency, on the theory that the organizational structure used to conquer space would also be effective in conquering cancer. The idea was sufficiently attractive and gained enough support that, although it was not formally adopted, a compromise was reached that gives NCI unusual autonomy within the

HEW-PHS-NIH hierarchy. (NCI is one of eleven institutes in the National Institutes of Health, under the administration of the Public Health Service, which is headed by the assistant secretary of HEW for Health.) The NCI director submits his budget directly to the president, with only the "comments" of the secretary of HEW.

HEW has decentralized some of its activities to the ten regional offices, where the regional directors carry out departmental policies, establish and maintain liaison with the states and local communities, and supervise HEW activities in the areas to which they are assigned. Some functions performed in the HEW regional offices have utility for all governmental grant operations. For example, the regional HEW comptroller has been delegated authority to negotiate the applicable indirect costs rates for colleges and universities in each region. Many HEW programs listed in the *Catalog of Federal Domestic Assistance* (CFDA) indicate that applications are to be submitted to the regional offices or suggest preapplication consultation with staff of those offices.

The regional offices are an important source of information, assistance, and guidance for grant seekers. The addresses of the offices, areas of coverage of each region, and current directors' names are indicated in Appendix III.

The major HEW divisions that make grants to states and other governmental subdivisions and support biomedical and behavioral research and other activities at academic and nonprofit institutions through grants and contracts are:

- I. Public Health Service
- II. Education Division
- III. Office of Human Development
- IV. Social and Rehabilitation Service

PUBLIC HEALTH SERVICE (PHS)

When PHS was still part of the Federal Security Administration (the forerunner of HEW), it made a policy decision with respect to the conduct of biomedical research which still prevails and which has led to a very high level of grant-making activity. It decided that biomedical research could thrive best where the most talented research people were found and where most of them wanted to remain—on university campuses, in teaching hospitals, and in nonprofit research institutes. It determined that the most effective way to utilize the talents of such people was by making grants to the institutions with which they were affiliated in support of work the institutions could not otherwise afford.

The origin of the Public Health Service was a 1798 act authorizing funds for marine hospitals for the care of American merchant seamen—the scope of its activities has broadened considerably during the intervening years.

In 1973 HEW made significant changes in the organization of its health programs, the effect of which was to consolidate those programs known collectively as the Public Health Service (PHS) into six major agencies:

A. The National Institutes of Health (NIH)
B. Alcohol, Drug Abuse, and Mental Health Administration (ADAMHA)
C. Health Resources Administration (HRA)
D. Health Services Administration (HSA)
E. Food and Drug Administration (FDA)
F. Center for Disease Control (CDC)

National Institutes of Health (NIH)

The mandate of the NIH is to improve the health of the nation by increasing knowledge of health and disease through the conduct and support of research, research training, and biomedical communications. Biomedical research constitutes nearly 90 percent of the federal health research and development and most of it is carried out by the NIH. Close to 90 percent of the NIH budget goes to help support research and training in nonfederal institutions. The range of research activities supported by NIH can best be comprehended by noting the titles of the forty-four review groups or study sections established to screen applications for scientific merit:

Allergy and Immunology	Biomedical Communications
Applied Physiology and Bioengineering	Biophysics and Biophysical Chemistry
Bacteriology and Mycology	Cardiovascular and Pulmonary
Biochemistry	Cardiovascular and Renal

Cell Biology
Communicative Sciences
Computer and Biomathematical
   Sciences Research
Dental
Development Behavioral
   Sciences

Endocrinology
Epidemiology and Disease
   Control
Experimental Psychology
Experimental Therapeutics
Experimental Virology
General Medicine
Genetics
Hematology
Human Embryology and
   Development
Immunobiology
Immunological Sciences

Medicinal Chemistry
Metabolism
Microbial Chemistry
Molecular Biology
Molecular Cytology
Neurology
Nutrition
Pathobiological Chemistry
Pathology
Pharmacology
Physiological Chemistry
Physiology
Population Research
Radiation
Reproductive Biology
Surgery
Toxicology
Tropical Medicine and
   Parasitology
Virology
Visual Sciences

There are now eleven institutes, including the new Institute on Aging. The largest in staff and budget is the National Cancer Institute (NCI), and the next largest is the Heart and Lung Institute (NHLI). Together their budgets total more than that of all the other institutes combined.

The National Cancer Institute (NCI) plans, directs, conducts, and coordinates a national research program on the detection, diagnosis, cause, prevention, treatment, and palliation of cancers, and specifically:

a. Conducts and directs research performed in its own laboratories and through contracts.
b. Supports and coordinates research projects by scientific institutions and individuals through research grants.
c. Supports training of manpower in fundamental sciences and clinical disciplines for participation in basic and clinical research programs and treatment programs relating to cancer by fellowships, and career awards.

   d. Supports construction of laboratories and related facilities necessary for research on cancer.

   e. Supports demonstration projects in cancer control.

   f. Collaborates with voluntary organizations and other institutions engaged in cancer research and training activities.

   g. Encourages and coordinates cancer research by industrial concerns where such concerns evidence a particular capability for programmatic research.

   h. Collects and disseminates information on cancer.

   i. Consults with appropriate individuals and agencies in the development, coordination, and support of cancer research programs in other countries.

The National Heart and Lung Institute (NHLI) supports basic and clinical research concerned with the structure and function of the cardiovascular and pulmonary systems and with the prevention, diagnosis, and treatment of diseases that afflict them. Major areas of research are arteriosclerosis, including coronary heart disease and cerebrovascular disease; peripheral vascular diseases; cardiac diseases, including congenital and rheumatic heart diseases; arrhythmias and heart failure; hypertension and kidney disorders; pulmonary diseases, including emphysema and other chronic obstructive lung disorders; and thrombosis, hemorrhagic diseases, and other diseases, including sickle cell disease.

The National Institute of Allergy and Infectious Diseases (NIAID) supports world-wide research activities on causes, diagnosis, treatment, and prevention of infections and allergic and other immunologically mediated diseases. Specific aspects of these activities are made the subject of institute-initiated and directed contract programs. Ongoing special emphasis programs of NIAID are:

   a. Allergic and immunologic diseases: asthma and allergic disease centers; cell-mediated versus humoral antibody responses; clinical immunology and immunopathology; lymphocyte biology.

   b. Bacterial and fungal diseases: biology of venereal disease; hospital-associated infections; mechanisms of resistance to antimicrobial agents; streptococcal disease and sequelae.

c. Viral diseases: antiviral substances (interferon); chronic and degenerative diseases of man; clinical virology; influenza; viral hepatitis.
d. Parasitic diseases: biological regulation of vectors; immunity to animal parasites.

The National Institute of Arthritis, Metabolism, and Digestive Diseases (NIMDD) supports research into the causes, prevention, diagnosis, and treatment of the various arthritides; the rheumatic and collagen diseases; the metabolic diseases, such as diabetes; other inborn errors of metabolism, such as cystic fibrosis; and digestive diseases. It supports work in orthopedics, dermatology, hematology, nutrition, endocrine disorders, energy and mineral metabolism, urology and kidney diseases, and development of the artificial kidney machine. NIMDD is interested in artificial kidney methodology, such as better attachment systems, improved membranes for dialysis, etc.

The National Institute of Child Health and Human Development (NICHD) supports programs in areas related to maternal health, child health, human biology, embryogenesis, perinatal biology, and causes of infant and fetal mortality. The aging studies formerly administered by NICHD have been transferred to the National Institute on Aging.

The National Institute of Dental Research (NIDR) supports investigations into the causes, means of prevention, diagnosis, and treatment of oral diseases including dental caries, periodontal diseases, lesions of soft and hard tissues, and oral/facial abnormalities such as cleft lip and palate.

The National Institute of Environmental Health Sciences (NIEHS), located in Research Triangle Park, North Carolina, supports fundamental research concerned with defining, quantifying, and understanding the effects of chemical, biological, and physical factors upon biological systems in relation to the health and well-being of man. NIEHS is also interested in research designed to elucidate and predict the health effects of pollutants and other potentially hazardous by-products associated with the various energy technologies and conservation proposals being developed in connection with the nation's drive for energy self-sufficiency.

The National Eye Institute supports research on the cause, natural history, prevention, diagnosis, and treatment of disorders of the eye and the visual system.

The National Institute of General Medical Sciences (NIGMS) supports research in the sciences basic to medicine, in the behavioral sciences, and in certain clinical disciplines. Specific research fields of interest are anesthesiology, the behavioral sciences in relation to organic disease, biochemistry, biomedical engineering, biophysics, cellular biology, clinical chemistry, diagnostic radiology, genetics and genetic chemistry, molecular biology, pathology, pharmacology, and toxicology.

Research and research training projects which have relevance for two or more of the institutes and do not fit specifically into any one are handled by NIGMS. Support by this institute is given in individual grants, program-project grants and center grants. Program-project grants emcompass several research topics on a central theme and often serve as the intermediate step leading to the establishment of a center. NIGMS centers receive about 25 percent of the total support of this institute. They are geographic in nature and usually involve several institutions and many departments. Applications for center grants require a cluster of individual grants plus a core program that shows how they fit together.

A new program was set up in NIGMS by passage of the fire-prevention law, which authorized the establishment of a program on research, care, and rehabilitation of burn victims. The first burn center was set up at Massachusetts General Hospital.

The training of medical scientists has long been a concern of NIGMS and its current plans call for setting up a multidisciplinary predoctoral fellowship program for training in cellular and molecular biology; genetics and regulation; and all biomedical areas, including the behavioral sciences. As of this writing the postdoctoral program in anesthesiology, pathology, and behavioral and biological sciences seems assured but the predoctoral program is still uncertain.

The National Institute of Neurological and Communicative Disorders and Stroke (NINCDS) research center project and clinical research center programs stimulate and support investigations in the neurological, sensory, communicative, and related fields. Support is provided for fundamental studies of the development, structure, and function of the nervous system, the neuro-muscular apparatus, and human communication.

The National Institute on Aging (NIA) was established in 1974 by the Research on Aging Act to support biomedical research on aging. Several agencies of the PHS, as well as the Administration on Aging, will work closely with the NIA in implementing the new act. The programs will be built around the Gerontology Research Center and the Adult Development and Aging Branch, both elements to be transferred from the NICHD. The budget request for 1975 was $14.4 million.

The Institutes account for about 85 percent of the total NIH budget of $2 billion annually. The remainder supports the National Library of Medicine, Research Resources programs, and the Fogarty International Center.

The National Library of Medicine supports projects for research, development, and demonstration in medical library science and biomedical communications.

The Division of Research Resources develops and supports specialized research facilities, e.g., clinical research units, animal resources and primate centers, and biotechnological areas such as mass spectrometry and high voltage electronmicroscopy.

The Fogarty International Center of the NIH administers a Scholars in Residence Program for advanced study in the health sciences and promotes discussion, study, and research on development of science internationally as it relates to health.

The General Research Support (GRS) program, which provides general funds to institutions in proportion to the amount of their federally funded biomedical research, was omitted from the president's budgets for 1974 and 1975, but in both years Congress voted to continue the program. The appropriations committees of both houses, however, have directed NIH to review the formulas and guidelines under which GRS funds are awarded and used. The primary purpose is to strengthen the research capability of institutions where substantial biomedical research is carried on with federal support.

Annual listings of NIH grants and awards have been prepared by the Division of Research Grants since 1946. Research contracts were added to this series in 1970. The listings also include grants and awards made by other health agencies of the Department of Health, Education, and Welfare in order to provide an overall accounting of DHEW's stewardship.

The listings are tabulated by principal investigator or project director as well as by the state and city of the organization having responsibility for the work. This report, *Public Health Service Grants and Awards,* is a good indicator of the kind of projects the various HEW agencies support. It may be ordered from the Superintendent of Documents, U.S. Government Printing Office, Washington, D.C. 20402. The cost was $1.95 at this writing.

The *Guide to Grant and Award Programs* (DHEW Publication No. (NIH) 73-33) may be ordered in single copies from the National Institutes of Health, Division of Research Grants, Bethesda, Maryland 20014. Multiple copies are $.60 each and must be ordered from the Superintendent of Documents, U.S. Government Printing Office, Washington, D.C. 20402.

Another useful NIH document is the *NIH Research Contracting Process* (DHEW Publication No. (NIH) 73-491) and may be ordered from the U.S. Department of Health, Education, and Welfare, Public Health Service, NIH, 3000 Rockville Pike, Bethesda, Maryland 20014.

Alcohol, Drug Abuse, and Mental Health Administration (ADAMHA)

ADAMHA conducts and supports programs to deal with the socio-medical problems of alcohol and drug abuse and to promote and sustain mental health and prevent mental illness. It administers programs of research on addictive drugs, and in the fields of behavioral and clinical psychopharmacology and the behavioral and biological sciences. It was established in 1973 and consists of the National Institute of Mental Health (formerly in the NIH and also formerly in the Health Services and Mental Health Administration (HSMHA)), the National Institute of Drug Abuse (NIDA), and the National Institute on Alcohol Abuse and Alcoholism. (NIAAA) The National Research Act of 1974 revised the federal policy on research training programs of ADAMHA and NIH. (See NIH section.)

Total funding for ADAMHA is in the range of $700 million annually, 50 percent of it allocated to general mental health programs and 33 percent to drug abuse programs. Of the remainder, about 14.5 percent goes to alcoholism studies, divided evenly between grants to states and project grants and contracts to institutions and individuals for community programs and for research.

National Institute of Mental Health (NIMH). NIMH has had so many organizational changes that it has not issued a program booklet since 1972. A description of current programs is in preparation and should be available in the spring of 1975. The 1975 budget for research grants is expected to be about $66 million. Training programs will continue under the policies of the 1974 National Research Act, which provides for support of training in certain fields and in return for a commitment to a period of service in a governmentally approved assignment.

Current program concentration is in the following areas:

a. Behavioral research: basic principles underlying behavior.
b. Child mental health: Intervention programs and applied research: work with social agencies, communities, and families—
   - psychological investigation of child development
   - nonintellective aspects of child development; effects of television on behavior
   - biological-behavioral (genetic-environmental) studies
   - problems of adolescence and youth
   - base-line indicator studies
c. Crime and delinquency—
   - studies leading to more knowledge about crime and delinquent behavior
   - development of intervention models
   - mental health and the legal system
d. Minority group mental health programs (black, Spanish-speaking, and native Americans)—
   - ethnological studies
   - racism and mental illness
   - strengths of the family re mental health

The Community Mental Health Center Program, through which a total of 626 centers were established with federal financing, expired on June 30, 1974 and was not proposed for extension. The basic staffing for existing centers is expected to continue as well as support of the specialized child mental health grants programs.

For information on other sources of support of mental health programs, the following publications may be consulted:

> Silber, Stanley C., ed. *Handbook: Foundation Support for Mental Health and Related Services.* Rockville, Maryland: National Institute of Mental Health, 1974. v, 89p. 5600 Fishers Lane, Rockville, Maryland 20852.
>
> Silber, Stanley C., ed. *Multiple Source Funding and Management of Community Mental Health Facilities.* Selected papers from NIMH Regional Office Funding Conferences 1970–72. Rockville, Maryland: National Institute of Mental Health, 1973. viii, 84p.

National Institute of Drug Abuse (NIDA). This program is coordinated by the White House Drug Abuse group. NIDA supports research on narcotic antagonists; marijuana; opiate substitutes for treatment; psycho-social aspects of drug abuse; heroin; drugs and youth; medical aspects of drug abuse; and the development of a uniform reporting system on drug use and abuse. The budget for 1975 is expected to be about $21 million for research.

During the past few years, a full range of community-based drug abuse treatment and rehabilitation programs was supported by federal funding with the government assuming primary responsibility for developing a national network of community treatment facilities. But the orientation is now shifting to a new approach that will stress more the prevention of addiction and shift operational responsibility for treatment service to the states. Indications are that project grants and contracts made by the federal government to institutions for drug treatment programs will decrease and that formula grants to the states for drug abuse programs may increase. Research emphasis will continue to be on clinical studies of new pharmacological therapies (i.e., chemicals that negate the effects of narcotics use and also long-acting therapeutic drugs) and studies in the sociological and psychological and physiological aspects of drug abuse.

National Institute on Alcohol Abuse and Alcoholism (NIAAA).
Federal project grant and contract funds for alcoholism
programs have declined since several alcoholism treatment projects
started in 1971 were completed. Federal support for the future will be
primarily in the area of demonstrations to test potentially effective
treatment modalities. Some incentive contracts are being initiated
with business organizations to develop programs for the identification, counseling, and treatment of workers with alcoholism problems. Research support includes such areas as clinical research—
hemodialysis, the rapid removal of alcohol from the bloodstream, and
physiological effects of alcohol—increasing the metabolism rate for
alcohol or preventing its absorption into the body.

Health Resources Administration (HRA)

HRA is responsible for health planning, manpower training, and
research and evaluation for health resources and needs. Current
planning programs and evaluation studies are looking toward the
National Health Insurance concept with special interest in cost control and training of the necessary manpower. HRA administers programs to increase the supply and effectiveness and the availability of
health manpower; supports and evaluates state and areawide health
planning programs; supports research and development directed at
containing the rate of increase of medical care costs and at developing
community-based health services systems. Many of its programs are
administered through state agencies and by the federal regional
offices. HRA currently supports more than fifty regional medical
programs across the country—area-wide organizations of health care
providers and consumers attempting to bring about more accessible,
efficient, and high quality health care to the public.

Legislation pending in Congress includes plans for the initiation
of a rational approach to delivery of health care; establishment of a
national health council; establishment of national health service areas;
health systems agencies to formulate plans for the future; a health
resources development fund; and a coordinating council to develop
plans formulated by the systems agencies and to review the federal
formulae for grant funding.

Minority recruitment for the health professions is one program that is being substantially supported for the next few years.

HRA publishes *Health Resources News*, twelve issues per year, free on request to HRA, Public Health Service, HEW, 5600 Fishers Lane, Rockville, Maryland 20852.

Health Services Administration (HSA)

This agency is responsible for the improvement of delivery of health service to the nation. It operates a program of comprehensive health services for American Indians and Alaskan natives; provides training for health personnel; administers grant programs for health care services for mothers and children; advises Social Security on medical care standards, policies, and procedures for the Medicare program.

Food and Drug Administration (FDA)

The mandate of FDA is to protect the health of the nation against impure and unsafe foods, drugs, cosmetics, and other potential hazards. The National Commission on Product Safety, set up by Congress in 1972, took over from FDA the responsibility for protecting the public against hazardous consumer products such as unsafe toys, flammable fabrics, fireworks, etc. FDA's research program is divided into four main areas: microbiology and immunology; analytical chemistry; pharmacology and pharmacokinetics; and toxicology. Microbiology and immunology includes studies on hepatitis in shellfish; serum hepatitis; detection of bacterial contamination in food and parenteral drugs; activity of allergenic extracts and identification of active principles; immunologic clinical studies of "new vaccines;" fate of bacteria and other organisms in food and drugs; and improvements in sterilization procedures for foods, drugs, and devices. Analytical chemistry encompasses drug, pesticide, and hormone residues in foods; heavy metals in foods; analysis of microfibers (e.g. asbestos) in food, beverages, and drugs; and improved analytic methods for drugs. The pharmacology and pharmacokinetics area is concerned with metabolic effects of drugs in adults, children, and pregnant women; bioavailability; adverse reactions, toxicity; drug interactions;

and epidemiologic surveys on drug use. Toxicology includes carcinogenicity; mutagenicity; teratogenicity; rapid screening for toxins; aerosol toxicity; mycotoxins; and studies of cells in culture.

FDA conducts research in its own laboratories and also supports a significant number of external research projects at colleges and universities. Individual researchers who are interested in collaborating with FDA, with or without direct support, should contact the Associate Commissioner or Deputy Associate Commissioner for Science, Food and Drug Administration, 5600 Fishers Lane (RM 14-57), Rockville, Maryland 20852.

Center for Disease Control (CDC)

CDC is located in Atlanta, Georgia. It administers national programs for the prevention and control of communicable and vector-borne diseases and other preventable conditions.

Being one of the oldest of the federal agencies, and having gone through so many reorganizations and metamorphoses, PHS recognizes the importance of making information about its programs available. In addition to the seven-part series, *Public Health Service Grants and Awards*, mentioned earlier as a source of information for NIH and other HEW agencies, the PHS publishes a *Grants Policy Statement* (DHEW Publication No. (OS) 74-50,000) which provides potential applicants with a compilation of the salient features of policies applicable to PHS grants. It sets forth the basic framework within which grantee institutions and PHS agencies are expected to operate. For detailed information on PHS programs, write to the addresses indicated in Appendix IV.

EDUCATION DIVISION

The Education Amendments of 1972 split the functions of the Office of Education (OE) in three parts. The Office of Education (OE) and the National Institute of Education (NIE) are in HEW's Education

Division; the Fund for the Improvement of Postsecondary Education (FIPSE) is directly within the office of the assistant secretary, HEW, which has the responsibility also for the Education Division. NIE was assigned primary responsibility for educational research. FIPSE was given the mandate to improve the effectiveness and quality of postsecondary education.

Office of Education (OE)

OE administers about 100 programs and spends approximately $6 billion annually. The outlook for federal support of education is unclear in the light of the fiscal 1975 presidential budget message, but some trends can be recognized. A consistent anti-institution viewpoint is evident in a number of entries and omissions. Direct student aid is favored over institutional support for college students; institutional grants are almost entirely abolished; even the traditional authorizations for the land grant colleges were recommended for elimination. A kind of "educational revenue sharing" is suggested, particularly in the elementary and secondary education budget through the proposed consolidation of former categorical programs. Although the consolidation, which would give greater autonomy to the states in administration of education grants, has not been approved by Congress, it is a concept that has executive level support and is entirely consistent with the philosophy of the New Federalism. This approach has the potential for seriously affecting national education not only from the obvious standpoint of funding, but also as to policy decisions on interpretation of federal laws which, if left up to the states, may reflect local priorities and prejudices rather than the legislative intent.

The revision to the Elementary and Secondary Education Act which was signed into law in August, 1974 authorized continuation of many programs already in existence and establishment of several new programs. The Compensatory Education program was continued through fiscal 1978, but the formula for distribution of funds was changed to give more local input from the schools and school districts receiving the funds. Bilingual education was continued with a provision that recipients of grants for bilingual education include in their curriculum a program of English-language instruction for students with limited English-speaking ability. The Ethnic Heritage Studies

Centers authorization was extended through fiscal year 1978. Adult education, handicapped education, and Indian education programs were revised and extended. A new National Center for Educational Statistics was authorized and placed in the HEW Office of the Assistant Secretary of Education, thus removing statistics from OE.

The new legislation also placed limits on future appropriations to OE, setting the figures at $7.5 billion for fiscal 1975; $8 billion for 1976, and $9 billion for 1977. This limitation does not apply to the Guaranteed Student Loan Program, the Higher Education Facilities Program and the Emergency Insured Student Loan Act or other uncontrollable expenditures. The law also provides that the funds appropriated in one fiscal year, but not spent, will carry over to the next fiscal year.

The presidential budget message of 1975 asserted that "the goal of equality of educational opportunity has the greatest funding priority in higher education," but a look at the figures makes it clear that the word "undergraduate" is implied. Federal graduate student support has been declining rapidly, the only exception being made for American Indian graduate students. The National Board on Graduate Education reports that the number of fellowships and traineeships awarded in 1973 was 6,600 compared with 51,446 in 1967! There are no signs that this will change.

Support of education in the medical professions has been reduced. Even undergraduate support has been decreased in the areas of education professions development and in some manpower fields, e.g., nursing training. The National Research Act of 1974 provides for support of professional training in those health fields where personnel shortages exist, to be repaid by assigned service or in cash.

The individual undergraduate college student who is eligible for assistance through the Basic Educational Opportunity Grant program or for one of the loan programs will be reasonably well off compared with others through fiscal 1976.

National Institute of Education (NIE)

The National Institute of Education was created in 1972 to build an effective educational research and development system and, as one writer phrased it, "to wrest educational research from the arid bureaucracy of the Office of Education." The institute was born under a cloud; educators and education supporters were suspicious of the administration's efforts to boost educational research while money for education programs was being reduced and impounded. The first year's budget was $142.6 million, but the following year trouble developed between the agency and the House Appropriations Committee with disastrous results. The budget request for fiscal 1974 was $162 million but when the battle smoke cleared away only $75 million remained, scarcely enough to meet existing obligations. Rumor had it that fences were being mended for 1975 but if they were, they soon broke down again. The 1975 request for $130 million was slashed to $80 million by the House, and the Senate eliminated it entirely. The $80 million was restored by the Senate-House committee, but the outlook for this agency is very gloomy. It looks as if those who objected to removing the research component from OE may soon succeed in having it returned—or in abolishing government support of educational research entirely. The founding director, Thomas K. Glennan, Jr., resigned after these repeated budgetary rebuffs; a new director may be able to turn the tide but it is doubtful.

By law, NIE is required to expend 90 percent of its funds through grants and contracts for basic and applied research surveys, evaluations, experiments, and demonstrations in education. One of the major research objectives is to explore the relationship between various types of learning and working capabilities.

Fund for the Improvement of Postsecondary Education (FIPSE)

In following its mandate to improve the effectiveness and quality of postsecondary education, the Fund established two main goals: diversity and cost effectiveness. It also formulated eight purposes for which grants and contracts are to be awarded:

1. Encouraging the reform, innovation, and improvement of postsecondary education and provision of equal educational opportunity for all.
2. The creation of institutions and programs involving new paths to career and professional training and new combinations of academic and experimental learning.

3. The establishment of institutions and programs based on the technology of communications.
4. The carrying out in postsecondary educational institutions of changes in internal structure and operations designed to clarify institutional priorities and purposes.
5. The design and introduction of cost-effective methods of instruction and operation.
6. The introduction of institutional reforms designed to expand individual opportunities for entering and reentering institutions and pursuing programs of study tailored to individual needs.
7. The introduction of reforms in graduate education, in the structure of academic professions, and in the recruitment and retention of faculties.
8. The creation of new institutions and programs for examining and awarding credentials to individuals, and the introduction of reforms in current institutional practices related thereto.

The Fund operates through three programs: a *Comprehensive Program*, under which applicants may submit proposals related to any or all of the purposes for which the Fund makes awards; a *Special Focus Program*, which accepts proposals related to a particular educational need or approach identified as an important and timely "target of opportunity" for concentrated support; and a *National Projects* competition, which accepts proposals describing projects of national significance. Detailed information on the Fund's programs is available upon request from Program Announcement, Fund for the Improvement of Postsecondary Education, Department of Health, Education, and Welfare, 400 Maryland Avenue, S. W., Room 3141, Washington, D. C. 20202.

The following publications may be consulted for information on HEW's Division of Education programs:

American Education, the official journal of the Education Division, publishes an annual guide to HEW education programs, usually in the Spring issue.

The guide is a comprehensive listing that tells the type of activities supported, the total appropriation for each, who may apply, and where to apply, and gives the authorizing legislation and overall objective of each appropriation. It is organized in programs. The most recent listing is grouped as follows:

Group I
  Elementary and Secondary Education
  Strengthening Organization Resources
  Postsecondary Education
  Education for the Handicapped
  Support of Overseas Educational Programs
  Occupational, Adult, and Vocational Education
  Desegregation Assistance and Impact Aid
Group II
  Teacher and Other Professional Training and Student
    Assistance
Group III
  Research
Group IV
  Construction

Individual copies of the guide may be obtained free upon request to American Education, P.O. Box 9000, Alexandria, Virginia 22304. Subscriptions to *American Education*, which is published ten times a year, are $9.95 a year.

Educational Researcher is published seven times a year and carries a listing of current and proposed educational research. It may be ordered from: American Education Research Association, 1216 Sixteenth Street, N.W., Washington, D.C. 20036. Subscription cost: $5 a year.

OFFICE OF HUMAN DEVELOPMENT

The Office of Human Development in the office of the secretary, HEW, administers programs in child development, youth development, aging, and special programs for native Americans. The expenditure level is approximately $700 million annually, of which more than half is in child development.

Programs for the aging, authorized by the Older Americans Act, and programs for youth development were transferred to the Office of Human Development from the Social and Rehabilitation Service in 1974.

Aging programs are funded at approximately $200 million annually to improve the state and local nutritional programs, and for enhancing the capability of state agencies to launch or strengthen action programs for service delivery to older persons. A portion of the budget is for research on the effects of isolation on the physical and mental well-being of the elderly, the provision of recreational facilities for the aged populations, the development of effective methods of increasing the elderly's use of preventive and ambulatory care, and their housing and transportation needs.

Youth development programs are funded at about $10 million annually for community youth service programs for prevention, treatment, and control of juvenile delinquency. A special appropriation of $5 million was added in fiscal 1975 for the problems of runaways.

Special programs for native Americans, i.e., American Indians, are funded at approximately $30 million annually primarily for community service activities.

Information on programs of the Office of Human Development may be directed to the appropriate regional office or directly to the office of the secretary, HEW.

SOCIAL AND REHABILITATION SERVICES (SRS)

Since its inception in 1965, SRS has administered the "public assistance" programs of the Social Security Act, which offer aid to the states to finance programs for the aged, the blind, and dependent children, and for the permanently and totally disabled. The federal government makes grants to the states for these purposes on a three-for-one matching basis—three federal dollars for every local one. This turned out to be such a bonanza for the states and such a drain on the federal coffers that in fiscal 1973 Congress put a $2.5 billion limit on federal grants for social services. This was one of the administration moves called "welfare reform" to deal with what was being referred to as "the welfare mess."

SRS expends approximately 12.5 percent of the total HEW budget for the main objective of preparing disabled people for gainful employment, independent living, or greater self-care and for public assistance staff training. The philosophical impetus for this program is both altruistic and pragmatic. A study in the late 1940s indicated that the cost of rehabilitating each disabled person and returning him or introducing him to the ranks of the employed would eventually be repaid ten times over in tax returns to the federal treasury—not in every case, but on the average. SRS funds may be used for planning, administration, improvement of services, construction of facilities, and staffing rehabilitation facilities.

In each of the HEW regional offices, there is a Social and Rehabilitation Services staff which coordinates activities of SRS in each state.

The Department of Health, Education, and Welfare publishes a manual that is the basic guide on all aspects of administration and financial management of grants made by all agencies of HEW unless a specific exception is made. The *DHEW Grants Administration Manual* may be ordered from the Superintendent of Documents, U.S. Government Printing Office, Washington, D.C. 20402.

OTHER GOVERNMENT DEPARTMENTS

Department of Agriculture (USDA)

Through the Agricultural Research Service (ARS), the USDA conducts research programs in close cooperation with the states, other federal agencies, industry, foundations, and private groups for the purpose of providing new knowledge and technology that will improve methods and increase efficiency of food production and conserve the environment. Through the Cooperative State Research Service (CSRS), federal grants are administered for research in agriculture, agricultural marketing, and rural life, and for cooperative forestry research. The funds are made available through the state Agricultural Experiment Stations and other designated state institutions in the fifty states and Puerto Rico, Guam, and the Virgin Islands. CSRS administers a grant program for basic scientific research, a portion of which is earmarked for the 1890 land grant colleges. The current level of funding for the research and extension programs of USDA is between $500 and $600 million, out of total departmental expenditures of approximately $10 billion.

For information:

    ARS   Information Service
            Agricultural Research Service
            Department of Agriculture
            Washington, D.C. 20250
    CSRS   Division of Information
            Office of Management Services
            Cooperative State Research Service
            Department of Agriculture
            Washington, D.C. 20250

Department of Commerce

The National Oceanic and Atmospheric Administration (NOAA) conducts the Sea Grant Program to expand research in development of coastal management plans and research to increase the production and utilization of marine resources.

The Economic Development Administration (EDA) aids the development of public facilities and private enterprise to help create new jobs in areas with severe unemployment and low family income problems. Funds for this program are allocated by direct formula grants to the states on the basis of emergency conditions.

Commerce's National Bureau of Fire Prevention supports fire service education programs, including fire extension programs at state universities for research and development. The fire extension program incorporates some of the activities formerly conducted through the National Science Foundation and the National Bureau of Standards fire research programs.

The current funding level of the Department is between $1.5 and $2 billion.

For information:

EDA　Office of Administration and Program Analysis
Economic Development Administration
Department of Commerce
Washington, D.C. 20230
There are many regional offices of EDA and a complete listing with addresses is found in the *United States Government Manual* and the *Catalog of Federal Domestic Assistance* (CFDA)

NOAA　Office of Public Affairs
National Oceanic and Atmospheric Administration
Department of Commerce
Rockville, Maryland 20852

Other　Office of Organization and Management Systems
Department of Commerce
Washington, D.C. 20230

Department of Defense (DOD)

A large part of DOD's research and development is assigned by contract, and the department makes extensive use of the *Commerce Business Daily* (CBD) to invite bids or proposals.

The three services—Army, Navy, and Air Force—all have grant and contract programs through which they support research at colleges, universities, and other nonprofit as well as not-for-profit institutions.

The Office of Naval Research (ONR) which pioneered the university research contract, is the oldest scientific contracting agency of the federal government. It was set up on August 1, 1946, the same day the Atomic Energy Commission (which passed out of existence in 1974) was signed into law. Beginning in 1970 ONR support has been limited to research relevant to Navy needs and covers a wide range in the areas of material sciences, psychological-behavioral sciences, and ocean science and technology. All emerging technologies are limited by materials and ONR is especially interested in studies on polymer chemistry; structural mechanics relevant to underwater shock problems and laser damage; rocket fuels; and ceramics. In the behavioral field they are interested in studies on group living; stress caused by separation from home and family; and engineering psychology (fitting knobs to people). ONRs ocean science and technology program includes underwater acoustical studies; noise reduction on submarines; sensitivity devices; electro-optic devices (immune to electromagnetic radiation); statistics and probability; plasma physics; and fluid dynamics.

They give some support to biomedical sciences in very specific fields, predominantly related to underwater stress and effects of nonionizing radiation. There is also interest in amphibious medicine, i.e., delivery of health care afloat.

The contract is a major mechanism used by ONR for research but they also support some activities, such as conferences, through grants. The annual budget is around $57 million and ONR manages an amount nearly equal to that for other agencies. The largest portion of the budget, approximately $44 million, goes to universities; about $2 million goes to other nonprofit institutions; and $3 million is spent on intramural research. Only about 20 percent "turnover" occurs each year; the remainder is committed to continuing projects. The main criteria are: 1) relevance to Navy needs; 2) quality of the applicant, based on past performance; 3) new ideas—or an idea whose time is right, e.g., welding of alloys or work on laser physics.

Inquiries about possible ONR support should be directed to one of their branch offices located in Chicago, Boston, Pasadena, New York, or San Francisco. Formal proposals should be written only after discussion with a member of the ONR scientific staff. Information on ONR programs is available in two publications:

ONR-1   *How to Get a Contract*
ONR-17   *Opportunities for Research*

Requests for these should be directed to the scientific officer at one of the branch offices or to:

> Office of Naval Research
> Department of the Navy
> Ballston Tower #1
> 800 N. Quincy Street
> Arlington, Virginia 22217

The primary Air Force agency for the extramural support of fundamental scientific research is the *Air Force Office of Scientific Research* (AFOSR) in the Air Force Systems Command. AFOSR sponsors basic research with emphasis on fields that are likely to have the greatest impact on the Air Force. AFOSR has a budget of about $25 million annually and supports approximately 2,000 investigators on 900 projects at 200 universities, other nonprofit institutions, and not-for-profit institutions. For projects totaling less than $100,000, the grant mechanism is used; the contract is used for larger ones. Support is given for basic work in physics, chemical sciences, mathematical and information sciences, electronic and solid state sciences, aerospace sciences, and the life sciences.

The AFOSR encourages telephone calls, preliminary letters, or visits to their offices to discuss proposal ideas. An Air Force representative will also arrange to visit an institution to discuss a proposed research plan if a request is made for such a visit and it seems appropriate.

About 50 percent of all applications submitted are funded. The criteria are: (1) Does the proposal meet an Air Force need? (2) quality of the science; (3) investigator's qualifications; (4) reasonable cost.

Trends for the future indicate increased emphasis on relevance and a decrease in programmatic and institutional funding. No new institutional grants are being made, although some continuing ones are being maintained. Plans are to encourage awards that involve *partial* support, and to emphasize cooperation between in-house and extramural research.

The brochures *USAF Grants for Basic Research, USAF Contracts for Basic Research,* and *Proposer's Guide to the AFOSR Research Program* can be ordered from AFOSR/XP, 1400 Wilson Boulevard, Arlington, Virginia 22209.

Researchers whose investigations are outside the AFOSR areas of interest may direct proposals to other Air Force Systems Command organizations. A list of those organizations, together with a functional statement of each activity, is contained in the publication *AFSC Guide for Unsolicited Proposals*, obtainable on request to: HQ AFSC/ PPPR, Andrews AFB, Washington, D. C. 20334.

The *Army Research Office* (ARO), located on the campus of Duke University, combines some of the previous functions of the Army Research Office in Arlington, Virginia, which has been abolished, and those of the former Army Research Office–Durham. ARO sponsors basic research at universities, colleges, institutes, and industrial laboratories and conducts its own in-house programs in chemistry, electronics, engineering, geosciences, life sciences, mathematics, physics, and metallurgy and materials.

ARO's budget is approximately $14 million annually. Grants and contracts go predominantly to educational institutions (92 percent) and average about $25,000 each. The grant mechanism is used for approximately 77 percent of ARO awards and the contract for 21 percent. Awards to other government agencies account for the remainder.

Examples of specific ARO interests are: physiological studies related to adaptation to climatic extremes; materials sciences, especially chemistry of polymers; mechanics and aeronautics, e.g., studies relevant to helicopter structural vibration and noise control.

Evaluation of applications is based on relevance of the proposed activity to needs of the Army, scientific merit, qualifications of the applicant, and availability of facilities to do the work.

ARO sometimes asks the National Research Council of the National Academy of Sciences to provide reviewers for their applications or they may select as reviewers individual scientists known to be specialists in the subject field of an application.

ARO has a scientific service program under which researchers from academic institutions spend a summer or a semester working full time in an ARO laboratory. If the project is not completed by the end of the assignment, a grant may be given for continuation of the study for one academic year, after which the faculty member returns to the ARO laboratory and completes the project.

Army also has programs in the behavioral and social sciences and in the medical sciences. Inquiries may be addressed to the following:

Basic Research	U.S. Army Research Office Box CM, Duke Station Durham, North Carolina 27706
Behavioral and Social Sciences	Director, U.S. Army Research Institute for Behavioral and Social Sciences 1300 Wilson Boulevard Arlington, Virginia 22209.
Medical Sciences	Commander, U.S. Army Medical Research and Development Command (SGRD-ID) Washington, D. C. 20314.

Department of Housing and Urban Development (HUD)

The mandate of HUD is to develop the nation's communities and metropolitan areas. Research and technology programs are conducted through grants and contracts with industry, nonprofit research organizations, and educational institutions, and through agreements with state and local governments and other federal agencies, aimed at finding new approaches in the housing and community development area.

The first major housing measure to pass Congress since 1968 was given final approval in August, 1974. It calls for seven existing grant programs to be combined into a new $8.6 billion, three-year program of community development block grants. The grants will be distributed on the basis of population, overcrowding, and poverty, and will include the purposes formerly assigned to model cities, urban renewal, and similar programs.

HUD spends about $60 million annually on research and technology relevant to the housing field. Total annual spending of the department approximates $5 billion.

Information requests on HUD programs should be directed to the area offices; there are several area offices within each federal region. The address of the nearest area office is available from the

Catalog of Federal Domestic Assistance, from the Federal Information Centers listed in Appendix V, and in the *United States Government Manual*.

A booklet entitled *Guidelines for Submitting Unsolicited Proposals* can be requested from: Office of Policy Development and Research, Department of Housing and Urban Development, 451 Seventh Street, S.W., Washington, D.C., 20410.

Department of the Interior

The Department of the Interior is one of the four federal agencies most affected by the increased emphasis on energy research and the consolidation of all energy programs under the Energy Research and Development Administration (ERDA). Interior's fossil fuel research and development, metallurgy, coal research, and coal gasification pilot plant will be transferred to ERDA. The Secretary of Interior was named chairman of the Energy Resources Council. The Department of Interior has been active in research and technology on fossil fuels, with emphasis on conversion of coal to synthetic liquid fuels and on stimulating greater oil and gas recovery from known fields. Geothermal energy, power transmission, and energy conservation have also been Interior concerns in the past, but it now appears that these programs will devolve upon the new agency ERDA.

The Office of Coal Research has contracts with more than sixty organizations operating pilot plants and conducting research in coal gasification and liquefaction—methods that will make coal products available in nonpolluting forms and through nonpolluting delivery systems. The research activities of this office and the Bureau of Mines have been moved to ERDA.

Interior's Bureau of Land Management plans to initiate a series of studies to determine the impact of oil and gas development on the outer continental shelf.

The Department budget runs to about $3.5 billion annually, which includes ongoing energy research and development programs. The 1975 budget request included an additional $311.6 million for energy, but that will probably move into ERDA along with the Interior energy programs.

The Office of Water Resources Research supports research by private firms, consultants, nonprofit institutions, and colleges and universities on solving energy problems, land use problems, and efficient allocation and conservation of scarce water and water-related resources compatible with environmental conditions.

The National Park Service (NPS) makes grants-in-aid to states on a matching basis for special historic preservation projects in a Bicentennial-related program applicable to major cities which figure prominently in Revolutionary history.

Interior's Bureau of Indian Affairs (BIA) supports Indian education at the level of about $200 million annually. Special education projects such as scholarships grants for Indian students enrolling in colleges and universities, adult education services, and vocational training are some of the activities sponsored by BIA. Education support for Indian students is also included in programs of HEW's Office of Education.

Information requests may be directed to the appropriate office or program director, Department of the Interior, Washington, D.C. 20240. Program directors should be contacted before sending in unsolicited proposals.

Department of Justice

The Department of Justice traditionally represents the government in all legal matters, sees to the enforcement of the federal laws, and construes the laws under which other departments act. Justice was catapulted into the grants business by the Omnibus Crime Control and Safe Streets Act of 1968, which established the Law Enforcement Assistance Administration (LEAA) under the general authority of the attorney general. "Law enforcement" as defined in the act encompasses all activities pertaining to crime prevention or reduction and the enforcement of criminal law. LEAA's operations include a grants program which provides technical assistance to the states through the regional offices. The current level of appropriations for LEAA is just over $900 million, of which 85 percent is distributed by formula grants to the states to improve and strengthen law enforcement and the remaining 15 percent allocated for projects determined by the national office. The principles followed in administration of this program adhere to the New Federalism philosophy; reallocation and use of grants is left to the discretion of each state.

A *Guide for Discretionary Grant Programs* that provides information about programs and projects for which discretionary funds are available from LEAA can be obtained from the agency's regional offices. Regional office addresses are listed in the *Catalog of Federal Domestic Assistance* (CFDA).

LEAA's manpower development program expends about $45 million for education development, internships, and training in the latest law enforcement and criminal justice techniques and methods.

The Law Enforcement Education Program (LEEP) makes student loans and grants to law enforcement officers and other criminal justice system personnel for training on a full- or part-time basis in degree programs, mostly at the undergraduate level.

Requests for information on LEAA or LEEP programs should be directed to the appropriate regional office. For further information, write to: National Criminal Justice Reference Service, Law Enforcement Assistance Administration, Department of Justice, Washington, D.C. 20530.

Department of Labor

The Labor Department supports activities relevant to its programs through grants and contracts, under its Manpower Research and Development Program, and doctoral dissertation and small-grant research projects, under its Manpower Development and Training Program. Both programs are administered by the Manpower Administration (MA).

Research interests of the MA include the use and development of manpower; manpower program planning and administration; and studies of specific industries, occupations, population groups, and areas. Specific interests are topics such as training and work experience for prisoners and ex-offenders, welfare recipients, and young people; job creation and supported employment; upgrading and job restructuring; studies of the labor market; work incentive programs; and projects to facilitate the utilization of selected manpower.

Under the Manpower Development and Training Program, small grants and doctoral dissertation grants are given for research that falls within the Department's area of interest.

Through MA's Comprehensive Employment and Training Act (CETA), grants are made to states and local "prime sponsors" (cities and counties with populations in excess of 100,000; for smaller communities, the state is the "prime sponsor") for public employment programs, summer youth employment, job placement services, remedial education, and vocational education and counseling. Decisions on programs are made at the prime sponsor level, which is at the mayors' or county commissioners' offices for populous communities and at the governors' offices for others.

Some CETA programs are administered federally, such as special programs for older workers, criminal offenders, persons of limited English-speaking ability, migrant workers, Indians, and the Job Corps, as well as technical services, research, and demonstration and evaluation projects. The MA disburses about $2 billion annually of which over $40 million is for the national special programs and the remainder for grants to prime sponsors.

General information on Department of Labor programs may be obtained from Manpower Administration, U. S. Department of Labor, Washington, D. C. 20210. Regional directors are responsible for coordination of all grant and contract programs. Information requests should be directed to the appropriate regional office; addresses are given in the *Catalog of Federal Domestic Assistance* (CFDA) or may be obtained from the Federal Information Centers.

Department of State

The Department of State through its Bureau of Educational and Cultural Affairs manages programs for exchanges of students, teachers, and other educators between this and other nations. It brings leaders in government, politics, social welfare, and other fields to consult with colleagues in the United States and to observe American society and institutions in their fields of interest. It also sends American groups and individuals in the areas of the performing arts and athletics abroad to advise, coach, or give performances. The Educational and Cultural Exchange program is funded at a level of about $50 million annually.

Information on Fulbright-Hays awards is distributed by Information and Reference Division, International Institute of Education (IIE), 809 United Nations Plaza, New York, New York 10017.

The State Department publishes a *Directory of Contacts for International Educational, Cultural, and Scientific Exchange Programs*, which is a useful guide to sources of information about international programs. It is distributed by Office of Policy and Plans, Bureau of Educational and Cultural Affairs, U.S. Department of State, Washington, D.C. 20502.

Intercultural Studies Information Service, published by the Foreign Area Materials Center nine times a year, contains information on foreign area studies and intercultural and international education. It is distributed by Foreign Area Materials Center, 60 East 42nd Street, New York, New York 10017.

Far Horizons, published quarterly by the State Department, gives information on research funding, research conferences, new research centers, new publications for U.S. government-supported and private research dealing with foreign areas, international relations, and foreign policy. Order from Superintendent of Documents, U.S. Government Printing Office, Washington, D.C. 20402. Subscriptions: $3.00 per year.

The Agency for International Development (AID) publishes a quarterly booklet, *AID Research and Development Abstracts* (ARDA), listing current research findings in various institutions and international research centers. Its function is to promote exchange of ideas and useful information among nations on topics of mutual interest. To receive ARDA, send name, title, and address to Department of State, AID, Technical Assistance Bureau, TA/RIG, Editor of ARDA, Washington, D.C. 20523.

Department of Transportation (DOT)

In 1972 the DOT inaugurated the University Research Program aimed at enlarging the role of universities in assisting the department to achieve its objectives by utilizing the resources of the higher education community more effectively in dealing with transportation problems. The stated purposes of the program include support of university-based seminars and conferences to bring university, government, and industry representatives together for joint studies of transportation problems. The main objectives are: to stimulate relevant, high-quality, and innovative transportation research at universities for the creation of new concepts, techniques, and knowledge; to encourage the use of modern tools of analysis, planning and management, and new technology, and of professionally trained people by state, regional, and local transportation agencies; to stimulate industry and local, state, and regional agency sponsorship of university-based transportation research.

Eligible applicants include any accredited nonprofit institution of higher education within the United States which offers baccalaureate and/or graduate degrees. Principal investigators must be full-time faculty members (whose duties must include teaching). Student participation is encouraged. Universities are encouraged to seek cooperation with state and local governments or with industry in performing the research. Criteria for consideration of proposals include: the relevance of the solution of important transportation problems, professional merit of the proposed research, and qualifications of the investigator.

In 1974 the National Mass Transportation Assistance Act was passed. It is a 6-year, $11.8 billion federal commitment to the support of mass transportation for both urban and rural areas. Funds may be used for construction and systems improvement grants and operating subsidies. This is the first federal legislation to include *operating* expenses for urban transportation facilities, and the first to provide any support to rural areas.

The Urban Mass Transportation Administration (UMTA) has been dispensing about $75 million annually for research, development, and demonstration projects through grants and contracts in urban transportation testing, and development of new techniques, facilities, etc. It is impossible to estimate what portion of the new appropriation will go into research and development since it will be distributed to cities and communities to be used for operating as well as new construction and development purposes. Grants will be made to cities and apportioned by categories: 54 percent to large metropolitan areas that already have mass transit systems in operation; 41 percent to cities with populations of more than 50,000 who do not have systems in operation (26 percent for construction grants or capital projects and 15 percent for operating or capital expenditures); the remainder will go to urban areas of less than 50,000 population and rural areas. Research and development grants and contracts resulting from this program will be administered through the cities to which the block grants are made.

The University Research and Training Program for interdisciplinary studies that combine professional training in urban transportation and related fields, and the Managerial Training Program, which provides fellowships for one year of advanced training for managers, technicians, and professionals in the urban mass transportation field, are budgeted, together, for about $4 million.

Projected annual expenditures for the DOT during the next five years are $10 to $12 billion.

For information on transportation research opportunities for universities under the Program of University Research, write to: Office of University Research (TST-60), Office of the Secretary, U.S. Department of Transportation, Washington, D.C. 20590.

For general information, write to the specified office at: U.S. Department of Transportation, Washington, D.C. 20590, or to Information Center, Department of Transportation, 400 Seventh Street, S.W., Washington, D.C. 20590.

Independent and Specialized Agencies

Among the approximately forty independent offices, commissions, agencies, and boards are some whose functions are solely regulatory or administrative; for example, the Federal Power Commission, the U. S. Tariff Commission, or the Federal Deposit Insurance Company. However, a number of them support research and other activities through grants, and some of their programs are quite extensive.

The National Science Foundation (NSF), the Energy Research and Development Administration (ERDA), National Aeronautics and Space Administration (NASA), and the Environmental Protection Agency (EPA) support scientific research. The bulk of federal support for the arts and the humanities is dispensed through another independent agency, the National Foundation on the Arts and the Humanities (National Endowment for the Arts, NEA, and National Endowment for the Humanities, NEH).

National Science Foundation (NSF)

The National Science Foundation supports research in the sciences, both basic and applied; awards scholarships and graduate fellowships in the sciences; and supports development and uses of computer and other scientific methods and technologies applicable to research and education in the sciences. NSF also provides a central clearinghouse for the collection, interpretation, and analysis of data on scientific and technical resources; collects information on the amount of federal funds received by universities and other nonprofit organizations for the conduct of scientific research, both basic and applied; and reports on this to the president and to the Congress.

During the fiscal year 1973, NSF made a total of 10,561 grant awards, totaling $605.9 million. Of that number, 6,138 were in support of fundamental research in all scientific disciplines and 1,630 went for graduate student support and science education improvement. The discipline receiving the most research awards was biological sciences (1,584) and the next three, in order, were mathematics (758), chemistry (675), and engineering (663). The remainder went to physics, atmospheric sciences, earth sciences, oceanography, astronomy, engineering, and scientific materials research, with 635 going to the social sciences.[7]

Social sciences programs at NSF received scanty attention until the mid-1960s, when recognition of the nation's mounting social problems resulted in a great deal of pressure for the establishment of a National Social Sciences Foundation equivalent in size to the NSF. The proposal was rejected, but beginning in 1968 there has been a

---

[7] National Science Foundation, NSF 74-3, January, 1974.

formal social sciences program within NSF which has grown steadily both in support levels and range of disciplines included. The program came in for severe criticism by the congressional subcommittee in charge of NSF appropriations during the deliberations on the 1975 budget. It seems to have survived without serious damage with a budget at the same level as the previous year, approximately $42 million.

Within the social sciences division there are programs for anthropology, economics, geography, history and philosophy of science, law and social science, sociology, social psychology, and science policy research.

NSF's remaining 2,793 awards for 1973 went to support programs directed to carrying out specific tasks, i.e., programs with defined goals toward which research can be directed, such as the Research Applied to National Needs (RANN) programs (616) and International Cooperative Scientific Activities (674).[8]

More than 50 percent, approximately $330.3 million, was spent for fundamental research and education activities, and $275.6 for everything else. The number of awards can be misleading as a gauge of support level because many international awards were very small travel grants. On the other hand, the size of awards made under the RANN program ranges from a few thousand to more than $1 million.

In comparison with HEW or even with only one of its agencies, the National Institute of Health, NSF is a small agency—its current budget is less than $800 million—but its impact on scientific research and education has been far greater than the size of its budget might indicate. There is scarcely an institution of any size in the nation that has not been directly or indirectly a recipient of NSF support for science education, and many students and scholars around the world have been the beneficiaries of one or the other NSF program. NSF support of basic scientific research has been the backbone of research programs for many universities and nonprofit research institutions whose development and accomplishments in their particular areas would have been impossible otherwise.

The Division of Advanced Energy Research and Technology supports research in nuclear, solar, geothermal, and other advanced

[8] National Science Foundation, NSF 74-3, January, 1974.

energy systems, but in January, 1975, the focus of advanced solar and geothermal research was shifted to the newly established Energy Research and Development Administration (ERDA). NSF will continue to make available to ERDA results of longer-range basic and applied research supported by NSF.

The energy research programs of NSF are an integral part of the RANN program, which includes, in addition to the Division of Advanced Energy Research and Technology, three other major programs:

Advanced Environmental Research and Technology Division— regional environmental systems; environmental aspects of trace heavy metals, nitrate contamination, atmospheric contamination, and analytical methodology; weather modification; environmental effects of energy; and disaster and natural hazard research.

Advanced Productivity Research and Technology Division—municipal systems and services; human resources and services; social data and evaluation; public regulation and economic productivity; technological opportunities in advanced industrial processing; enzyme technology; industrial automation; excavation technology; and instrumentation technology.

Office of Exploratory Research and Problem Assessment—technology assessment; consumer and marketplace; minority group problems; societal implications of an aging population; and technology-related transnational problems.

An overview of all NSF programs, contained in *NSF Guide to Programs*, is easy to obtain, well written, clear, and understandable. There are separate brochures for every sizable program. Information requests should be directed to: Public Affairs Office, National Science Foundation, Washington, D. C. 20550.

The *National Science Foundation Bulletin*, issued monthly except in July and August, disseminates information on programs, policies, and activities of the NSF. Request it from: NSF Bulletin, Resource Office, National Science Foundation, Washington, D. C. 20550.

Energy Research and Development Administration (ERDA)

In the past 25 years, 75 to 80 percent of federal energy research has been in nuclear science, administered largely through the Atomic

Energy Commission (AEC), which has been in the vulnerable position of being both the promoter and the regulator of nuclear energy.
The Energy Reorganization Act of 1974 abolished the AEC and established three new federal entities: the Energy Research and Development Administration (ERDA), the Energy Resources Council, and the
Nuclear Regulatory Commission. The purpose of this measure was to
consolidate all federal research and development in order to more
effectively direct the efforts to achieve national energy independence,
and to ensure neutrality among the competing technologies thereby
precluding domination of the field by nuclear energy R & D.

The Energy Resources Council, which formulates the nation's
energy policy, is chaired by former Secretary of Interior Rogers C. B.
Morton, and has as members the Secretary of State, the administrator
of ERDA, the administrator of the Federal Energy Administration, the
director of the Office of Management and Budget, and others. The
Council will be responsible for coordinating the energy research and
development programs run by different federal agencies.

The Nuclear Regulatory Commission will be concerned with the
licensing of nuclear facilities and other regulatory functions. The
Commission's Office of Nuclear Regulatory Research will be responsible for developing an independent capability for evaluating technical information relating to reactor safety, safeguards, and environmental protection in supporting the licensing and regulatory process.
It is probable that some of the research involving effects of different
technologies upon the health and ecology of the nation, formerly in
the domain of the Environmental Protection Agency, will be taken
over by the Office of Nuclear Regulatory Research.

ERDA will assume all the functions of the AEC except the regula-
tory activities. It will also absorb the Department of Interior's Office of
Coal Research, the fossil fuel research and development activities of
Interior's Bureau of Mines energy centers and coal gasification pilot
plant, some of the metallurgy research, and the National Science
Foundation's programs in advanced solar and geothermal studies.
ERDA will also take over the Environmental Protection Agency's
program on alternative automotive power systems.

The major divisions of ERDA are headed by assistant administrators who are expert in the following research fields: nuclear power;
fossil fuels; environment and safety; conservation; solar, geothermal

and advanced energy systems; and national security. The research emphasis will be in physics and environmental and biological sciences, and the program will include extension of scientific capabilities to support all energy fields.

A comprehensive Solar Energy Research Development and Demonstration Act was also passed in 1974, calling for an intensive program aimed at advancing the commercial development of various solar energy technologies. Research will be concentrated in the fields of thermal energy conversion; bioconversion of organic materials to useful energy or fuels; photovoltaic or other direct conversion processes; ocean thermal power conversion; solar heating and cooling of buildings; direct solar heat as a source of industrial processes; and energy storage. The act calls for the establishment of a Solar Energy Research Institute to be located at an existing or a new federal laboratory.

These new energy programs are scheduled to begin operations early in 1975, and guidelines should be available by that time.

National Aeronautics and Space Administration (NASA)

The prospects for NASA grants and contracts to colleges, universities, and nonprofit research institutions have never been so poor since NASA was created in 1958. In 1965–66 NASA spent approximately $46 million in university programs, through major predoctoral fellowship and traineeship programs, multidisciplinary research, and grants for facilities related to both types of programs. NASA spending at universities had declined to $2 million by 1974 and to only $400,000 for 1975. Clearly, *that* heyday is over.

NASA is redirecting some of its research and technology programs toward reduction of petroleum energy requirements and the search for fuels other than those based on petroleum. Emphasis is also being placed on reducing the undesirable environmental effects of civil and military aircraft. Some of the research in these areas may well be assigned to universities and research institutions through grants and contracts, but it is not likely to be a lucrative source of funding for the immediate future.

For information: NASA Headquarters Information Center, Washington, D.C. 20546.

Environmental Protection Agency (EPA)

EPA supports research and development and demonstration efforts on a wide variety of subjects primarily related to pollution sources and effects, environmental sciences, and pollution control technology. It is primarily a regulatory and enforcement agency, and its scientific and technological programs are aimed at analysis, data collection, and confirmation on environmental effects of pollutants— studies that provide the technology for EPA to fulfill its mission.

The main program interests are: effects on health and ecology of environmental pollutants; essential technology to control pollution and provide the public with the means of meeting the EPA requirements; and the development of technology to enable EPA to perform its monitoring functions.

EPA programs are administered through four National Environmental Research Centers at Cincinnati, Ohio; Corvallis, Oregon; Las Vegas, Nevada; and Research Triangle Park, North Carolina.

Specific areas of interest are:

1. Air—health and ecological effects of air pollution and control technology, for example, smokestack effluents.
2. Water—marine ecology, primarily related to ocean dumping and outfalls in coastal areas; water quality health effects; sludge problems; waste water treatment plants; and water supply—health effects, especially development of small purification systems for small communities.
3. Pesticides—the scientific basis for the cancellation of DDT use, for example.
4. Radiation—verification and maintenance of information for the new Office of Nuclear Regulatory Research.
5. Noise—effects of noise on the environment—this program is being reduced.
6. Interdisciplinary program—the National Center for Toxicological Research in Pine Bluff, Arkansas has responsibility for interdisciplinary research relevant to protection of the environment.
7. Overhead monitoring.
8. Toxic substances.

The role of EPA in the new energy programs is not clearly defined, but it will be concerned with health and ecological effects associated with increased energy sources, such as coal mining and stimulated production of oil and gas.

Control technology interests of EPA include studies of hydrocarbons that are carcinogenic; stack gases; alternate methods of combustion or removal of particulates; alternate methods of removing fossil fuels from the earth; and cleaner uses of energy.

The nation's economic difficulties are making it apparent that in the conflict between economic development and environment, the environment will probably come out second. It was, therefore, encouraging to hear the former secretary of the interior, Rogers C. B. Morton, chairman of the Energy Resources Council, state before the American Mining Congress late in 1974 that: "The people of the United States are not going to see the resources of this nation locked up and left unused—but the people of America are also intelligent enough to know that they must weigh the costs of each action and the results of that action. The American public is not going to be stampeded into environmental disaster by the energy shortage scare—they will not buy the slogan, 'Let them freeze in the dark.' We want to have light and have heat and still be able to see through the air and drink the water."

EPA announces the availability of Requests for Proposals (RFPs) in the *Commerce Business Daily* (CBD) and also accepts unsolicited proposals for both contracts and grants. Grant applications for demonstration or research projects may be submitted at any time, but prospective applicants are advised to communicate with the appropriate personnel in one of the National Environmental Research Centers before submitting a final proposal. Scientific/technical merit review of proposals is conducted by both intramural and extramural evaluators.

Information on EPA programs is available at the National Research Centers and at EPA's ten regional offices, addresses listed in the *Catalog of Federal Domestic Assistance* (CFDA). Requests may also be sent to Allowance Staff (RD-674), Office of Research and Development, Environmental Protection Agency, 401 M Street, S. W., Washington, D. C. 20460.

National Foundation on the Arts and the Humanities

The National Foundation on the Arts and the Humanities consists of the National Endowment for the Arts (NEA), the National Endowment for the Humanities (NEH), and the Federal Council on the Arts and Humanities. Each endowment has its own council, composed of the endowment chairman and twenty-six other members. The councils advise the two chairmen on policies and procedures, review applications for financial support, and make recommendations for action on them. In the last instance, decisions on proposals are the responsibility of the chairmen, but the broad-based knowledge and collective wisdom represented by the council membership carries great weight.

The federal government's entry into the fields of the humanities and the arts in 1965 with the establishment of the National Foundation on the Arts and Humanities was greeted by both cheers and jeers. The jeers were mostly from professionals in the arts fields— "Like a gorilla trying to thread a needle," was the way painter Larry Rivers phrased it. But after ten years, the cheers have become louder and the jeers barely audible. Writing in the *New Yorker* magazine, August 5, 1974, art critic Harold Rosenberg stated, "This season, not a single museum was able to mount a major exhibition without contributions from the National Endowment for the Arts. . . ." The Metropolitan Opera was saved from reducing its 1974–75 season by four to six weeks because of a timely infusion of funds through a $1 million matching grant from the Arts Endowment which, since it is a fifty-fifty matching grant, will result in an additional $2 million for operating money to the Met.

Dr. Ronald Berman, chairman of the Humanities Endowment, is proud to be head of "the only place in the world giving money to the humanities." Dr. Berman closed a speech to the American Council of Learned Societies in 1974 by saying, "I see in this room those who have formed the intellectual life of a nation . . . if we don't restore the humanities and make them new in all their integrity, in this culture, there is no one else who will."

The two endowments operate quite independently, although there is a shared staff for administrative functions. There is some overlap in programs, and applications are occasionally referred from one to the other. Both contribute to film programs and museums and they both support writing projects. In an effort to define the difference between the literary programs, one Humanities staff member is quoted as saying (facetiously, of course): "Arts deals with people who can write but can't spell; Humanities supports those who can spell but can't write."

In sharp contrast to many federal programs, National Endowment budgets have consistently been recommended for substantial increases each year in the president's budget presentation to Congress. They have usually been trimmed in both the House and the Senate but the annual budgets have increased steadily. It is expected that following the Bicentennial celebration in 1976 funding for the Humanities Endowment may level off at approximately the current figure, in the neighborhood of $75 million.

National Endowment for the Humanities (NEH). NEH was established out of concern that the United States' position of world leadership be based on achievement in the realm of ideas and of the spirit as well as on superior power, wealth, and technology. In setting up this new agency, Congress was responding to an increased awareness on the part of educators, legislators, and the general public that the humanities required sustained and widespread federal support. Although a few large foundations have consistently supported the humanities to a limited extent and at least one has expressed the intention to increase support in that area, the National Endowment is the major source of support for the humanities in the United States, or for that matter in the world.

The act establishing the endowment defined the humanities as including, but not limited to, the following fields: history, philosophy, languages, linguistics, literature, archeology, jurisprudence, history and criticism of the arts, ethics, comparative religion, and those aspects of the social sciences employing historical or philosophical approaches. The last category includes cultural anthropology, sociology, political theory, international relations, and other subjects concerned with values and nonquantitative matters.

NEH does not provide funds of a "formula" or "program" nature; its grants are awarded competitively and on individual merit. However, the Public Programs Division has established a state-based program through which groups in each state act as regrant agencies in support of Public Programs projects. The Public Programs activities involve individual academic humanists from universities and non-academic institutions such as museums and libraries in programs designed to develop instruments suited to broad national dissemination, increased understanding of the humanities, and discussion of public issues from the humanistic viewpoint. In fiscal 1974, 40 percent of the NEH expenditures went into state, community, and public programs which, for the most part, were selected by state or local committees that determine which programs are most suitable for their geographic areas.

In addition to the Public Programs Division, the other major divisions of NEH are the Division of Education, Fellowships Division, and Research Grants Division.

The Education Division supports projects and programs to renew and strengthen the impact of teaching in the humanities, both in liberal arts and in vocational and professional curricula.

The Fellowships Division provides stipends to enable individual scholars, teachers, and nonacademic humanists to study areas which may be directly related to the work they characteristically perform.

In fiscal 1974, the Research Grants Division funded 175 grants for a total of $6.5 million in program funds and $5 million in matching funds, for research in the humanities with substantial emphasis on matters of national concern, to centers for research in priority areas, and to the editing of significant humanistic texts.

Through the Research and Fellowships programs NEH disbursed approximately $18 million in 1974 for scholarly research and study in the humanities.

The Endowment also has a Youthgrants in the Humanities Program, which operates through the Endowment's Office of Planning and supports projects designed and conducted specifically by young people who need not have either academic affiliation or an academic degree to apply. Applicants should preferably be not more than thirty years old and may apply directly or through nonprofit organizations.

NEH accepts applications from universities; four-year colleges; junior and community colleges; elementary and secondary schools; educational, cultural, and community groups; museums and histori-

cal societies; libraries; public agencies; and radio and television stations. Applications are accepted from United States citizens or nationals and from foreign nationals who have been living in the United
States or its territories for at least three years at the time of application. Support *may* be afforded to any individual or organization
whose work, in the judgment of the National Council (or the chairman acting in their behalf), promises significantly to advance knowledge and understanding of the humanities in the United States.

National Endowment for the Arts (NEA). The mandate of the
NEA is to foster growth and development of the arts, to preserve and
enrich the nation's cultural resources and to provide opportunities for
wider experience in all the arts.

Grants are made to individuals and nonprofit organizations in
the fields of architecture and environmental arts, dance, education,
expansion arts, literature, museums, music, public media (radio,
television, and film), theater, and the visual arts. Awards are made in
the form of fellowships to individuals of exceptional talent; program
funds to organizations for up to one-half the total cost of the project,
the other half provided by the applicant organization; and Treasury
Fund awards, funded jointly by NEA, a nonfederal contributing
donor, and the applicant organization. A portion of the funds appropriated annually for the NEA is allocated to state and regional arts
committees, who have complete independence in determining activities they will support.

The Arts and the Humanities budgets have been maintained at
very similar levels. The Director of NEA since 1969, Nancy Hanks,
has the wisdom, charm, wit, beauty, genius, or whatever it requires
to persuade Congress to approve NEA budgets, and it appears that
future appropriations for the Arts Endowment will continue to rise or
at least remain stable as long as she remains at the head of the agency.

NEA gets its greatest publicity from large grants made to national
opera, music, or dance groups, but a great deal of its support goes to
grass-roots activity in small towns and inner cities. Abandoned rail-
road stations have been converted into local cultural centers; children
have received instruction in clowning techniques; and arts and crafts
"heritage weekends" in West Virginia have been supported with

NEA funds. Grants have been given to jazz clubs, pottery work-shops, and street theaters. The Arts Endowment likes projects that travel around. One theater company received grants in 1973 and 1974 to float on a raft down the Mississippi River and perform for field hands and townsfolk at landings along the way.

The gorilla may not get the thread through the eye of the needle every time, but like the dog that sings off key, the astounding thing is that he does it at all.

The NEA has compiled a list of federal funding sources for the arts entitled *Cultural Directory: Guide to Federal Funds and Services for Cultural Activities,* which can be ordered from Associated Council of the Arts, 1564 Broadway, New York, N. Y. 10036 for $4.00.

The staffs that have been assembled for both Endowments are unusual for their enthusiasm, their diligence to the assigned task, and the friendly spirit with which requests for information and assistance are received. Telephone or mail requests for information are an-swered promptly and no visitor is turned away without attention. The atmosphere in the Endowment offices is different from that of many federal agencies. Dignity and competence are not lacking but the atmosphere is casual, easy, and relaxed. A visitor wandering in off the street would not be likely to make the mistake of thinking himself to be in the Pentagon.

Both Endowments have brochures describing their entire range of programs, and many of the divisions publish their own program descriptions and guidelines.

For information, write to: National Endowment for the Arts, or National Endowment for the Humanities, Washington, D.C. 20506.

INFORMATION SOURCES—GOVERNMENTAL PROGRAMS

The Public Information law, often called the Freedom of Informa-tion Act, became effective on July 4, 1967 and was amended and strengthened in 1974. It requires each governmental agency at every level to be free with information and advice and to make available to the public information regarding its organization, procedures, functions, general policy interpretations, and all amendments, revisions, or repeal of those elements, except for highly classified security material. This statute makes it incumbent upon every federal agency with grant funds at its disposal to announce its programs and to be cooperative, even generous, in responding to requests for information, forms, instruction, or guidance.

Federal agencies take this requirement seriously and most programs that offer grant possibilities have printed information, guidelines, application forms, and other appropriate materials which they willingly distribute upon request.

In order to facilitate the dissemination of information on all aspects of the federal government, including programs and services, Federal Information Centers are maintained throughout the country by the General Services Administration. Any individual may visit, telephone, or write the Centers and ask for information. For a complete list of Federal Information Centers and the cities they are located in, including the tie-line telephone numbers which serve some localities, see Appendix V.

Bill Status System—Legislative "Hot Line"

One of the best ways to keep up with the latest information on federal programs is to follow closely the progress of appropriations bills through Congress. This can be a confusing and difficult task, but in order to make it easier Congress has instituted a system called the Bill Status System. It provides information to any member of Congress or to the public on legislation past and pending during current sessions of Congress.

Telephone information can be obtained over the legislative "hot line" (the number during the ninety-third session of Congress was (202) 225-1772 and may still be the same), by giving the operator the bill number, author, or subject. Written information may be requested from Bill Status System, House Information Systems, Committee on House Administration, U.S. Congress, Washington, D.C. 20515.

Depository Libraries for Government Publications

Large public libraries and libraries of major universities where there is a graduate school may be and often are designated as depositories for government publications. These depositories render an invaluable service by keeping government publications and making them permanently available to residents of every state, the District of Columbia, Guam, Puerto Rico, and the Virgin Islands. Distribution is made to libraries by the Office of the Superintendent of Documents and publications are retained permanently even after their stocks have been exhausted or they are permanently out of print and can no longer be ordered from the superintendent of documents.

Designated regional depositories are required to receive and retain one copy of all government publications made available to depository libraries either in printed or microfacsimile form. Some libraries are "restricted" depositories and they are allowed to select the classes of publications best suited to the interests of their clientele.

The *Catalog of Federal Domestic Assistance*, as well as the *Federal Register* and other documents containing information about federal funding programs, can be found in all designated regional depositories and in many of the restricted depositories. Information about the governmental holdings of any library can be obtained from its information service. A listing of all government depository libraries of the United States can be ordered from: Chief of the Library, Department of Public Documents, U.S. Government Printing Office, Washington, D.C. 20402.

United States Government Manual

The official handbook of the federal government, an annual publication, the *United States Government Manual* (formerly the *Government Organization Manual*) is in itself a lavish, but concise and well-organized, source of information, and the 1973–74 edition added a special section called "Guide to Government Information" to indicate some of the media which can help the individual citizen keep abreast of government activities and requirements. The "Guide" explains how to keep in touch with U.S. Government publications, discusses the Code of Federal Regulations, the *Federal Register*, and other information sources. The main body of the *Manual* contains descriptions of all federal agencies and the current edition emphasizes the activities of each one rather than the internal agency structure. The write-ups of agencies that have grant programs include addresses to which requests for grant information may be directed.

Order from: Superintendent of Documents, U.S. Government Printing Office, Washington, D.C. 20402. Price: $5.75.

Federal Register

This is the medium for making available to the public federal agency regulations and other legal documents of the executive branch, covering a wide range of government activities. The *Register* includes proposed changes in regulated areas, many of which presage the announcement of new grants programs or changes in current programs. Published daily and found in all Federal Depository libraries and Federal Information Centers.

Order from: Superintendent of Documents, U.S. Government Printing Office, Washington, D.C. 20402. Subscription: $45.00 yearly; $5.00 monthly.

Catalog of Federal Domestic Assistance (CFDA)

Specifically in order to assist the grant seeker in identifying the purposes for which federal assistance is available, the government has taken a leaf from the Sears Roebuck catalog, so to speak, and put out a catalog of its own, *Catalog of Federal Domestic Assistance* (CFDA).

CFDA is a comprehensive listing and description of federal programs and activities which provide assistance or benefits to the American public. It gives information on grants, loans, loan guarantees, scholarships, mortgage loans, and insurance or other types of financial assistance. It also lists sources of assistance in the form of or provision of federal property, facilities, equipment, goods, or services—including the donation of surplus, real, or personal property.

The CFDA is organized into three indexes: a functional index, a subject index, and an agency program index. Detailed program descriptions in the center portion of the catalog are listed in the same order as the agency program index, alphabetically by name of the agency.

Continuous updating keeps the catalog as current as possible, but the rapidity with which federal programs are wiped out and new ones established is such that it cannot be assumed that any listing is completely accurate at any given time. The catalog should be used, therefore, only as a guide to indicate which agencies to approach for information on a program that appears to be of interest and appropriate.

The last section of the catalog provides addresses of regional and local federal offices that can be contacted for additional information on listed programs and on application procedures. This last section is very important because many programs are handled through state agencies, and the regional and local offices can provide assistance and guidance to applicants for those programs or in other cases refer the inquirer to the appropriate Washington, D.C. agency.

The CFDA, a publication of the Executive Office of the President, Office of Management and Budget, may be ordered from: Superintendent of Documents, U.S. Government Printing Office, Washington, D.C. 20402. The cost of the 1974 issue was $14.30.

This catalog is also available on magnetic tape, 7 track, 556 and 800 BPI, odd and even parity; or 9 track, 800 BPI, odd parity, for those who have computer equipment available. The taped version may be ordered from: National Technical Information Service, U.S. Department of Commerce, Springfield, Virginia 22151. Stock No. is PB-207823. Price (as of this writing) is $97.60.

A sample page from the CFDA will be found on p. 98 annotated to indicate the significance of each element of information included in each entry.

Commerce Business Daily (CBD)

CBD, published by the Department of Commerce, is the medium through which the federal government announces bidding opportu-

ENVIRONMENTAL PROTECTION AGENCY

OFFICE OF AIR AND WATER PROGRAMS

66.001   AIR POLLUTION CONTROL PROGRAM GRANTS

(1) **FEDERAL AGENCY:** OFFICE OF AIR AND WATER PROGRAMS, ENVIRONMENTAL PROTECTION AGENCY

(2) **AUTHORIZATION:** Sections 105 and 106, Clean Air Act of 1963; Public Law 88-206 as amended by Public Law 91-604; 42 U.S.C. 1857c.

(3) **OBJECTIVES:** To assist State, local, regional, and interstate agencies in planning, developing, establishing, improving, and maintaining adequate programs for prevention and control of air pollution or implementation of national primary and secondary air quality standards.

(4) **TYPES OF ASSISTANCE:** Project Grants.

(5) **USES AND USE RESTRICTIONS:** Grant funds may be used for costs specifically incurred in the conduct of a project in accordance with the purposes enumerated in the approved application. These include personnel costs, supplies, equipment, training of personnel, travel, and other necessary expenditures during the approved project period. Funds may not be used for construction of facilities, not for expenses incurred other than during each approved award period.

(6) **ELIGIBILITY REQUIREMENTS:**
Applicant Eligibility: Any local, regional, State, or interstate agency with legal responsibility for air pollution control is eligible for grant support provided such organization furnishes funds for the current year in excess of its expenditures for the previous year for its air pollution program.
Beneficiary Eligibility: Same as applicant eligibility.
Credentials/Documentation: The application must supply evidence of legal authority for air pollution control; evidence of the availability of non-Federal matching funds; and a workable program officially adopted for the agency. A State Plan, coordinated with the Governor's office, is required under Part III of OMB Circular No. A-95 (revised).

(7) **APPLICATION AND AWARD PROCESS:**
Preapplication Coordination: Applications should be reviewed under procedures in Part I of OMB Circular A-95 (revised). Prior to approval of any grants, the official State air pollution control agency must coordinate local efforts. The standard application forms as furnished by the Federal agency and required by OMB Circular A-102 must be used for this program.
Application Procedure: Requests for application forms and completed applications should be submitted to the Grants Administration Division, Environmental Protection Agency, Washington, DC 20460. Application must meet the requirements of the grant regulations and will be reviewed to determine merit and relevancy of the proposed project.
Award Procedure: Notification of grant award must be made to the State Central Information Reception Agency and required by OMB on SF 240.
Deadlines: None.

Range of Approval/Disapproval Time: 90 to 120 days.
Appeals: None.
Renewals: None.

(8) **ASSISTANCE CONSIDERATIONS:**
Formula and Matching Requirements: For pre-maintenance programs in State, interstate and regional—an approved State Implementation Plan—up to 75 percent Federal; others 66⅔ percent Federal. For maintenance grants: State Implementation Plan—up to 75 percent Federal; others 66⅔ percent Federal. For maintenance grants: 10 percent of the funds available shall be granted for air pollution control programs in any one State.
Length and Time Phasing of Assistance: The term of grant shall be determined at time of grant award.

(9) **POST ASSISTANCE REQUIREMENTS:**
Reports: As specified in grant award (usually quarterly interims and final progress and expenditure reports).
Audits: Subject to inspection and audit by EPA and Comptroller General.
Records: Financial records, including all documents to support entries on the accounting records and to substantiate charges to each grant, must be kept available to personnel authorized to examine EPA grant accounts in an institution. All such records must be maintained for 3 years after the end of each budget period, and if questions still remain, such as those raised as a result of audit, related records should be retained until the matter is completely resolved.

(10) **FINANCIAL INFORMATION:**
Account Identification: 20-00-0108-0-1-404.
Obligations: (Grants) FY 72 $40,400,000; FY 73 est $46,000,000; and FY 74 est $48,300,000.
Range and Average of Financial Assistance: $1,200 to $2,780,000; $132,000.

(11) **PROGRAM ACCOMPLISHMENTS:** During fiscal year 1972, 240 grants, totaling $40,400,000, were awarded to State, local, and regional air pollution control agencies to develop, establish, improve and maintain air pollution control programs.

(12) **REGULATIONS, GUIDELINES, AND LITERATURE:** Title 42 CFR Part 35.

(13) **INFORMATION CONTACTS:**
Regional or Local Office: Contact appropriate EPA Regional Administrator listed in appendix.
Headquarters Office: For program information: Deputy Assistant Administrator, Air Quality Planning and Standards, Air and Water Programs, Environmental Protection Agency, Research Triangle Park, NC 27711.

(14) **RELATED PROGRAMS:** 66.002, Air Pollution Fellowships; 66.003, Air Pollution Manpower Training Grants; 66.501, Air Pollution Control Research Grants; 66.005, Air Pollution Survey and Demonstration Grants; 11.404, Weather Forecasts and Warnings.

66.002   AIR POLLUTION FELLOWSHIPS

FEDERAL AGENCY: OFFICE OF AIR AND WATER PROGRAMS, ENVIRONMENTAL PROTECTION AGENCY
AUTHORIZATION: Section 103 of the Clean Air Act, 42 U.S.C. 1857b, Public Law 88-206, as amended by Public Law 91-604.
OBJECTIVES: To encourage and promote the specialized training of individuals as practitioners in pollution abatement

and control. Agency fellowships are awarded to present or prospective employees of a regional, State or local environmental pollution control or regulatory agency to provide training for and upgrading of personnel in the areas of pollution abatement and control. Special fellowships are awarded to individuals for study in speciality areas which

(1) FEDERAL AGENCY
The name of the agency responsible for the program.

(2) AUTHORIZATION
Reference to the legislation that created the program. For more detailed information, the act itself can be read. Evidence of familiarity with the provisions contained in the legislation by references to specific portions of it may strengthen a proposal. Copies of legislative acts can be found in federal depository libraries, ordered from the U. S. Government Printing Office, or requested from a congressman.

(3) OBJECTIVES
Defines the purposes for which the program was established; provides one basis—perhaps the main basis—for determining if the proposed activity fits within the program.

(4) TYPES OF ASSISTANCE
One element in determining eligibility for the program. For example, block grants and formula grants are made to governmental subdivisions; project grants and research grants may be made to educational and other nonprofit institutions and to individuals. This item with item (6) will usually clear up any question of eligibility.

(5) USES AND RESTRICTIONS
Describes what the money can be used for—indicates what budget items may be requested. Also states specific purposes for which the funds may *not* be used.

(6) ELIGIBILITY REQUIREMENTS
Indicates specifically what categories of applicants are eligible to apply and to serve as administrators of the funds; also who may benefit by the disbursement of the funds; and what documentation must be submitted in evidence of eligibility.

(7) APPLICATION AND AWARD PROCESS
Information on preapplication consultation and procedures; application deadline dates; submission procedures; and information on the procedures that will be followed for award announcements. Estimate of the time lag between submission data and award announcement; provisions for appeals or renewals.

(8) ASSISTANCE CONSIDERATIONS
Defines the timing and method of payment of the award; requirement for matching funds, or any special stipulations that must be agreed to or qualifications to be met.

(9) POSTASSISTANCE REQUIREMENTS
Accounting, reporting, and auditing procedures to be followed.

(10) FINANCIAL INFORMATION
A very important entry—indicates the amount of funds available in the program for fiscal year of record. This item can never be considered up-to-date, and the data, if significant, should be confirmed with the regional or national office administering the program.

(11) PROGRAM ACCOMPLISHMENTS
Reports on activities already funded; a guide to the kind of proposal acceptable under the program.

(12) REGULATIONS, GUIDELINES, AND LITERATURE
Those listed may be ordered directly from the agency shown in (1); worth ordering for any programs of interest to the applicant not only as a guide for preparation of a specific application, but as an addition to a basic library on federal programs.

(13) INFORMATION CONTACTS
Regional and national offices to which queries should be directed or applications submitted; the first approach is usually made to the regional office—a good idea in any case, as acquaintance with the staff may be helpful in future contacts.

(14) RELATED PROGRAMS
A system of cross-referencing the CFDA. May indicate other sources of grants, fellowships, training grants for the applicant's area of interest and activity.

nities for procurement of equipment, services, materials, or research through contracts; subcontracting leads; contract awards; sales of surplus property; and foreign business opportunities. Civilian agency projects expected to be as much as $5,000 and defense agency projects expected to cost as much as $10,000 must be advertised in CBD and instructions given for obtaining the Request for Proposals (RFP).

CBD notices inform the reader whether response may be in the form of a request to be included among a list of possible contractors who will each be sent a formal RFP or whether potential contractors should respond with a resume of experience, qualifications, and capabilities to provide the advertised service, material, or research. In the latter case, the RFP will be sent only if the qualifications are considered suitable for the proposed project. Announcements of awards are also published in CBD. Subscriptions: Administrative Services Office, Department of Commerce, 433 West Van Buren Street, Chicago, Illinois 60607. $40.00 annually (plus $30.25 for airmail service).

Request for Proposals (RFP)

RFPs are sent to institutions and organizations that respond to announcements of contracting opportunities and to other sources that are known to be interested in and capable of performing the proposed activity.

The RFPs include: (1) statement of the required work; (2) desired performance schedule; (3) available government-furnished property, if any; (4) applicable provisions to be included in the contract if awarded; and (5) criteria that will be used to evaluate proposals received. They also include useful guidance to offerors as to how to present the technical portion of proposals and how to prepare pricing information. They always specify a required date for submission of offers.

Requests to be placed on a list for routine receipt of announcements of availability of RFPs may be sent directly to the agency that issues them.

Commercial Guides to Government Programs

Commercial publications also provide subscribers with information on federal programs in specialized areas. One of the best known and most widely used is that of the Commerce Clearing House, Inc. (CCH) entitled *College and University Reporter*, which lists programs with an educational focus. Primarily a publisher of reports on tax and business law, CCH, in cooperation with nineteen institutions of higher learning and the American Council on Education (ACE), puts out this report on federal programs of special interest to educators. It includes information on institutional, teacher, and student programs; government procurement; taxes; federal laws affecting institutions of higher learning; and a section on "Federal Agencies Sponsoring Research." This last section, organized by federal department and agency, lists the type of research done, and gives the organizational and telephone directories of those agencies with which institutions of higher education are likely to have frequent dealings.

Subscribers receive two loose-leaf volumes of basic data on federal programs, with information as to where to apply for funds or grants, how to apply, forms to be used, and federal personnel involved, along with their office addresses, titles, and phone numbers. The basic information is organized by Topical Index, Finding Lists, Case Table, and Current Case Table. The basic report is supplemented by weekly reports covering current developments affecting higher education, including congressional action, court decisions, availability of new research funds, and regulation changes. A separate weekly summary is available which highlights the contents of the weekly reports. For information write to: Commerce Clearing House, Inc., 4025 W. Peterson, Chicago, Illinois 60646. Price: $570 a year for subscriptions for two years; $625 a year for one-year subscriptions. Subscriptions include weekly issues, legislative dispatches, and two loose-leaf basic volumes.

Another well-known reference service used by many organizations, especially academic institutions, is the *Guide to Federal Assistance for Education*, published by New Century Education Corporation (formerly Appleton-Century-Crofts).

The basic information is in two volumes which are updated monthly. They are organized by sections labeled for users: Individuals; Elementary and Secondary Schools; Institutions of Higher Education; State Agencies; and Other Users. The "Other Users" section is for groups that do not meet the qualifications of the other four, such as business, labor, professional, health, and welfare organizations, private employers, research institutions, and local political subdivisions (not including school systems). Within each section, programs are grouped by major areas, and a functional index indicates the group and page location for each subject or activity.

Order from: New Century Education Corporation, 440 Park Avenue South, New York, New York 10016. Subscription price: $375 a year.

A new information service is currently being offered to colleges and universities by Frank H. Cassell and Associates, Inc., who started *Federal Research Report* (described on the next page under Periodicals). It is called *College Resources Development Service* (CR) and offers to provide the following services:

1. A monthly bulletin with announcements of government grant programs, program deadlines, legislative priorities; analysis of target agency funding patterns; and an addendum tailored for the subscriber's specific needs.
2. Assistance in proposal preparation; an annual workshop on the subscriber's campus.
3. Grants management counsel.
4. Assistance in connection with trips to Washington to explore grant possibilities.
5. A Washington "hot line" for use by the subscriber to make inquiries, ask for information, etc., from CR's staff.

The fee for this service has not been set, but the plan is to make services available on a package basis and to establish an annual fee according to the level of the subscriber's need.

If the quality of service developed by CR is the same as the quality of information provided through the *Federal Research Report*, it may well turn out to be the best service available for information and assistance on government funding. But publishing a semimonthly report and providing a service tailored to the needs of a multitude of institutions of varying sizes, purposes, and needs are quite different undertakings and time will tell how this works out.

Information on the new service may be obtained by writing to: Mr. John Morrow, Director, College Resources Development Division, Frank H. Cassell and Associates, Inc., 104 South Michigan Avenue, Room 725, Chicago, Illinois 60603.

Another recently introduced grants information service, *Vital Grants Information*, is offered by the National Center for Government Grants. It is designed for postsecondary academic institutions interested in federal funding sources. A one-year subscription costs $89.50 for which the member receives: the Vital Grants Information Series, consisting of interviews with key government agencies and specialists; *Guide to Proposal Writing*, a reference manual; two cassettes (with binder), "Insider's Guide to Washington," and "How Others can Support your Proposal." This service is too new to evaluate. For detailed information, write to: National Center for Government Grants, P. O. Box 2413, Chicago, Illinois 60690.

A new publication, the *Washington Energy Directory*, lists key policy and program people associated with energy research and development in the Federal government and the private sector in Washington, including the Federal executive departments and independent agencies, the Congress, international agencies, and significant private and national organizations. It contains names of organizations and titles of approximately 780 key people in 55 different Federal and private Washington agencies and more than 45 Congressional committees and subcommittees concerned with making energy-related policy or administering energy R & D funds.

Subscriptions for 1975–76 cost $25.00. The Directory will be updated during the year and a new issue published annually. Order from: Center for Policy Process, Suite 401, 1755 Massachusetts Avenue N.W., Washington, D.C. 20036.

Periodicals

There are some excellent periodical publications that provide subscribers with information on federal grant programs, guidelines, new appropriations, and forecasts. Some of the best ones are for a restricted clientele, that is, prepared by Washington representatives for internal distribution within one institution.

Two good publications that anyone may subscribe to are *Federal Research Report*, published by Business Publishers, Inc., and *Federal Notes*, a publication of the University of Southern California, Los Angeles.

Federal Research Report, a semimonthly publication, reports on government activities related to funds for research, education, and associated areas. Each issue has a listing of upcoming grant deadlines. It is concise, clear, and accurate. It may be ordered from: Federal Research Report, P.O. Box 1067 Silver Spring, Maryland 20910. Subscription cost: $32.00 for one year; $58.00 for two years; $82.00 for three years.

Federal Notes, also a semimonthly, provides information on sources of federal funds for education, on current legislation, program plans of federal agencies, time-schedule application information, highlights on regulatory notes from the *Federal Register*, and notes on upcoming programs.

Address: Office of Federal Notes, University of Southern California, University Park, Los Angeles, California 90007. Subscription cost: $48 a year.

Science, a weekly publication of the American Association for the Advancement of Science, is reliable, complete, up-to-date, and well written. Its coverage of federal programs and current legislation as they relate to the scientific community is unmatched by any other publication. Its reporting on Washington activities is so thorough that, although the focus is science, it is useful to project planners and researchers in every field. The federal budget coverage is excellent, as are the background and interpretive articles.

Announcements of the availability of Requests for Proposals (RFPs) are frequently published in *Science*. A subscription to *Science* is included with membership in the American Association for the Advancement of Science. For others, it is $40.00 a year. Address: Science, 1515 Massachusetts Avenue, N.W., Washington, D.C. 20005.

Other periodicals that specialize in one area:

FASEB, the newsletter of the Federation of American Societies for Experimental Biology, an excellent source of current information on federal legislation and programs of interest to scientists. Subscription is included with membership in any of the Federation societies. Nonmember subscriptions are $5.00 a year. Address: FASEB Newsletter, 9650 Rockville Pike, Bethesda, Maryland 20014.

Science & Government Report with the subtitle of "The Independent Bulletin of Science Policy," is published in Washington approximately every two weeks, "22 times a year." The publisher and editor is Daniel S. Greenberg, who is well known in the scientific world from his former association with *Science* where he was one of the most respected and widely read writers. *Science & Government Report* is concerned mainly with the policies that result in legislation creating federal programs, but the background information is an excellent way of keeping up with current trends in federal funding, and factual information on federal spending in research and development is also included. Subscriptions are $58 a year or $110 for two years. Complimentary copies and further information may be requested from: Science & Government Report, Northwest Station, Box 6226A, Washington, D.C. 20015.

Science News, published by: Science Service, Inc., 231 West Center Street, Marion, Ohio 43302. Subscription: $10.00 a year.

A publication launched in 1974 called *Government R & D Report* promises to report on federal research and development projects for profit and nonprofit institutions, emphasizing programs of engineering, technology, and development of systems and hardware performed under contract. Address: Government R & D Report, M.I.T. Station, P.O. Box 284, Cambridge, Massachusetts 02139. Subscription: $70.00 a year.

In the area of community development, a good bimonthly publication is the Federal Programs *Monitor*, an information service of the Center for Community Change, a nonprofit, tax-exempt organization which assists local community development groups in low-income urban and rural areas. It is available free upon request to: Monitor, Center for Community Change, 1000 Wisconsin Avenue, N.W., Washington, D.C. 20007.

Publications that cover both government and foundation programs are listed in the section on Basic Sources of Information.

How to Find Out About Grants and Who Gives Them

FOUNDATION GRANTS

Philanthropy has been a powerful weapon in gaining influence and attracting adherents ever since human societies were sufficiently differentiated to admit of rich and poor. And ever since wealthy individuals began to set up formal organizations and endow them with funds to support favored causes and purposes, they have aroused the suspicions of those who sought to gain or hold power.

Modern foundations are the institutional descendants of a variety of charitable and philanthropic organizational forms that have for centuries interposed themselves between the people and the state. In ancient Greece, philanthropic institutions were suspect for political and economic reasons. Plato's "foundation"—an arrangement, established upon his death in 347 B.C., under which his properties were held in perpetuity for the support of his academy—managed to survive until the sixth century, when it was abolished by the Byzantine Emperor Justinian I for "spreading pagan doctrines." But that did not prevent Justinian's wife, the illustrious Empress Theodora, from establishing an institution to provide for the needs of former

107

prostitutes and endowing it with a liberal income to insure its continued support.[9]

During the Middle Ages, philanthropy was dominated by church and state, more or less in turn, each using charity and other forms of generosity to challenge the domination of the other. The Church established monasteries, chantries, and schools, and when Henry VIII sought to reduce religious influence in his kingdom, one of his first moves was to dissolve the monasteries and close up the schools and chantries—an act which, whatever the other effects may have been, deprived many poor people of their only opportunity to get an education.

The creation of any community, college, ecclesiastical, or lay organization without royal authorization was prohibited in Lower Austria (Bavaria) in 1753. French royalty also saw the formation of wealthy associations as a threat and took steps to submit them to royal authority. And even after the revolution the right of private persons to establish *foundations* was abolished in France and *associations* were placed under severely restrictive statutes. Under the Constitutional Regime, associations and foundations existed only by a special concession, a favor that the state might or might not grant.

The cornerstone of Anglo-Saxon law concerning philanthropy was laid in 1601 toward the end of the reign of Elizabeth I by the enactment of a Statute of Charitable Uses, which recognized that a charitable trust has a function that is both public and private for which the participation of neither church nor state is essential. Nevertheless, in the United States in the latter part of the twentieth century there is no clearly definable separation between the spheres of governmental and private philanthropy as they constantly meet and overlap in what Waldemar A. Nielsen calls "the endless, ambiguous interface."[10] In fact, foundations in this country have become an

---

[9] Demetrios J. Constantelos, *Byzantine Philanthropy and Social Welfare*. New Brunswick, N. J.: Rutgers University Press, 1968.

[10] Waldemar A. Nielsen. *The Big Foundations*. New York: Columbia University Press, 1972. Copyright The Twentieth Century Fund.

endangered species—they were threatened with extinction by a proposed amendment to the 1969 Tax Reform Act that would have forced them to phase out their activities and close their doors within the next forty years. Senator Albert Gore's proposed amendment failed, but the danger has not entirely vanished.

Out of a concern for the future of foundations in this country and a recognition that some changes in their role may be necessary as the society changes, John D. Rockefeller III in 1969 asked Peter G. Peterson, chairman of Bell and Howell, to form a commission to study American philanthropy and make recommendations for the future. Basically a fact-finding study, the commission was expected to obtain information upon which rational policy recommendations could be made. Its report, published in 1970, concluded that there is a continuing and growing need for private philanthropy in the country, but that some changes are needed in the characteristics and programs of foundations and other charitable organizations, and called for a government tax policy that would stimulate an increased flow of private resources to philanthropy.[11] These recommendations conflict with some of the provisions of the Tax Reform Act, particularly those that place limitations on tax deductions for contributions to private foundations.

Again, in 1973, four years after the tax reforms went into effect, Mr. Rockefeller initiated the formation of a group to make a study and develop recommendations on ways of strengthening the private, nonprofit sector. It is called the Filer Commission, after its chairman, John H. Filer of Aetna Life and Casualty Company, and is currently examining such issues as the methods of supervising, regulating, and classifying charitable institutions; the impact of tax considerations on private philanthropy; and alternative means of achieving the results sought by the present structure of private philanthropy in the United States.

These studies are a response not only to legislative actions that have altered the financial and operational bases of foundations but

---

[11] See *Foundations, Private Giving and Public Policy: Report and Recommendations of the Commission on Foundations and Private Philanthropy*. Peter G. Peterson, Chairman. Chicago: University of Chicago Press, 1970, pp. 123–188.

also to attacks against philanthropic foundations by congressional leaders and others in recent years that have grown increasingly hostile.

Public attitude in this country towards foundations has been characterized by inconsistency and ambivalence. They have been viewed alternately with the respect and admiration normally accorded the rich and powerful, and with the traditional suspicion and cynicism borne by philanthropic institutions through the ages.

Foundations have been eulogized by Warren Weaver,[12] satirized by Kurt Vonnegut, Jr.,[13] and criticized by Joseph C. Goulden, who said they were ". . . institutions which exist to benefit the rich and the near-rich . . . administered by philanthropoids who build cuckoo clocks and try to pass them off as cathedrals."[14]

The Walsh Commission in 1915 decided foundations were dangerously reactionary; private studies in the 1930s concluded that they were a means whereby the capitalistic class maintained power and control over the economic system; and in the 1950s, Senator Joseph McCarthy suggested that they were all communistic. David Merrick, theatrical producer, at the First Annual Congress of Theatre at Princeton University in 1974, made the statement that "All foundations are just tax dodges, anyway, including my own."[15]

In short, foundations have been accused of everything. They have even been, according to Merrimon Cuninggim, former President of the Danforth Foundation, "caught in the act of helping."[16]

How did this come about? How can an institution engender such widely different opinions, arouse public admiration on the one hand while incurring deep hostility on the other? Many reasons have contributed but the explanation for the most part can be divided into

[12] Warren Weaver. *U. S. Philanthropic Foundations: Their History, Structure, Management, and Record.* New York: Harper and Row, 1961.
[13] Kurt Vonnegut, Jr. *God Bless You, Mr. Rosewater.* New York: Dell Publishing Co., Inc., 1965. Copyright by Kurt Vonnegut, Jr.
[14] Joseph C. Goulden. *The Money Givers.* New York: Random House, 1961, pp. 317–318.
[15] Source: *The New York Times,* June 16, 1974.
[16] Merrimon Cuninggim. *Private Money and Public Service.* New York: Mc-Graw Hill Book Co., 1972, p. 267.

three specifics: First, foundations got off to a bad start in this country; second, nobody is quite sure what a foundation is; and third, foundations have up until recently surrounded themselves with an aura of mystery and awe that made it difficult to obtain factual information from them or about them.

Foundations became significant in the United States only after the nation's economic development advanced sufficiently that individuals were able to amass great wealth, but the spirit of philanthropy, inspired by natural kindliness, a nascent sense of social justice, religious belief, or merely the sense of well-being that accompanies benevolence, was abroad in the land long before that.

Benjamin Franklin founded the American Philosophical Society in 1743, which had many of the characteristics of a foundation, but according to some authorities the first United States foundation was established in 1800 as the Magdalen Society of Philadelphia, with the stated aim of ameliorating the distressed condition of "that class of females who have been unhappily seduced from the path of innocence and virtue and who at times seem desirous of a return thereto." The trustees voted in 1918 to broaden the purposes of the foundation (could there have been a dearth of unhappy females desirous of returning to the path of innocence and virtue?) and also changed the name at that time to the White-Williams Foundation.

During the nineteenth century a number of philanthropic societies and associations were established, but the modern foundation movement really started early in the twentieth century with Andrew Carnegie and John D. Rockefeller, Sr. in the lead. Before the turn of the century, in 1886, Carnegie had already endowed a public library in Pittsburgh and ten years later formally established the Carnegie Institute of Pittsburgh. And Rockefeller in 1889, while he was President of the Standard Oil Trust, gave the American Baptist Education Society $600,000 of the first million necessary to found the University of Chicago. Between 1901 and 1911 Carnegie set up four foundations in England and Scotland, his birthplace, and four in the United States. The Carnegie Corporation of New York, founded in 1911, was the largest in size and scope, and aside from the United Kingdom Trust is the only one without functional or local limitations.

In 1901 the Rockefeller Institute for Medical Research was founded, and in 1908 its charter was extended to enable it to carry on educational activities.

The Rockefeller Foundation applied to the United States Congress for a corporate charter in 1910, and a more unpropitious time for such a request would be hard to find. The "Progressive Era" launched by Theodore Roosevelt was in full swing with President William Howard Taft faithfully carrying out Roosevelt's "trust-busting" policies. One of the trusts up for busting was the Standard Oil Company. The Supreme Court decision against it and the powerful American Tobacco Company was rendered in May, 1911, while debate on the foundation's charter application raged in Congress—a debate that was punctuated with cries of "robber barons," "the kiss of Judas Iscariot," and "tainted money," echoing the note struck by Ida Tarbell in her 1902 *McClure's Magazine* articles on the Standard Oil Company and how it grew.

After three years of congressional controversy over the application, it was withdrawn, and the foundation applied to New York State instead. The state charter was promptly issued in 1913, and the Rockefeller Foundation has continued to operate under it since that time. Most foundations, as a matter of fact, operate under state charters, and one wonders at this point why the Rockefeller Foundation sought a federal charter in the first place.

But that was not the end of the Rockefeller Foundation's troubles. A year later the Rockefeller-controlled Colorado Fuel and Iron Company became involved in labor difficulties that culminated in the infamous Ludlow Massacre, which ended only when federal troops were brought in. Suspicion fell upon the foundation because some of its board members were also directors of Colorado Fuel and Iron and because the foundation had launched a study in the field of industrial relations shortly before the strike occurred.

The industrial relations program was abandoned and the foundation turned to public health and the control of disease, specifically hookworm, malaria, and yellow fever. Since then the Rockefeller Foundation has, in addition to the medical sciences, supported programs in the natural sciences, the social sciences, the humanities, and agriculture all over the world. Beginning in the sixties the foundation entered the areas of university development, population stabilization, equal opportunity, cultural development, conquest of hunger, and the quality of the environment. The name Rockefeller—once associated with "robber barons" and "tainted money"—has come to mean untold generosity and benefactions throughout the world. In South America, Rockefeller means medical research, health care, and agricultural development; in the Far East, it means hospitals, public health services, and high-yielding, long-grain rice. It means the new Bodleian Library at Oxford University, the School of Medicine in Paris, the restoration of Versailles. The Rockefeller family has donated more to philanthropic enterprises than any other family in the history of this country. One has to go back to the Medici family in Renaissance Italy to find anything to compare with it.

In May, 1974, the Rockefeller Foundation published its general guidelines stating seven major program areas. Five are continuations of existing programs and two—The Arts, the Humanities, and Contemporary Values and Conflict in International Relations—are enlargements of old interests; but they represent significant new commitments. The other five are: Conquest of Hunger; Education for Development; Equal Opportunity for All; Population and Health; and Quality of the Environment.

The troublesome debut of the Rockefeller Foundation and the objections that arose through associating the foundation with the philosophy and practices imputed to the Standard Oil Company may have put a damper on the foundation movement which proceeded at a steady but modest pace until after World War II.

Danforth, Kresge, Charles Stewart Mott, Charles F. Kettering, and John A. Hartford Foundations and the Duke Endowment were established in the twenties. During the thirties, Eli Lilly, Kellogg, Nemours, Alfred P. Sloan, Longwood, Houston, Irvine, Sid W. Richardson, and Henry J. Kaiser were the large entries in the field. These foundations, following the lead of Rockefeller and Carnegie, supported programs in health, education, and improvement of social conditions. It does not overstate the case to say that foundations were a critical force in the advancement of scientific research in this country. In the years prior to World War II, support for the independent researcher who wanted to be relieved of academic or other institutional responsibilities to spend full time on research came mainly from the foundations. This fact has been almost forgotten, having been reduced to relative insignificance by the torrent of governmental assistance later made available to scientists for both training and research.

Unlike Rockefeller, the Ford Foundation was fifteen years old before its troubles began. It was established in 1936 as a means for supporting the Ford family's favorite charities and as a device to avoid payment of estate taxes by heirs of deceased family members. The Ford Motor Company was in a shambles and it was hard to believe that a foundation whose holdings consisted of Ford stock could survive very long. But in the mid-forties, Henry Ford II and his mother, Mrs. Edsel Ford, wrested control of the company from the unscrupulous Harry Bennett and dragged it back from the brink of bankruptcy to a profit-making level in less than two years. They then turned their attention to the foundation and decided to make it into something worthwhile. And what a stir that caused!

Under the leadership of Paul G. Hoffman, the Ford Foundation in 1950 enunciated a five-point program:

1. The problem of world peace
2. The problems of democracy
3. Problems of the economy
4. Problems of education
5. The scientific study of man

Hoffman brought in other activists like Robert M. Hutchins; Marshall Plan ambassador to Europe Milton Katz; and Chester A. Davis, an experienced administrator of agriculture programs. Within two years it had launched several foreign economic development programs, the largest one in India; established the Center for Advanced Study in the Behavioral Sciences in Palo Alto; founded two quasi-independent agencies, the Fund for the Advancement of Education and the Fund for Adult Education; set up grant programs in both eastern and western Europe; and incurred the implacable wrath of Senator Joseph McCarthy. Hoffman's successor, Rowan Gaither, who took over in 1953, was forced to spend the next two years defending the foundation's policies against public and congressional criticism.

In the meantime, Ford Motor Company profits were increasing at such a rate that the foundation had difficulty in disposing of its income. In 1955 it started selling off its auto shares and at the same time made several large grants to private colleges—$50 million was distributed in one package—and in the same year, a special distribution of $550 million was made to colleges and universities, hospitals, and medical schools.

Ford had become the giant in the field in less than five years after announcing its program plan and has remained in that position ever since. By 1968 its assets reached $3.7 billion, an amount equal to one-third of the assets of the top thirty-three foundations and to one-sixth of those of all other foundations combined. Its resources then were four times as great as those of Rockefeller and twelve times those of Carnegie. After the divestiture of the auto stock and the extraordinary outlays of 1955, foundation earnings leveled off and disbursements stabilized. In 1957, it gave away $162 million and reached a peak of $365 million in 1966, the year McGeorge Bundy became president.

Bundy moved immediately to revive some of the spirit of the foundation's first days and concentrated on controversial social and political change. The foundation had survived the McCarthy onslaught but the congressional subcommittee on tax reform, under the leadership of Congressman Wright Patman of Texas, was just getting into its stride. The Ford Foundation's extensive assets and its support of liberal and controversial causes made it a natural target, especially in conservative circles. It is apparent that the subcommittee singled out Ford for intensive investigation and placed great emphasis on the significance of certain grants such as those made to former aides of presidential candidate Robert Kennedy following his assassination.

There is little doubt that the Ford Foundation was a major target of the regulatory provisions of the 1969 Tax Reform Act restricting expenditures for projects directed toward influencing legislation through attempts to affect the opinion of the general public. Depending upon the interpretation of this provision, it could conceivably prevent foundations from doing almost anything the Internal Revenue Service did not approve. As *Science*, the publication of the American Association for the Advancement of Science phrased it, this provision could encompass ". . . almost everything worth studying, for almost any study worthy of foundation support might directly or indirectly influence a decision of some governmental body."

So far the effects of this legislation are hard to assess. The Ford Foundation has continued its progressive programs to seek solutions to troublesome social problems. In addition to education, which has always been one of the areas it supported most generously, international affairs, and civil liberties, it launched programs in the arts and the humanities in the 1960s and joined the Rockefeller Foundation in giving increasing attention to problems of world population growth and food shortages.

But the ancient conflict between private philanthropic organizations and the state came into clear focus with the enactment of the 1969 Tax Reform Act, indicating that the struggle has abated not one whit since the "foundations" were suspected of being involved in the Catiline conspiracy in the first century. This would be less puzzling if the record of foundations in this country were less impressive. Foundations have helped make possible many of the most important advances of the twentieth century. Foundations have liberated thousands of gifted individuals from the limitations of inadequate education; promoted international understanding and the cause of peace; trained leadership for business and government; aided developing and emerging nations. They can be identified with sponsorship of studies leading to the elucidation of the "genetic code" mechanism, the discovery of the first polio vaccine, the development of high-yield food grain, and early rocket research. They have spearheaded a nationwide drive against loan-shark practices; established a pension system for college and university faculties; and brought enjoyment of the arts to millions of people. Whatever the original impetus for the foundation movement in this country may have been, and there is ample evidence of mixed motives, foundations have provided leadership in early recognition of social problems and of scientific and intellectual potentialities that prompted the government with its far greater resources to assume responsibility in moving the nation ahead in social, educational, and scientific fields.

There is little doubt, however, that war-time profits and rising taxation were factors in the sudden population explosion that occurred among foundations following World War II. When Congressman Patman launched his investigation into their financial behavior in the sixties, there were at least 25,000 foundations in existence, *95 percent of which had been set up since 1945.* Before the war the establishment of a private foundation was thought to be the prerogative of the super-rich, but afterwards the moderately rich and even the only slightly rich began to find purposes that could best be served through such organizations. And so, foundations proliferated and their assets ranged from a few thousand dollars to billions. Their purposes varied widely, too, but the majority adopted the catchall general purpose phraseology which indicated that they supported welfare, social, religious, charitable, or educational causes—one or more or all of these. This terminology left them free to dispense their monies for almost any philanthropic purpose they chose and some of them interpreted the meaning of philanthropy very broadly. Congressman Patman found during his investigations that foundations were being used to recruit football players, to maintain tax-free residences, to underwrite banquets, and to support widows, divorcees, and mistresses. Although such uses and abuses of the tax-exempt privilege were not representative of those foundations holding the overwhelming percentage of foundation assets, Patman's investigation resulted in a number of tax and regulatory provisions aimed at ending such practices.

The 1969 Tax Reform Act may curtail or even prevent the use of foundations as tax dodges, but if Patman's committee had continued to be as assiduous in its investigations in the seventies as it was prior to 1969, it would have had to look no further than the White House for evidence of attempts to use foundations for other than eleemosynary purposes.

In a memorandum to President Nixon dated March 3, 1970, Special White House Consultant Patrick Buchanan recommended that "The President should direct an in-house group of people preferably outside the Administration to quietly undertake a study of the top 25 foundations in this country; to identify both their leadership and power structure; and to indicate which are friendly, which are potentially friendly, which can be coopted to support projects the President supports. . . . This group would be charged with reporting to the President specific options on how we could either influence, take over or create a major institution to accomplish Administration objectives. . . . All the high rollers we know would be passed the word that of the charities the President prefers, this one is the best. The Big Supporters would find themselves on White House Guest Lists."[17]

No mention is made of tax-exempt or other advantages but it is difficult to believe Mr. Buchanan expected these "high rollers" to go along just to have a meal at the White House. There is no evidence that the suggestion was acted upon—it may have been one of the dreams that drowned in Watergate—but it was exactly the kind of abuse Congressman Patman was dedicated to prohibiting. In a letter to Mr. William C. Archie, executive director of the Mary Reynolds Babcock Foundation, Inc., late in 1973, Patman stated, "If the impression is abroad in the land that I have not been friendly to private foundations, it is because I have made the decision that I will be the spokesman for the intended beneficiaries of private foundations, the American public. Private philanthropy plays a necessary and vital role in our country . . . it is only in those instances when personal gain is placed ahead of public welfare that I speak out to criticize the Foundation community."[18]

Patrick Buchanan's recommendation demonstrates amply the confusion in the minds of many about foundations, especially on the question of their nature and purpose, a prime factor in the misunderstanding and mistrust directed at foundations; that is, *nobody is exactly sure what a foundation is.* The name is applied loosely to a group of organizations that are not managed in the same way, do not function alike, and have different objectives. Therefore when statements are made that "foundations do this or that," the truth or falsity lies in the speaker's interpretation of the word "foundation." The most widely accepted general definition of a foundation is that of F. Emerson Andrews, president emeritus of The Foundation Center, in the introduction to *The Foundation Directory,* fourth edition. He describes a foundation as "a nongovernmental, nonprofit organization with funds and program managed by its own trustees or directors, and

[17] *Foundation News,* January/February, 1974, p. 6–8.
[18] *Foundation News,* January/February, 1974, p. 9.

established to maintain or aid social, educational, charitable, religious, or other activities serving the common welfare."[19]

Mr. Andrews also said: "The prestigeful name *foundation* has been adopted by many organizations which . . . have no proper right to its use. These include agencies which solicit contributions instead of disbursing from an established fund, and some which are trade associations, pressure groups, or outright rackets."[20]

In an attempt to establish a legal identification for foundations and to distinguish between their privileges and responsibilities and those of other organizations serving the public welfare, the 1969 Tax Reform Act decreed that religious, educational, scientific, cultural, and charitable organizations—501(c)(3) organizations—are either private foundations or they are not. The law also establishes the criteria that determine such classification, and 501(c)(3) organizations are being reviewed to determine their status. As of September 30, 1973, 31,000 organizations had been classified as private foundations and at least 6,000 were still awaiting classification. These figures were given in testimony before the Senate Subcommittee on Foundations on October 1, 1973, by Dr. Robert Goheen, chairman and chief executive officer of the Council on Foundations, Inc., who said the final number of private foundations could be as high as 37,000.[21]

Those organizations that meet the criteria for private foundations fall into two general categories: *operating* and *nonoperating* foundations. An *operating* foundation is one that uses its income to run its own program or support its own institution. Typical examples are research institutes, homes (such as orphanages or homes for the aged), and some museums. The name of an organization, however, is not sufficient to identify it as an operating or nonoperating founda-

[19] Marianna O. Lewis, ed. *The Foundation Directory*. Edition 4. New York: Columbia University Press, 1971, p. vii.

[20] F. Emerson Andrews. *Philanthropic Foundations*. New York: Russell Sage Foundation, 1956, p. 12.

[21] Ref: Hearings before the Subcommittee on Foundations of the Committee on Finance, United States Senate, Ninety-third Congress, First Session on the Role of Private Foundations in Today's Society and a Review of the Impact of Charitable Provisions of the Tax Reform Act of 1969 on the Support and Operation of Private Foundations, October 1 and 2, 1973.

tion; the determination is based on such things as source of income and degree of grant-making activity—there are privately endowed "homes" that have ceased to maintain residential establishments and now have active grant-making programs.

It is the nonoperating foundations that are the major sources of grant support, and those might be loosely placed into three groupings: the independent foundations; community foundations or trusts; and company-sponsored foundations.

By far the largest group is that of the independent, privately endowed foundations, currently estimated to number more than 30,000. The range in size is from very large, e.g., Ford, Carnegie, Rockefeller, Kellogg, Sloan, Robert Wood Johnson, and others, to the very small ones with assets of a few thousand dollars, usually bearing the name of the individual or family donor. All are governed by a board of trustees. The large ones are administered by trained professional staffs and address themselves to the basic problems in the fields in which they operate. Some cover a wide range of fields and are called "general purpose" foundations, but many foundations—large and small—have decided to focus their efforts in one particular kind of activity and are sometimes referred to as "special purpose" foundations.

Most of the small foundations operate quite informally and have no professional staff. Their grant making is usually directed to institutions and organizations in which the donors have a personal interest.

All community foundations or trusts are classified as "charitable organizations," i.e., in the 501(c)(3) category for IRS purposes, and most but not all meet the criteria for "private foundation." There are about 240 community foundations in the United States, and they hold about 3 percent of foundation assets. Some of them have exercised remarkable leadership in the improvement of their immediate geographical areas through surveys and experimental projects and in support of essential community services. Their boards of directors are broadly representative of the communities in which they are located, and their grant programs are usually restricted to the community. The Cleveland Foundation is the oldest in this group—just over sixty years old—but the New York Community Trust recently passed it in size with assets of $200 million and disbursements of $10 million annually. Other examples of organizations in this category are the San Francisco Foundation, the Chicago Community Trust, and the Permanent Charity Fund of Boston.

Company-sponsored foundations account for about 6 percent of all foundation assets in this country. There are approximately 1,800 of them and most are not heavily endowed. The new tax laws have created some uncertainty as to the future of this group of foundations—one study indicates a possible attrition rate of as much as 10 percent between 1970 and 1973. They are the mechanism used by companies to provide a stable fund for the annual philanthropy. Foundation contributions can be reduced in poor earnings years and replenished during good profit years, allowing the philanthropic activities to be maintained at the same level.

Company foundations typically support programs that corporations are expected to support, such as community chests, education, hospitals, and, more recently, arts and urban affairs. Their grants or gifts are often restricted to the communities in which the companies have plants or offices. Among the large company-sponsored foundations are Alcoa Foundation in Pittsburgh; Ford Motor Company Fund, Detroit; Exxon Education Foundation, New York; and Sears Roebuck Foundation, Chicago.

It is foundations themselves that are responsible for the third cause of rampant ignorance and misinformation about them. Although there are outstanding exceptions, *they have not as a group made it easy for individuals or organizations to acquire information about their activities.* They are just beginning to understand their responsibility regarding the dissemination of information and in the past have been sluggish or downright uncooperative in responding to requests for information.

In a sense it is understandable. Any organization with money to give away deserves and requires protection from those promoters, entrepreneurs, operators, or con men whose major talents lie in the ability to ferret out vulnerable benefactors for fraudulent causes. They must also protect themselves from time wasters, those otherwise honorable people who simply want to talk about an idea that is only half-formed and for which they have conceived no presentable plan of action.

But the experience reported by one nonprofit, tax-exempt organization that sought to accumulate information about foundations for its library is discouraging, to say the least.

In 1973, The Grantsmanship Center, in Los Angeles, California, requested information from all foundations listed in the 1971 *Foundation Directory*—those with assets of $500,000 or more, or who made grants of as much as $25,000 during the year of record. Beginning in August, 1973, 5,454 letters were mailed out over a six-week period explaining that The Grantsmanship Center was a nonprofit, educational institution and requesting information for its library. A statement in the letter clearly explained that it was *not a request for funds*.

As of April, 1974, the Center had received a total of 759 responses, 431 letters had been returned and 4,264 were still unanswered. Of those that responded, 40 flatly refused to send information, 75 merely acknowledged receipt of the letter, 59 said they had terminated operations, and 113 turned down a request for funds! Only 337 replied by sending copies of the annual report or other literature or wrote that their IRS 990-AR form was available for review in their offices, and 135 sent an informative letter about the foundation.

One "termination" reply read: "Your letter addressed to me as President of —— Fund has been received. Thanks to the efforts of Mr. Wright Patman to discourage private foundations, —— Fund distributed its assets and closed its doors last year."[22]

In all, 4,264, more than 80 percent of those who received the letter, did not reply at all! This can be partially explained by the fact that only 5 percent of all foundations have any full-time staff, and only 20 percent have any paid staff at all, including secretaries. Less than 3 percent of foundations distribute separately published annual reports, and not all of those are printed in sufficient quantities to be sent out upon request. They are sometimes distributed only to a selected list of libraries and other information-gathering organizations and to a few individuals.

That is no way to run a ship, one might say. But the fact is that a foundation is no ordinary ship. Its goals and purposes may best be

[22] *Grantsmanship Center News,* April-May, 1974.

served by procedures and practices that would be suicidal for a profit-oriented business enterprise. A foundation is engaged in the business of disbursing money for worthy purposes. And any monies used for administrative staff, public relations, and printing and distribution of information materials will reduce by the amount of their cost the funds available for grant-making purposes. Viewed in that light it may seem that those foundations that keep overhead to the minimum are making maximum use of their resources for their announced purposes.

The matter of public disclosure of foundation activities is one of the subjects dealt with by the 1969 Tax Reform Act. That law requires the preparation of an annual report to be published or made available for inspection at the foundation's offices. Additionally, the Internal Revenue Service forms which private foundations file—990-PF and 990-AR—have been revised to require fuller information than did past forms. Foundations are also required when they file their IRS forms to place simultaneously "in a newspaper having general circulation" a notice that the form is available for inspection by the public for 180 days.

As of this writing, foundations appear to be complying with the letter of the law if not always the spirit. A large number of foundations have chosen the *New York Law Journal* for their notices. With a circulation of less than 9,000 and a rather specialized readership, the *Law Journal's* qualifications as a "newspaper having general circulation" are doubtful, but this choice is defended by those who claim that subscribers to the *Law Journal* represent the group most likely to have an interest in foundation reports.

More than ten years before the Tax Reform Act, executives in some of the larger foundations had begun to come to grips with the problem of dissemination of information to the public and supported the establishment of The Foundation Center in 1956, an organization whose sole mission is to gather and disseminate factual information on foundations. Although the Center is supported by foundation grants, the task of collecting up-to-date information from foundations is by no means an easy one. The communications barriers that exist between foundations and individuals who seek information are only slightly more formidable than those that impede The Foundation

Center in the accomplishment of its mission. Again, the fact that so few foundations have any professional staff means that it is hard to nail down the board member or part-time director who has the information, and even then the material is not assembled in a format that makes it usable for the Center's purposes. Data obtained directly from the Internal Revenue Service are a year or a year and a half behind at the best. The mission of educating foundation executives and donors to the importance of making information available to the general public was one of the first to be faced by the Center and is still a major objective. They report that each year an increasing number of foundations cooperate in providing them with information.

Foundations in this country are in trouble and it is certain that many of their operational characteristics and programs will change during the next few years. What the McCarthy and the Patman committees have failed to do may, unless the tide soon turns, be accomplished by the flagging economy of the nation. By 1973, the Ford Foundation's expenditures had leveled off at about $200 million per year and its capital assets were estimated at more than $3 billion. Then the effects of the Arab oil embargo and other things reached Wall Street in 1974 and the market value of the foundation's assets fell to $2 billion within a year. The foundation announced a cut in its grant programs that may be as much as 50 percent. This is a serious blow to grant seekers, not only for the loss it represents but because of the effect it might have on other foundations that have come to regard Ford as a kind of polestar in the field.

Soon after the Ford announcement, the Carnegie foundation reported a drop in its assets from $336 million to $210 million and announced a $500,000 reduction in its grant-making program, which was $14 million in 1973. Others that are experiencing similar declines in market value of assets are beginning to hint at a possible reduction in their grant programs. The Rockefeller decline is estimated at more than one-third. Other foundations—Mott, Kettering, Duke, and Luce among them—have lost as much as 50 percent of their market value. And even the newer foundations that were expected to boost foundation largesse have experienced market value losses, including Clark (based on the Avon Products fortune) and Rowland (Polaroid). The biggest losers will be colleges, universities, hospitals, and private welfare agencies, which receive more than 60 percent of the total annual foundation disbursements. And the more venturesome organizations such as civil rights movements, environmental organizations, and other activist groups that have received the major portion of their support from foundations will be very hard hit, indeed.

It is difficult to determine how much the current talk about slashing grant programs is really the result of a reduction in market value of assets—earnings have held up rather well—and how much is part of the continuing pressure foundations are bringing for a reduction in the excise tax on foundation investment income. The excise tax not only blurs the definition of a "tax-exempt" organization but it is clearly excessive for its purpose as stated. It was said to reflect congressional determination that "private foundations should share some of the burden of paying the cost of government, especially for more extensive and vigorous enforcement of the tax laws relating to exempt organizations." In other words, it was to make the foundations pay for the enforcement of tax laws against them, a debatable proposition at best. But even if the principle is accepted, the collections so far have been in excess of what is needed for auditing purposes. Most foundations probably would not object to audit fees scaled to the assets of each organization and to the actual cost of enforcement.

One of the many myths about foundations and one that contributed to the belief that financial regulation of their activities was necessary is that they control a tremendous percentage of the nation's wealth, but the facts did not bear this out even before the 1974 decline. Charles Schultze of the Brookings Institution calculated the ratio of foundation holdings in 1968 to total holdings of stocks, bonds, and mortgages and found that foundations control a *very small and declining proportion of the nation's financial wealth.* By using two different methods of computation, Mr. Schultze showed that in 1968, foundation holdings were between 1.29 and 1.39 percent of the nation's total holdings—compared to the somewhat higher figures in 1958, when foundations held between 1.47 and 1.57 percent of the national total.[23]

[23] See *Foundations, Private Giving and Public Policy, op. cit.,* p. 51.

In dollar amounts, total assets of foundations in the United States, at the end-of-1973 market value, were estimated to be between $26.5 and $27 billion. If current estimates of the decline in assets in 1974 are accurate, the amount could now be more than 30 percent less—nearly $10 billion less! Foundation disbursements during 1972 and 1973 amounted to approximately $2.36 billion annually, less than two-tenths of 1 percent of the 1973 Gross National Product, and less than 10 percent of all philanthropic giving in the country during both years. Two and one-half billion dollars sounds like a lot of money, but it is only about half as much as Americans spend annually on cosmetics and beauty treatments; half as much as they spend on pet food; one-fifth as much as they spend on tobacco products; and about one-tenth as much as the nation spends on liquor, beer, and wines. And it seems probable that foundation grant-making in the immediate future will not even reach the $2.36 billion level.

Foundations are wrestling with problems other than those surrounding their financial base. The Tax Reform Act, in spite of its name, goes a great deal further than imposing additional tax obligations on foundations. It also includes a number of provisions that restrict the kinds of programs foundations can support and requires the foundations to ensure that their grants are used only for the specific purposes intended—and they may be penalized severely for any failure to do so. This, in effect, puts the Internal Revenue Service—a tax collecting agency—in the role of censor over the substantive programs of foundations. A narrow interpretation by the IRS of the 1969 legislation could force some foundations to abandon programs they have traditionally supported and with which they have become identified. They are, therefore, reviewing all of their ongoing activities and inaugurating new ones only after meticulous consideration of their suitability for the overall foundation purposes and for their invulnerability to IRS criticism. Consequently, only current information on foundation programs can be considered accurate, and potential grant seekers must make special efforts to ascertain that the interests of a foundation to be approached have been recently researched.

Although specific program interests and activities are subject to change, the distribution of their support in broad, general areas has remained fairly consistent over the years. Education claims the major portion of foundation monies, with health not far behind. Social welfare and international affairs are other areas receiving foundation support. The latest available figures on foundation spending indicate distribution in this order: [24]

Education	36%
Health	24%
Sciences	12%
Welfare	9%
International Affairs	9%
Humanities	8%
Religion	2%

Within these general areas—and there is no indication that there will be any radical shifts from these categories—foundations, especially the larger ones, are tending more and more to establish their own priorities, to focus on particular activities or aspects of a problem. This is consistent with grant making through the ages—their beneficence is directed toward the achievement of the ends they most desire and now, since 1969, consistent with the necessity to stay in the good graces of the Internal Revenue Service.

The Filer Commission has its work cut out for it, especially in the pursuit of its stated purpose to explore alternative means of achieving the results sought by the present structure of private philanthropy. It may be that only with a new structure incorporating some aspects of the present system but altering, in fundamental ways, the foundation–government relationship will resolutions be found for some of the present ambiguities and conflicts.

Sources of information on foundations are considerably more abundant than they used to be, but candidates for foundation grants still need to exercise a good deal of initiative in order to find out which foundations are most likely to be receptive to a particular proposal.

[24] Source: *Giving USA*. 1974 Annual Report.

INFORMATION SOURCES—FOUNDATIONS

Finding out what a foundation is interested in and likely to support can be a frustrating task. Myths abound, word-of-mouth information is unreliable, and, as The Grantsmanship Center discovered, the direct approach of writing to the foundation doesn't work at all well.

Once the decision has been reached to explore foundation sources for project funds, the first names that spring to mind are the largest, best-known ones, the thirty or forty that are responsible for one-third of all grants, or the hundred largest from which one-half of all foundation giving comes. But the very fact that a few foundations account for a disproportionately large share of foundation spending results in their receiving a disproportionately large share of applications. For example, the Robert Wood Johnson Foundation, which is interested in improving health care in the United States, has total assets exceeding $1 billion and in 1973 gave away $53 million. However, the foundation received *3,500 proposals requesting more than $600 million. If they had been able to fund only those proposals that were within the scope of their concerns, $361 million would have been required—* nearly seven times the amount awarded. The Johnson Foundation, one of the largest, is able to support approximately 15 percent of the applications sent to them.[25]

The grant candidate should not limit his search to the larger foundations but will find it worth the effort to explore possibilities from among the medium-sized or smaller foundations, especially for individual grants, scholarships, or institutional grants for well-defined, modest-sized programs.

"Smaller" foundations refers to those with active grant-making programs and not to those that seldom or rarely make grants outside the circle of family or friends.

The most important element in singling out a foundation as a possible source of support is its grant-making record. The statement of purpose, objectives, or total assets—all are irrelevant if the organization has not made a significant grant within the past year or two (providing, of course, that there isn't some plausible explanation). The pattern of giving is as important as the number and amount of

[25] The Robert Wood Johnson Foundation Annual Report for 1973, pp. 32–33.

grants awarded. A foundation that makes awards to the same organizations year after year or the same type of organizations—for example, community chests, religions of one sect, or for research on a specific disease—would not be a good possibility for a theater or dance group. Or a foundation that has a record of supporting very conservative, standard programs is not a good prospect for a women's liberation organization.

For exploration into the world of foundations, all the general sources may be helpful, i.e., libraries, journals, the daily press. There are some subscription services that provide information on a routine monthly or quarterly basis, and many publications that serve as guides to foundation funding sources.

The most abundant and reliable information on foundations is gathered and disseminated by The Foundation Center.

Research to uncover possible foundation funding sources should be conducted with these points in mind:

1. The project or activity must fall within the known scope of interest of the foundation to be approached.

2. Some foundations prefer to support specific types of organizations, e.g., schools for the handicapped or for people with a particular handicap, but not "educational institutions" in general.

3. Some foundations restrict their grant making to certain geographic locations.

4. Certain foundations support programs affecting specific populations, i.e., low-income groups, women, preschool children, members of minority groups, etc.

5. All foundations have some limitations and/or restrictions on the grants they make. Some will fund construction projects, others do not; a few will provide support for ongoing operating costs, most do not; and they all have limits on the dollar amounts of their grants, although they vary among foundations and from program to program even within the same foundation.

6. Few foundations have application deadlines as a rule, but may set them for special competitions or fellowship awards. It is important to know if there is a deadline date and what it is.

One of the best summaries of the interests of foundations as indicated by the activities they have supported is given in Merrimon Cuninggim's *Private Money and Public Service*, in the chapter "Counter-Attack: The Record of Achievement," under the following headings: [26]

1. The Work of Large Foundations
2. Accomplishments of Selected Middle-Sized Foundations
3. An Incomplete Honor Roll of Smaller Foundations
4. Community Funds, Company Foundations and Clusters

Although foundation programs are not immutable, their general areas of interest remain fairly stable, and changes are often only in the degree of emphasis. Mr. Cuninggim's brief summaries provide an excellent guide for the totally disoriented applicant in the beginning stages of identifying possible sources of foundation funds for a specific project.

THE FOUNDATION CENTER

The Foundation Center was established in New York in 1956 for the sole purpose of collecting factual information on philanthropic foundations and making it available free or at very low cost to visitors and also by mail or telephone services. It is supported by foundation grants—at the end of 1973, eighty-nine foundations ranging in size from very large to small and located in all areas of the country had contributed to its support.

One of the principal reasons foundations support the Center is to provide a public information channel and relieve each foundation of the necessity of distributing information about its programs upon request. This is one explanation for the seeming indifference on the part of some foundations to individual requests for information.

Services of The Foundation Center are available throughout the country in three national collections and, as of January, 1975, forty-nine regional collections in thirty-nine states. The national collections

[26] Cuninggim, *op. cit.*, pp. 135–175.

are located at:

> The Foundation Center
> 888 Seventh Avenue
> New York, New York 10019

> The Foundation Center
> 1001 Connecticut Avenue, N.W.
> Washington, D.C. 20036

> Donors' Forum
> 208 South La Salle Street
> Chicago, Illinois 60604

These collections, also called reference centers, have broad national collections of source materials on foundations and their grant-making activities. They are open to the public without charge every weekday excepting holidays.

National collections have standard reference works and books, reports, and guides relating to the foundation field, foundation annual reports on film, and foundation IRS information returns.

The forty-nine regional collections (eventually the number will be sixty) concentrate on records, reports, and information relevant to the area of their geographic coverage. A list of the regional collections in existence at this writing, indicating the state or area they cover, is given in Appendix VI.

All national and regional collections include *The Foundation Directory*, Edition 4 (1971)—and by mid-1975, Edition 5 should be on the shelves; the *Information Quarterly*, a supplement which updates information in Edition 4 of the *Directory*; foundation annual reports on film; the *Foundation Grants Index*, listing grants of $10,000 or more by subject field through 1972 ($5,000 or more beginning in 1973) with expanded descriptions, listed by state under foundation name, and with a key words index.

The policy of The Foundation Center is to make available to the public information about foundations; it does not direct applicants for funds to particular foundations, nor does it arrange introductions to foundation officials. Its policies expressly forbid staff members from making suggestions or referring inquirers to specific foundations. The

Center's functions are limited to the gathering and dissemination of information.

On January 1, 1975, The Foundation Center introduced a new Associates Program, designed for individuals and nonprofit organizations needing frequent access to foundation information services tailored to their special requirements. An annual fee of $150 gives Associates access to telephone and mail services, custom searches of computer files, and a library research service. The Associates Program does not affect the traditional free use of the Center's national or regional library collections by visitors. Non-Associates may order by mail any "off the shelf" item prepared by the Center for general use, such as the microfiche listing by subjects from the Foundation Grants Index, referred to here as the Computer Output Microfilm (COM).

The New York Center provides the basic collection for the regional libraries and makes new information available as it is published, but it cannot control the level and quality of services offered. The regional collections are located in public and college and university libraries, and a few are in foundation offices. The service provided by any regional library is likely to be similar to that offered by the institution where it is housed. Space and facilities may affect the quality and extent of the service available. Some libraries ask visitors to make an appointment to use the collection because of the limited space. It is a good idea to telephone beforehand to determine the opening and closing hours and to find out if there are any special restrictions on the use of the collection.

Some regional libraries have copying equipment available, but some do not, and the materials must be used in the library. Most of the collections are open Monday through Friday from 9:00 to 5:00, excepting holidays; some have more liberal hours. The one at the University of California, Los Angeles, for example, maintains the same schedule as the university research library which is coordinated with the academic year—hours are extended during final examinations and reduced during intersessions and holidays.

Following is a summary of the publications and services of The Foundation Center with notations as to which are available in the regional collections and which must be ordered from the New York Center.

The Foundation Directory

Prepared by The Foundation Center and distributed by Columbia University Press, Edition 4 (1971) lists 5,454 foundations with assets of $500,000 or more or which made grants of as much as $25,000 during the year of record. Edition 5 (1975) lists the approximately 2,500 foundations that have assets of $1 million or more or make grants of $500,000 or more annually. Edition 5 provides four indexes: (1) Fields of interest (revised and expanded for Edition 5); (2) State and city locations (new to this edition); (3) Personnel (names of donors, trustees, and administrators); and (4) Foundation names. Descriptive entries include: name and address of foundation, date and form of organization, name of donor, purpose and activities, limitations, assets, gifts received, expenditures, names of officers and trustees or directors. The *Directory* is in all Center libraries and also in many college and public library collections. It may be ordered from Columbia University Press, 136 South Broadway, Irvington-on-Hudson, New York 10533. Price of Edition 4: $17.50. (Price of Edition 5, also published by Columbia University Press: $30.00, which includes four supplements to be issued approximately twice a year beginning in 1975.)

Foundation Center Information Quarterly (October 1972–July 1974)

A supplement to *The Foundation Directory*, to update information in Edition 4, it includes information drawn from the latest available public records of foundations or from recent reports directly to The Foundation Center, such as changes in address, activities or purpose, officers, directors or trustees, and current financial data, including number and size of grants. The *Quarterly* also announces recent reports or publications received and new services available at The Foundation Center. The *Information Quarterly* ceased publication with the July 1974 issue and will be replaced by *Foundation Directory Supplements* beginning in 1975. The current issues of the *Quarterly* will, however, still be useful in conjunction with Edition 4 of *The Foundation Directory*. Edition 4 lists more than 5,000 foundations and will remain a useful reference volume even after the appearance of

Edition 5, which includes only the larger foundations—about 2,500. Individual issues of the *Quarterly* are $2.50 each and may be ordered from Columbia University Press, 136 South Broadway, Irvington-on-Hudson, New York 10533.

Foundation Grants Index, Bimonthly

This is a list of currently reported grants of $5,000 or more, arranged alphabetically, first by state in which the foundation is located, then by foundation name, and under that by name of the recipient. There is a separate index of recipients and an alphabetical index of selected key words from grant descriptions that help identify the specific subject matter of each grant reported by the foundation. The *Index* is a good indicator of current foundation interests and suggests possible funding sources for projects similar to those already funded. It is compiled by the staff of The Foundation Center in New York and issued as a removable section of *Foundation News.*

Foundation News

A bimonthly journal published by the Council on Foundations, Inc., it contains, in addition to the *Grants Index,* news and feature articles on the latest developments in foundation philanthropy and on pending legislation and tax matters, new developments in foundation program areas, book reviews, conference and meeting announcements. (The Council on Foundations, Inc., is a service organization to member foundations and major corporations with philanthropic programs. The current membership of over 650 represents 65 percent or more of all estimated assets of grant-making foundations.)

Major articles in *Foundation News* usually deal with issues of interest to foundation administrators and trustees, and there are also articles relevant to the interests of the potential applicant. The removable section containing *Foundation Grants Index* is an indispensable reference tool for those interested in foundation grant-making activities. *Foundation News* is available in all Foundation Center collections, national and regional, and is also found in many public and college libraries and institutional grants offices. Subscription orders may be sent to *Foundation News*, P. O. Box 783, Chelsea Station, New York, New York 10011. $10.00 a year to foundations; $15,00 a year to others.

Foundation Grants Index Annual

Grants Index listings from the six bimonthly issues of *Foundation News* for a given calendar year are cumulated and published in one volume. The annual and bimonthly editions of *Grants Index* are both available for reference at all Foundation Center national and regional collections. The annuals may be ordered from Columbia University Press, 136 South Broadway, Irvington-on-Hudson, New York 10533. 1972 *Index*: $10.00; 1973 *Index*: $12.00.

Foundation Grants Data Bank

A computer file of recent and retrospective grant records from nearly 2,000 foundations is maintained by the Center. Computer searches may be requested by Associates based on key words that identify the purpose for which funds are being sought, such as drug abuse, population studies, urban and inner-city programs, pollution, etc. Printouts may also be ordered by recipient name or by geographical location.

One satisfied client reported that she fed the words "bird life" into the bank and after ninety seconds of polite whirring it printed out five grants, three of which were given by foundations that appeared to be distinct possibilities for her. (With electronic thoroughness, the computer also printed out a grant to Blue Bird Circle in Houston to construct a new outlet store.) Another key word, such as "Audubon," might have turned up more possibilities.

Associates can order searches by mail from the New York Center. Request forms are available at all Foundation libraries. The cost, as of January, 1975, is $30.00 for any search containing fifty grant records or less, and $.30 for each grant record thereafter. Note particularly on the search form, "Request for Custom Search of Foundation Grants Data Bank,"[27] shown on the following page, the section titled

[27] Reprinted with permission of The Foundation Center, New York.

THE FOUNDATION CENTER

information on the philanthropic foundations: library service • research • publication

888 Seventh Avenue, New York, N.Y. 10019 / TELEPHONE: (212) 489-8610

REQUEST FOR CUSTOM SEARCH OF FOUNDATION GRANTS DATA BANK

SELECTION CRITERIA

Scope of Search: (Please describe fully the topic for which you desire grants information.)

Specific Inclusions: (If there are any descriptive or technical terms you wished used in your search, please list them below.)

Restrictions: (Enter any limitations or exclusions you wish applied to your search.)

PRICING AND VOLUME

There is a basic minimum charge of $30 for a listing of grant records up to a maximum of fifty. All records beyond the fiftieth are charge at the rate of 30¢each. Bearing in mind this pricing schedule, Please indicate the number of records you wish printed:

[ ] All   [ ] If not all, state maximum number:_____

* * *

SEQUENCE
(optional)

If you have a preference, please indicate the order in which you would like the grants arranged by checking one of the boxes below:

[ ] Alphabetically by state location of foundations
[ ] Alphabetically by state location of recipients
[ ] Alphabetically by foundation names
[ ] Alphabetically by recipient names
[ ] By dollar amount of grants, smallest to largest
[ ] By dollar amount of grants, largest to smallest

* * *

MAILING INFORMATION

Date of Request: _____

Name:_____

Title:_____

Organization: _____

Address: _____

_____

Telephone:_____May we reverse charges if we find it necessary to call you in order to clarify your search request? (Does not apply to area code 212)   [ ] Yes   [ ] No

* * *

AGREEMENT

I agree that the material furnished by The Foundation Center in response to this request is for my private use or for the internal use of my organization. I further agree to restrict its circulation to authorized persons within my organization, and that it shall not be adapted, reproduced, or sold for commercial gain.

Signature: _____

(For Foundation Center Use Only)

Date of search:_____No. of records printed:_____Amount Due:_____

"Restrictions"; attention to this section can prevent paying for information already known. For example, if the search subject is "American Indians" and foundations X, Y, and Z are already known to support American Indian programs but additional ones are needed, instructions should be given under "Restrictions" to "Omit X, Y, and Z Foundations." Or, if a search has already been done in one area, the restriction might be "Omit New York State foundations."

A custom search of Foundation Directory, Edition 5 Data Bank is also available to Associates. Searches of this data bank cost $85.00 per hour, with a minimum charge of $45.00 for each search; a price estimate is given to the requester before the search is conducted. Forms requesting searches from the Edition 5 Data Bank are available in all Center libraries or may be ordered from the New York Center. All requests are submitted to the New York Center. A replica of the form is shown on pages 140 and 141.

Foundation Information Returns

After a foundation has been identified through *The Foundation Directory* or the *Grants Data Bank,* and additional information is needed, its latest Internal Revenue Service return can be viewed free of charge in the Center's three national collections or in the geographically appropriate regional collection. Because of the filing cycle and processing requirements, returns are not available until one and one-half or two years after the close of the filing year; 1972 returns were first available in the spring of 1974. Aperture cards may be purchased by library visitors. Associates can order information returns filed by private foundations from The Foundation Center in New York. The filmed aperture cards (punched cards in which film is mounted) cost $.90 for the first card and $.45 for each additional card as of 1975. Most foundation returns require two cards. Entire sets of returns for all foundations in any one state can be ordered from the Internal Revenue Service.

Data Sheets

Full-size, hard-copy sheets containing the information from the IRS returns are available. They are more expensive than the returns filmed on aperture cards but do not require reading equipment. They are designed primarily to provide information on the smaller foundations and are not available for foundations that publish annual reports. They may be ordered from the New York Center for (at this writing) $4.00 each. Order from: The Foundation Center, 888 Seventh Avenue, New York, New York 10019.

Foundation Annual Reports

Very few foundations issue annual reports, only the larger ones as a rule, and not all of them. The Foundation Center films on microfiche (sheets of film 4″ × 6″ in size) all separately published reports they receive. These records may be reviewed at the three national collections and at the appropriate regional foundation libraries. They may also be ordered from The Foundation Center in New York. The cost is $.90 for the first microfiche card and $.45 for each additional fiche. (There are usually three foundations per fiche.)

Computer Output Microfilm (COM)

Selected topics likely to be of interest to many institutions and individuals have been searched by The Foundation Center computer and listings of grants recently made in those subjects put on microfiche. The COM lists are less expensive than the custom searches of the *Grants Data Bank* and the prepared listings cover all major fields and many subdivisions in each. COM listings may be ordered from The Foundation Center, 888 Seventh Avenue, New York, New York 10019. The subjects currently available and the cost for each list are shown in the table on p.142.

Information in The Foundation Center collections is recent and complete only to the extent that current information is provided regularly by the foundations themselves. There is a continuing increase in the flow of information to the Center from foundations, however, as more and more of them come to realize that in the long run they will benefit by the dissemination of accurate information about their programs and activities. Foundations are also increasingly aware that requests for information handled competently by the

FOR THE USE OF THE FOUNDATION CENTER
ASSOCIATES ONLY

THE FOUNDATION CENTER

information on the philanthropic foundations: library service • research • publication

888 Seventh Avenue, New York, N.Y. 10019
Entrances on 56th and 57th Streets
Tel. (212) 489-8610

This is a preliminary search request form. Please fill it out as carefully as possible, typing or printing clearly. When we receive your completed form, a member of our staff will contact you to work out the search strategy in detail.

REQUEST FOR CUSTOM SEARCH OF FOUNDATION DIRECTORY, EDITION 5 DATA BANK

Selection Criteria

Scope of search: (Please describe fully the topic for which you desire information.)

Specific Inclusions: (If there are any descriptive or technical terms you wish used in your search, please list them below.)

Restrictions: (Enter any limitations or exclusions you wish applied to your search.)

CHARTERED IN 1956 BY THE REGENTS OF THE UNIVERSITY OF THE STATE OF NEW YORK

Pricing

The charge for searches from the Foundation Directory data bank is $85 per hour, with a minimum charge of $45. When we have reviewed your search request, we will give you a more exact price estimate.

Fields to be Listed

Please indicate which data fields you would like listed for each foundation record by checking the appropriate boxes below. Please note that this is a listing of all possible fields. Not every foundation record contains all fields.

[ ] List all data fields

[ ] Foundation name	[ ] Asset type (Market	[ ] Scholarship amount
[ ] Former name	or Ledger value)	[ ] Number of Scholarships
[ ] Care of (Name)	[ ] Gifts received	[ ] Loan amount
[ ] Street	[ ] Expenditures	[ ] Number of loans
[ ] City	[ ] Grants amount	[ ] Names and titles of
[ ] State	[ ] Number of grants	officers and trustees
[ ] Zip code	[ ] Highest grant amount	[ ] Fields of interest
[ ] Establishment data	[ ] Lowest grant amount	[ ] Limitations
[ ] Donor name(s)	[ ] Program amount	[ ] Foundation type
[ ] Purpose and activities	[ ] Number of programs	[ ] IRS Employer
[ ] Fiscal year date	[ ] Matching gifts amount	Identification number
[ ] Asset amount	[ ] Number of matching gifts	

Mailing Information

Date of Request:_____

Name:_____

Title:_____

Organization:_____

Address:_____

_____

Telephone:_____ May we reverse charges if we find it necessary to call you in order to clarify your search request? (Does not apply to area code 212)
[ ] Yes   [ ] No

-----------------------(For Foundation Center Use Only)-------------------------

Date of search_____   Time charged_____
Printout mailed_____   Amount due_____

Subject	Number of grants	Number of fiche	Price per set
Education			
1 Primary & Secondary Education	734	3	$ 9.00
2 Educational Administration & Research	450	2	6.00
3 Student Aid	440	2	6.00
4 Libraries	379	2	6.00
Health			
5 Medical Education	625	3	9.00
6 Medical Research	531	3	9.00
7 Hospitals	1,011	4	12.00
8 Mental Health	414	2	6.00
Cultural Activities			
9 Visual Arts	190	1	3.00
10 Music	362	2	6.00
11 Dance & Theater	389	2	6.00
12 Museums	296	2	6.00
13 Historical Projects	146	1	3.00
14 The Media	170	1	3.00
Religion			
15 Theological Education	118	1	3.00
16 Churches & Temples	128	1	3.00
Physical Sciences			
17 Chemistry & Physics	226	1	3.00
18 Agriculture & Biology	174	1	3.00
19 Environmental Programs	267	1	3.00
Social Sciences			
20 Psychology & Sociology	239	1	3.00
21 Business & Economics	234	1	3.00
22 Government & Politics	154	1	3.00
23 Law & Justice	324	2	6.00
Welfare & Social Concerns			
24 Child Welfare	456	2	6.00
25 Youth Agencies	944	3	9.00
26 The Handicapped	280	2	6.00
27 The Aged	162	1	3.00
28 Minorities	1,015	3	9.00
29 Crime & Delinquency	234	1	3.00
30 Community Development	579	3	9.00
31 Alcohol & Drug Abuse	252	1	3.00

national and regional libraries appreciably reduces their information dissemination burden. Many of them encourage potential applicants to use the resources of The Foundation Center.

State Directories

Editions 4 and 5 of *The Foundation Directory* do not include information on foundations with assets of less than $500,000 or whose annual grant-making is under $25,000. Consequently, other sources must be researched for information on smaller foundations. A number of directories have been published which include foundations, charitable trusts, and similar organizations in one state. So far, directories are available for eleven states but others are being compiled and it is to be expected that many state listings will soon be published. Announcement of the issuance of new specialized directories and reviews of each appeared regularly in *The Foundation Center Information Quarterly* and in the future will appear in supplements to Edition 5 of *The Foundation Directory*.

Directories of foundations located within one state that have been compiled and are available at the national collections of The Foundation Center or at the regional libraries covering the subject state, as of this writing, follow.

CALIFORNIA. *A Guide to California Foundations,* by Peter D. Abrahams, Julie T. Casson, and Dennis B. Daul. Common College, Woodside, California, 1973. 116 pages, $2.50.

This publication includes chiefly northern California foundations. Information includes corporate name, address, telephone number, assets, total grants, person to contact, preferred form of contact, "funding cycle" (when proposals are acted upon), purpose statement, officers and trustees, and staff. There is no index of fields of interest.

CONNECTICUT. *A Directory of Private Foundations in the State of Connecticut,* edited by John Parker Huber. Eastern Connecticut State College Foundation, Willimantic, Connecticut, 1973. 131 pages, $3.00.

Lists 853 private foundations and charitable trusts in Connecticut. Its chief purpose is to make known the smaller foundations not listed in *The Foundation Directory* published by The Foundation Center. For each entry an attempt is made to include name, address, principal officer, net worth (usually at ledger instead of market value and at the beginning of the reported year), total expenditures (grants are not separated from administrative costs), and the chief field of interest and largest grant recipient. Special attention is given to grants for education. If the organization is also included in *The Foundation Directory* with its more complete information, this fact is noted.

This volume is being revised, and a new edition will soon be available.

DISTRICT OF COLUMBIA. *The Guide to Washington, D.C. Foundations*, by Margaret T. de Bettencourt. Guide Publishers, Washington, D.C., 1972. 62 pages, $8.00.

Identifies and describes 337 private foundations and foundation-like trusts located in Washington, D.C. Attempts to identify fields of interest for grants, using the seven classifications of *The Foundation Directory*: Welfare, Education, Humanities, Health, Religion, International, and Sciences. Records indicate that more than half of the grants went to the Washington metropolitan area, which includes neighboring portions of Maryland and Virginia, and 3 percent went abroad. Includes most of the Washington foundations listed in *The Foundation Directory* and many more smaller ones.

MAINE. *A Directory of Foundations and Charitable Trusts in the State of Maine*, edited by John Parker Huber. Eastern Connecticut State College Foundation, Willimantic, Connecticut, 1973. xv + 93 pages, $3.00.

Maine has relatively few foundations. Using a loose definition of "foundation," this publication lists 249 organizations—92 private foundations (of which 14 are operating foundations), 16 public foundations, and 141 trusts, 64 of which are in Augusta, and of those the Depositors Trust Company is trustee for 62. (One has assets listed as $747 and income for the year of $29!) The introduction gives sources for further information, makes suggestions on framing proposals to foundations, and provides for each organization its name, address, principal officer and trustees, areas of interest, net worth, and other helpful data.

MICHIGAN. *Directory of Selected Michigan Foundations and Charitable Trusts, Fourth Edition.* Michigan League for Human Services, Lansing, Michigan, 1973. 190 + 53 pages.

Includes 553 entries divided into organizations with assets of $50,000 or more and those under $50,000 that make disbursements of at least $1,000 annually. Appendices include an index of foundations by counties and a classification by purpose under seventeen subject headings and lists foundations that have suspended operations. This publication is not for sale but is available to Michigan League for Human Services members for a service charge of $8.50.

NEW HAMPSHIRE. *A Directory of Private Foundations in the State of New Hampshire,* edited by John Parker Huber. Eastern Connecticut State College Foundation, Willimantic, Connecticut, 1973. 127 pages, $3.00.

Includes 250 organizations under a very loose definition of "foundation"—eight of which have either no net worth or negative assets. This is the first volume of the New England Foundations Research Project designed to cover "private and selected public foundations and charitable trusts in the New England States." Directories have been published for Connecticut, Maine, Rhode Island, and Vermont. This volume contains a number of errors and omissions and some misleading information. It will presumably be revised and improved on the basis of the experience gained by compilation of the other New England directories.

OHIO. The *Charitable Foundations Directory, 1973* and its supplement, The *Ohio Charitable Foundations Directory, 1973.* Office of the Attorney General, State of Ohio, Columbus, 1973. xxvi + 95 pages, supplement 11 pages, $2.00.

Designed to benefit groups or individuals seeking assistance from charitable foundations, this volume was prepared by Attorney General William J. Brown with the aid of his staff and volunteers from the Junior League of Columbus. Since it lists all organizations reporting to the attorney general regardless of assets or distribution, there are some entries that grant seekers will find useless except for their amusement value; for example, the Steve Nagy Bowling Benefit Trust of Cleveland, which has as its single purpose to "aid distressed bowlers and families." Generally, the foundations listed are classified into eight categories: Aged or Infirm; Children; Education—General; Educational—Scholarship; General Purpose; Medical Research or Aid; Other; Religious. More than half of all entries are in the General Purpose category. The supplement, issued about a year after the basic volume, adds 200 additional trusts and lists 43 Ohio organizations that have terminated operation. The directory and supplement may be ordered from the Office of the Attorney General, State House Annex, Columbus, Ohio 43215.

OREGON. *Directory of Foundations and Charitable Trusts Registered in Oregon,* compiled and edited by Virgil D. Mills. Department of Justice, State of Oregon, Portland, Oregon, 1973. 76 pages, $5.00.

A listing of 331 foundations and trusts, of which nearly half, about 150, have student aid as a chief or sole purpose. Many of the organizations have very small assets—the Oregon Center for Creative Giving reported $34 in assets at the close of 1972. The listing is alphabetical with no breakdown by towns or counties; more than two-thirds of the organizations are in Portland. Each entry includes name, address, a brief statement of purpose, dollar amount of assets, and grants for the year of record for each organization. May be ordered from: Registrar of Charitable Trusts, Department of Justice, 555 State Office Building, 1400 S.W. Fifth Avenue, Portland, Oregon 97201.

RHODE ISLAND. *A Directory of Foundations and Charitable Trusts in the State of Rhode Island,* edited by John Parker Huber. Eastern Connecticut State College Foundation, P.O. Box 431, Willimantic, Connecticut, 1974. 73 + xvi pages, $3.00.

List of a total of 158 organizations: 126 private foundations (several are operating foundations), 12 public foundations (with one community trust, The Rhode Island Foundation), and 20 trusts. Twelve of the listed foundations have net worth of more than $1 million and account for over three-quarters of the total net worth, $85 million at the end of 1971. Thirty-seven made no grants at all during the latest year of record, 1971 in most cases. Entries include name, address, principal officer and trustees, chief fields of interest, net worth, three largest grants with amounts and recipients, and the smallest grant with amount and recipient for each organization. Also includes suggestions on proposal preparation. Listing is arranged by type of organization—Private Foundations, Public Foundations, and Trusts—making it necessary to check all three sections unless the category is already known.

VERMONT. *A Directory of Foundations and Charitable Trusts in the State of Vermont,* edited by John Parker Huber. Eastern Connecticut State College Foundation, Willimantic, Connecticut, 1973. 36 + xix pages, $2.00.

Vermont has very few foundations and only four met the qualification for inclusion in *The Foundation Directory,* Edition 4. This publication lists 70 organizations: 39 private foundations, 15 public foundations, and 16 trusts, with net worth ranging from over $1 million (3) to less than $10,000 (23). Also organized by type, i.e., Private Foundations, Public Foundations, and Trusts, which complicates the search for a particular foundation. There are four indices: A. geographical distribution, under towns; B. activity areas, under 18 classifications; C. rank by net worth; and D. rank by dollar value of grants.

VIRGINIA. *Virginia Directory of Private Foundations.* Division of State Planning and Community Affairs, Commonwealth of Virginia, Richmond, 1974. vi + 166 pages, $2.00.

A well-organized and selectively compiled listing which does not include foundations and trusts set up for specific purposes since they are not open to grant applications. There are 332 organizations listed, of which 137 or 41 percent are in Richmond. Each entry includes the organization's official name, address, principal officer, net worth at end of the taxable year, statement of purpose, and data on grants. Grants information includes number of grants, total amount in the year of record, and name and amount for both the largest grant recipient and the smallest. (The reader should be alerted that the assets of the Looney Foundation, listed at $45 *million*, should read $45 *thousand!*)

The Catholic Guide to Foundations

Another specialized directory in The Foundation Center's national collections covers all American philanthropic foundations whose grants suggest some preference for activities carried out under

Catholic auspices. It is *The Catholic Guide to Foundations*, Edition 2, by Francis G. de Bettencourt. Guide Publishers, Washington, D.C., 1973. 170 pages, $12.00.

This directory includes 336 foundations in 48 states—Alaska and Vermont had none that qualified—and the District of Columbia, which vary in size from 12 with net worth exceeding $10 million to 118 whose net worth is less than $100,000. The listing is broken down into four major categories: Religious—churches, shrines, monasteries, missions, etc.; Health—clinics, hospitals, nursing homes, health agencies; Educational—schools, colleges, scholarships, libraries; and Welfare—child care, homes for the aged, community funds, etc. A geographical locator is included with all foundations arranged alphabetically under the 48 states and the District of Columbia, and an index of officials keyed to their foundation.

Foundations Outside the United States

The Foundation Center's New York library has reference materials on philanthropic organizations in other countries, and reports and publications relating to philanthropic activity and legislation outside of the United States. Many of these publications and reports are also available in the Washington, D.C. collection.

The major fund of information on foundations in other countries and areas of the world is contained in directories of information similar to *The Foundation Directory* of United States foundations. Following is a list of foreign directories available in New York and Washington national collections of The Foundation Center or which may be ordered from the publishers.

AUSTRALIA. *Directory of Philanthropic Trusts in Australia.* Australian Council for Educational Research, Frederick Street, Hawthorn, Victoria 3122, Australia, 1968. 226 listings, 274 pages, Australian $5.50 or $6.05.

CANADA. *Canadian Universities' Guide to Foundations and Granting Agencies.* 3rd Edition. Information Division of the Association of Universities and Colleges of Canada, 151 Slater, Ottawa K1P 5N1, Canada, 1973. 300 listings, 161 pages, $7.50.

This directory includes U.S. foundations that support Canadian institutions. Comparable to the situation in the United States, few Canadian foundations publish reports. Of the 1,400-odd foundations currently active in Canada, only 18 are known to distribute their reports. Half of this total emanates from substantial, grant-making foundations, and these nine reports are available in the New York library of The Foundation Center. Although the activities of Canadian foundations are primarily provincial and rarely national in scope, the policies and range of interests of the major ones parallel those in this country. (The Foundation Center maintains files on many other Canadian foundations, as well as Internal Revenue Service microfilm records of the 1970 returns—990s and 990-ARs for those Canadian foundations which have U.S. investments.)

EUROPE. *Guide to European Foundations.* Prepared by the Agnelli Foundation. Columbia University Press, 136 South Broadway, Irvington-on-Hudson, New York 10533, 1973. 296 listings, 401 pages, $12.50.

FRANCE. *Fondations.* Published under the auspices of the Ministry of the Interior by Journaux Officiels, 26 rue Desaix, 75 Paris 15, France, 1971. 263 listings, 134 pages, 7.30 French francs or about $1.50. (In French)

GERMANY. *Deutsche Stiftungen für Wissenschaft, Bildung und Kultur.* Published by Nomos Verlagsgesellschaft, Baden-Baden, Germany, 1969. 629 listings, 428 pages, DM 35 or about $9.50. (In German)

INTERNATIONAL. *International Foundation Directory, The.* Published by Europa Publications, 18 Bedford Square, London WCIB 3JN, 396 pages, 550 listings for North America, Europe, South America, Japan, and parts of Asia. £7.95.

LATIN AMERICA. *Philanthropic Foundations in Latin America.* Available through Basic Books, Inc., Order Services Department, P.O. Box 4000, Scranton, Pennsylvania 18501, 1968. 777 listings, 215 pages, $7.50. Soft-cover, Spanish edition is available through the Pan American Development Foundation, 19th Street & Constitution Avenue, N.W., Washington, D.C. 20006. 283 pages, $1.50.

NEW ZEALAND. *Directory of Philanthropic Trusts.* Issued by the New Zealand Council for Educational Research, P.O. Box 3237, Wellington 1, New Zealand, 1964. 59 listings, 68 pages, available free upon request.

SWEDEN. *Svenska Kulturfonder.* Published by P. A. Norstedt & Soners forlag, Stockholm, Sweden, 1970. 700 listings (approximately), 288 pages, 19.50 kronor or about $3.75. (In Swedish)

UNITED KINGDOM. *Directory of Grant-Making Trusts.* Published by the National Council of Social Services, 26 Bedford Square, London WCIB 3HU, England, 1971. 2,000 listings (approximately), 854 pages, £5.30 or $13.25.

FOUNDATION INFORMATION SERVICES

Services offering information on foundations on a subscriber basis are usually established as sidelines of management and consultant firms. Their greatest usefulness is to institutional grants or development offices that require a constant flow of certain types of current materials and cannot or do not wish to do their own research.

Subscriptions to commercial services vary in cost but are fairly expensive for most institutions. They are a convenient means of keeping abreast of new developments, current programs, and activities in the large and active foundations; they are little or no help with the small foundations.

Foundation Research Service

One of the most reliable services has been Foundation Research Service (FRS), a subsidiary of Lawson & Williams Associates, Inc., a management consultant firm. In the past FRS dealt exclusively with the 1,000 largest foundations that account for 90 percent of all grants to all types of programs. They have just introduced a new fund-raising aid, called *The 1975 Foundation 500* described as a "no-nonsense index to the grants given by the top 500 foundations." This publication is a cross-referenced system that matches foundations with seventy detailed subject categories such as arts, education, health, religion, international, science, welfare, etc. It also provides recipient-by-state categories showing what foundations have given in which of the seventy categories and in which of the fifty states and the District of Columbia. The index retails at $19.50 and will, presumably, be updated from time to time. For information, write to Foundation Research Service, c/o Lawson & Williams Associates, Inc., 39 East 51st St., New York, New York 10022.

Taft Information System

The largest and best-known foundation information subscription service is the Taft Information System. Published by Taft Products, Inc., a subsidiary of J. R. Taft Corporation, a financial management and consulting firm, the Taft service is viewed askance (or worse) by many foundations because it focuses on "inside information" about the personal lives of foundation trustees and officers. This approach is based on the principle that knowledge of a board member's political, religious, or social affiliations; hobbies; prejudices; and partialities gives valuable clues to guide the applicant in directing his efforts towards the most promising organizations and styling them in the manner most likely to meet with receptivity. The type of information required for this approach can be obtained only through knowledge of many personal, sometimes intimate, facts about the lives of individuals with decision-making authority in foundations, and it is understandable that the acquisition of such information and its subsequent publication might create some resentment. Many foundation trustees or executives fail to see that their club memberships or the religion or political affiliations of their spouses are tidbits of information that should be made available to grant seekers. As a result of criticism on this point, recent Taft entries seem to soft-pedal this approach, but much personal information is still included. And, however it may be viewed by the foundations, or to whatever degree they express disapproval, it seems to work.

The Taft System is the oldest of the commercial foundation information systems in business and probably the best known. It lays claim to a high degree of satisfaction on the part of its subscribers, and while other similar services have entered the field, floundered, and died, Taft seems to roll merrily along.

Subscribers receive the *Foundation Reporter*, a directory of major foundations in America, updated every 120 days; the monthly *News Monitor of Philanthropy*; and the *Hot Line* news service, one or two pages "supplied as news occurs." Cost of a one-year subscription at this writing is $275, $495 for two years.

The 1973–74 edition of *Foundation Reporter* began with 230 foundations, to be supplemented with updates every three months (some of the update entries, however, read "No new information available").

Detailed information about the service with current subscription prices may be requested from: Taft Products, Suite 600, 1000 Vermont Avenue, N.W., Washington, D.C. 20005.

Two other services that offer information on foundations and other sources are described in the section on Basic Sources of Information. They are the ORYX Press Grant Information System and Funding Sources Clearinghouse, Inc. (See Index).

OTHER PUBLICATIONS BY AND ABOUT FOUNDATIONS

Foundation Newsletters

Some foundations issue newsletters that are available to institutional libraries upon request. This list gives those published by a few of the major foundations:

A/D/C Newsletter. The Agricultural Development Council, Inc., 630 Fifth Avenue, New York, New York 10020.

Carnegie Quarterly. Carnegie Corporation of New York, 437 Madison Avenue, New York, New York 10022.

CLR Recent Developments. Council on Library Resources, Inc., One Dupont Circle, Washington, D.C. 20036.

Danforth News and Notes. The Danforth Foundation, 222 South Central Avenue, St. Louis, Missouri 63105.

Ford Foundation Letter. The Ford Foundation, 320 East 43rd Street, New York, New York 10017.

Mirror. The Winston-Salem Foundation, 2230 Wachovia Building, Winston-Salem, North Carolina 27101.

New Ways. Charles F. Kettering Foundation, 5335 Far Hills Avenue, Suite 300, Dayton, Ohio 45429.

Resources. Resources for the Future, Inc., 1755 Massachusetts Avenue, N.W., Washington, D.C. 20036.

RF Illustrated. The Rockefeller Foundation 111 West 50th Street, New York, N.Y. 10020

Twentieth Century Fund Newsletter. Twentieth Century Fund, Inc., 41 East 70th Street, New York 10021.

Journals

In addition to *Foundation News,* other periodicals that provide information about foundations are:

Giving USA: A Compilation of Facts and Trends on American Philanthropy. Published by American Association of Fund Raising Counsel, Inc., 500 Fifth Avenue, New York, New York 10036. Annual subscription: $12.50.

Non-Profit Report: The Philanthropy Monthly. Published by Non-Profit, Inc., 205 Main Street, Danbury, Connecticut 06810. Annual subscription: $72.00.

Philanthropic Digest: Summary of News and Giving to Education, Health, Religion, Welfare and the Arts. Published by Brakely, John Price Jones, Inc., 6 East 43rd Street, New York, New York 10017. Annual subscription: $15.00.

Books on Foundations

American Foundations and Their Fields. Seventh edition. Edited by Wilmer Shields Rich. New York: American Foundations Information Service, 1955. 744 pages. The last of a series of directories begun by Twentieth Century Fund in 1921. Out of print.*

Andrews, F. Emerson (editor). *Foundations: 20 Viewpoints.* New York: Russell Sage Foundation, 1965. 108 pages. Twenty of the significant views on foundations which appeared in the first five volumes of *Foundation News.* Out of print.*

Andrews, F. Emerson. *Foundation Watcher.* Lancaster, Pa., Franklin and Marshall College, 1973. 321 pages. A reliable book, with brisk, incisive, and sometimes tough commentary.

* Out of print. Available in The Foundation Center's New York Collection.

Andrews, F. Emerson. *Patman and Foundations: Review and Assessment.* New York, The Foundation Center, 1968. 62 pages. Presents in brief the main findings of some 5,000 pages of six Patman reports and two hearings, together with an evaluation of his conclusions. Out of print.*

Andrews, F. Emerson. *Philanthropic Foundations.* New York: Russell Sage Foundation, 1956. 459 pages. Still basic in the field, this volume gives a full picture of foundation operations and problems, including legal, tax, and policy implications. Out of print.*

Commission on Foundations and Private Philanthropy. *Foundations, Private Giving and Public Policy.* Report and Recommendations of the Commission on Foundations and Private Philanthropy. Chicago, University of Chicago Press, 1970. 287 pages. Under chairmanship of Peter G. Peterson, this commission of private citizens was charged with studying "all relevant matters bearing on foundations and private philanthropy, and to issue a report containing long-range policy recommendations with respect to them."

Cuninggim, Merrimon. *Private Money and Public Service: The Role of Foundations in American Society.* New York: McGraw-Hill Book Co., 1972. 267 pages. An examination of recent criticism of foundations and a look at their achievements. Merrimon Cuninggim was chief executive officer of The Danforth Foundation for more than a decade.

Embree, Edwin R. and Julia Waxman. *Investment in People: The Story of the Julius Rosenwald Fund.* New York: Harper & Brothers, 1949. 291 pages. The full and final record of the Julius Rosenwald Fund. Out of print.*

Ford Foundation, The. *Report of the Study of The Ford Foundation on Policy and Program.* Detroit, The Ford Foundation, 1949. 139 pages. Prepared for the guidance of this foundation in its initiating period, an important document of general value. Out of print.*

Fosdick, Raymond B. *Adventure in Giving: The Story of the General Education Board.* New York: Harper and Row, 1962. 369 pages. The full and exciting history of the General Education Board, published as it concluded its operations. Out of print.*

Fosdick, Raymond B. *The Story of The Rockefeller Foundation.* New

* Out of print. Available in The Foundation Center's New York Collection.

York: Harper & Brothers, 1952. 336 pages. A semiofficial history of great general interest. Out of print.*

Glenn, John M., Lilian Brandt, and F. Emerson Andrews. *Russell Sage Foundation, 1907–1946.* Two volumes. New York, Russell Sage Foundation, 1947. 746 pages. The comprehensive history of the first forty years of the foundation largely instrumental in early organization of social work.

Goulden, Joseph C. *The Money Givers.* New York: Random House, 1971. 341 pages. A journalist examines all aspects of the tax-free foundations. Partly a diatribe against foundations, but contains much useful information.

Harrison, Shelby M., and F. Emerson Andrews. *American Foundations for Social Welfare.* New York, Russell Sage Foundation, 1946. 249 pages. General discussion of organization, finances, administration, fields of activity, with the first extensive (505) foundation directory. Out of print.*

Heimann, Fritz R. (editor). *The Future of Foundations.* The American Assembly, distributed by Prentice-Hall, Inc., Englewood Cliffs, N.J., 1973. 278 pages. Background papers prepared for the 1972 Arden House conference on problems of American foundations.

Hollis, Ernest V. *Philanthropic Foundations and Higher Education.* New York: Columbia University Press, 1938. 365 pages. Good report on early foundation support of higher education, with chapters on foundation history, policies, and organization. Out of print.*

Howard, Nathaniel R. *Trust for All Time.* Cleveland, The Cleveland Foundation, 1963. 111 pages. A history of both the earliest of the community foundations, The Cleveland Foundation, and the whole community foundation movement.

Jordan, W. K. *Philanthropy in England, 1480–1660.* New York, Russell Sage Foundation, 1959. 410 pages. The definitive history of philanthropy in England for its period, with extensive treatment of the many thousands of charitable trusts which then originated.

Katz, Milton. *The Modern Foundation: Its Dual Character, Public and Private.* New York, The Foundation Library Center, 1968. 26 pages. A lawyer's critique of various types of modern foundations. Out of print.*

* Out of print. Available in The Foundation Center's New York Collection.

Keppel, Frederick P. *The Foundation: Its Place in American Life.* New York: The Macmillan Company, 1930. 113 pages. The classic early discussion of the foundation, its varieties and functions, by the former president of Carnegie Corporation of New York.

Kiger, Joseph C. *Operating Principles of the Larger Foundations.* New York: Russell Sage Foundation, 1954. 151 pages. A study of the development of foundation doctrine based largely on material from foundations and their critics, prepared by the research director for the Select (Cox) Committee to Investigate Foundations. Out of print.*

Lindeman, Eduard C. *Wealth and Culture.* New York: Harcourt, Brace & Company, 1936. 135 pages. An early "study of one hundred foundations and community trusts and their operations during the decade 1921–1930," with views of the author on effects of distribution of wealth on American culture. Out of print.*

Macdonald, Dwight. *The Ford Foundation: The Man and the Millions.* New York, Reynal and Company, 1956. 186 pages. Sprightly account of the earlier years of The Ford Foundation. Out of print.*

Nielsen, Waldemar A. *The Big Foundations.* A Twentieth Century Fund study. New York, Columbia University Press, 1972. 475 pages. Critical examination of the thirty-three largest foundations by a former executive of The Ford Foundation, with sweeping recommendations for reform.

Owen, David. *English Philanthropy, 1660–1960.* Cambridge, Harvard University Press, 1964. 610 pages. British philanthropy from 1660 through passage of the Charities Act of 1960. Includes substantial treatment of foundations.

Pifer, Alan. *The Foundation in the Year 2000.* New York, The Foundation Library Center, 1968. 16 pages. A look into the future of foundations by the president of Carnegie Corporation of New York. Out of print.*

Reeves, Thomas C. (editor). *Foundations Under Fire.* Ithaca, Cornell University Press, 1970. 235 pages. A selection of twenty-four papers by major critics and supporters of foundations, dealing with public responsibility, venture capital, propaganda and politics, business and taxes.

* Out of print. Available in The Foundation Center's New York Collection.

Report of the Committee on the Law and Practice relating to Charitable Trusts. (Nathan Report) London, Her Majesty's Stationery Office, 1952. 251 pages. The historic report of the Lord Nathan Committee on British charitable trusts. Includes recommendations for the future.

Richman, Saul. *Public Information Handbook for Foundations.* New York, Council on Foundations, 1973. 95 pages. Deals with reports, news stories in various media, press conferences, speakers, other means of telling the foundation story to a wider public.

Savage, Howard J. *Fruit of an Impulse: Forty-Five Years of the Carnegie Foundation, 1905–1950.* New York, Harcourt, Brace and Co., 1953. 407 pages. History of a foundation important in the educational field, with material of general value. Out of print.*

The Story of The New York Community Trust—the first 50 Years. 1974. 36 pages. The New York Community Trust, 415 Madison Avenue, New York, New York 10017.

Weaver, Warren. *U.S. Philanthropic Foundations: Their History, Structure, Management, and Record.* New York, Harper & Row, 1967. 492 pages. An appraisal of present-day foundations by an experienced executive of the Rockefeller and Sloan foundations. Includes discussion by nineteen specialists of the value of foundation grants in their areas.

Whitaker, Ben. *The Philanthropoids; Foundations and Society: An Unsubsidized Anatomy of the Burden of Benevolence.* New York, William Morrow & Company, 1974. 256 pages.

Zurcher, Arnold J., and Jane Dustan. *The Foundation Administrator: A Study of Those Who Made America's Foundations.* New York, Russell Sage Foundation, 1972. 171 pages. A study under Foundation Center auspices. Extensive factual data on administrators—backgrounds, salary, duties, attitudes toward tasks.

Zurcher, Arnold J. *Management of American Foundations: Administration, Policies, and Social Role.* New York, New York University Press, 1972. 184 pages. Informed discussion of foundation operation by the former executive director of Alfred P. Sloan Foundation.

---

* Out of print. Available in The Foundation Center's New York Collection.

How to Find Out About Grants and Who Gives Them

BUSINESS AND INDUSTRY GRANTS

The corporate community is not a rich source of grant funds, but there are a few indications that this situation may be improving. A new concept of industry's social responsibilities is bringing about changes in business policies, organization, and operations. Companies are revising hiring and training policies, encouraging employee participation in community affairs, increasing dialogue with youth and minority groups. There is mounting pressure from within and without for greater corporate involvement in the solution of society's problems; the direction and volume of corporate philanthropy will probably go through some changes within the next few years—changes that could bring about an increase in sponsorship of the type of activity that can be supported through the grant mechanism.

Corporate philanthropy is both a response to and a defense against the crusade waged by private philanthropists to ameliorate the adverse effects of the industrial revolution on the lives of individuals and on the general well-being of the society. The main benefici-

159

aries of corporate philanthropy in the past have been health programs, charitable institutions and causes, and for the past twenty-five years, education.

Business and industrial executives began in the late 1940s to develop an understanding of the interdependence between the needs of the corporation and products of the nation's educational institutions, particularly of the universities. This changing attitude was reflected in a rise in support of higher education by some leading business concerns, surveyed by the Council for Financial Aid to Education, Inc., from $24 million in 1947 to $375 million in 1969. The 1970 earnings slump may be credited with the reduction that year to $340 million which carried through to 1971, when the total was $345 million. However, 1972 was not much better—$365 million. Considering the inflation of that period, these figures actually represent a sizable decrease after 1969. In 1973, when earnings reached an unprecedented high, the contributions of those same business concerns to education rose to $425 million—a hopeful sign until the 1974 slump cast a shadow over the future outlook, especially after the 1970–71 reaction.[28] Education is one area in which the business community recognizes that it has a stake, and if support of educational activities falls off, the outlook for other areas is dismal, indeed. But the whole economic picture of the nation is so uncertain that no one can predict the future. To be sure, the corporate community is going to continue to need training and skills that are best developed at educational institutions and there is some possibility that the bonds between the two will grow stronger.

Generally speaking, the past record of the United States business community in philanthropy is discouraging. In 1970 total corporate contributions to philanthropic causes was slightly more than $797 million, or 1.08 percent of pretax profits. Total contributions rose to an estimated $950 million in 1973 including funds turned over to company-sponsored foundations. This appears to be a substantial increase until it is noted that it was only 0.75 percent of pretax profits.[29]

This pattern has persisted over many years. When former presi-

[28] Source: Council for Financial Aid to Education, Inc., New York. *Aid to Education Programs of Some Leading Business Concerns.* 1972 and 1974 editions.
[29] Source: *Giving, USA.* 1974 Annual Report.

dent Lyndon Johnson was a member of the board of the Mayo Clinic, he once addressed a group of businessmen on the subject of philanthropic giving and told them that they apparently believed the government was better at dispensing their funds than they were. He cited statistics to show that businessmen were giving less than 1 percent of profits to charitable causes although they were allowed up to 5 percent as tax-deductible amounts for such purposes.

To be fair, it must be stated that the dollar contributions do not reflect the total participation of the business community in education, research, and social welfare. Many contributions are made in the form of "gifts-in-kind"—products donated to charitable institutions, hospitals, or for disaster relief, or pieces of equipment given to educational institutions.

Another factor to be considered is that although, as President Johnson stated, governmental regulations encourage the business community to support philanthropic causes, occasionally a seemingly arbitrary or incomprehensible legislative interpretation will impede corporations in activities that are of the most interest to them and in which they have made their best record.

In June, 1974, for example, an IRS ruling was made that could reduce corporate scholarship programs to as little as one-quarter of their former level. The new rule limits the number of scholarships that can be awarded to children of employees to not more than 25 percent of the "eligible applicants." This literally means that even if funds are available and eligible students have applied, at least three-fourths of the applicants must be turned down. There are other restrictions on corporate scholarship programs in the same ruling. The ruling is being contested and it remains to be seen what the ultimate outcome of this strange decision will be. It appears, on the surface, to be an attempt to reduce, or at least discourage, corporate support of education.

The company foundation is preferred by some corporations as a means of distributing their philanthropy because it offers certain advantages over the direct giving method. The chief advantages of the company-sponsored foundation are:

1. A company can stabilize its donations by divorcing them from fluctuations in annual earnings.

2. By vesting responsibility for grant making in specific individuals it makes for better management.
3. The foundation offers greater latitude for program development by facilitating long-range planning.
4. There are tax benefits.
5. It improves the public image of the corporation.

In the first shock wave that followed the enactment of the 1969 Tax Reform Act, there were predictions that the company foundation was a doomed institution. But a survey (published in 1973) conducted by The Conference Board, Inc. of 240 company foundations indicates that the majority can continue to function under the new legislation, although an estimated 10 percent of the approximately 2,000 company foundations closed their doors soon after the new law went into effect.[30] The study indicates, however, that the growth of such foundations may be halted because it is now costlier to set them up and the tax advantages have been reduced.

The company foundation was little known prior to World War II and many of them, perhaps as many as 50 percent of those currently in existence, were established during the high-profit years of the Korean War, 1950–1953.

Since the foundation is a separate legal entity, chartered to operate in the public interest, it may not legally make gifts which are of sole benefit to the sponsor. Therefore, many activities sponsored by company foundations have no association whatsoever with the product of the donor, and companies with foundations seldom dispense completely with direct grants.

Like all other foundations, the company-sponsored foundation prefers to make grants to tax-exempt organizations in preference to individuals. Some company foundation prohibit grants to private foundations, and, generally speaking, charitable institutions that are not classified as "private foundations" are those most likely to receive grants from company-sponsored foundations. Once the question of tax-exempt status has been clarified, foundation officials evaluate

---

[30] Source: *The Impact of the Tax Reform Act of 1969 on Company Foundations.* A research report from The Conference Board, by John H. Watson, III. 1973. (Conference Board Report No. 595)

applications by the following criteria: (1) the problem area, to determine if it fits into their program; and (2) the applicant organization itself and its plan for dealing with the problem. No matter how interested the foundation may be in the problem, it wants assurance that the applicant organization is qualified to carry out the plan of the proposal.

Company foundations stipulate the areas of their interest just as other foundations do, and information on this is available from the same sources as for all other foundations. The Foundation Center and/or its regional collections includes company foundations in its compilations and research resources. Company foundations seem to be more responsive to direct requests for information than foundations in general.

The procedures for approaching company foundations are also very much the same as for other similar organizations. Preliminary discussion before the submission of a formal application is extremely important, especially since 1969, when new factors must be taken into consideration.

In approaching corporations or businesses for *direct* grants, there is no standard procedure, because grant programs are administered in a variety of ways and every company is different. The office or individual designated to handle applications for grants may be relatively far down in the executive hierarchy or may be the president himself. It is sometimes possible to identify that individual by a telephone call to the main office or by requesting information of the philanthropic programs of the company by letter. The publication of the Council for Financial Aid to Education, Inc., *Aid to Education: Programs of Some Leading Business Concerns*, lists the offices and individuals responsible for philanthropy in the business concerns covered by the publication—many of the major ones. *Standard & Poor's Register of Corporations, Directors and Executives* lists United States and Canadian corporations with officers and directors followed by an alphabetical list of executives, indicating the area of responsibility of each. The *Register* is available in large reference and all business libraries, or may be ordered from Standard & Poor, 345 Hudson St., New York, N.Y. 10014. The cost is $140 per year; cumulative supplements are issued in May, July, and October.

As industry has become more mindful of its social responsibilities and of its dependence upon the academic sector for skilled personnel, it has also come to realize that its mission-oriented research can survive only through a steady infusion of new basic knowledge.

Dr. Herbert I. Fusfeld, director of research of the Kennecott Copper Corporation, speaking as president of the Industrial Research Institute before the Annual Meeting of the National Association of State Universities and Land Grant Colleges at Denver, Colorado, in November, 1973, said: "Industrial research is by definition mission oriented. . . . It may very well call for new basic scientific knowledge, either to make the program work at all, as in the case of fusion, or to guide and make more effective an otherwise long and costly experimental development. . . . Joint ventures can be set up under a variety of funding possibilities. . . . There are many ways for industry to provide funds for universities today."

A concordant note on this theme was sounded in the spring of 1974 at a meeting convened primarily to honor the three physics Nobel laureates for 1973. The dinner meeting was hosted by Frank Cary, chairman of the board of International Business Machines Corporation, and was attended by the presidents or chairmen of the boards of many of America's largest high technology companies. The principal speaker, Patrick E. Haggerty, chairman of the board of Texas Instruments, Inc., began by acknowledging the debt that his and other companies owed to fundamental advances in solid state physics and devoted a good part of the talk to a call for a new science and technology advisory apparatus in the executive office of the president. In commenting on the meeting, Philip H. Abelson, editor of *Science*, stated, "But academia now understands that it cannot count on government for sustained rational behavior. At the same time, industry needs a healthy university system . . . if anything is clear, it is that we cannot depend solely on the wisdom of politicians in the solution of long-range problems. We must find better ways. A closer cooperation of academic scientists and dynamic elements of industry could lead to effective actions."[31]

[31] *Science*, Vol. 183, 29 March 1974, p. 4131.

Unfortunately there is no central organization that collects and disseminates information about the research needs and interests of corporations, and the researcher or project director with a well-developed idea must deal directly with the corporation official responsible for research activities. The National Association of Manufacturers and the United States Chamber of Commerce can give information on the products of various industries which will indicate their specific interests. The *Trade Association Directory*, found in business libraries and some large general libraries, indicates which companies are interested in certain fields. There are trade associations for house trailers, pharmaceuticals, steel and iron, cosmetics, and many others. Professional societies in science and technology fields are also possible sources of information about corporate interest in certain types of research.

Research grants are made by corporations primarily on the basis of the companies' needs for segments of knowledge or for products that can be researched, studied, or developed at institutions or laboratories other than their own in a manner that is advantageous to the company. If some essential piece of information or item of equipment will require the building of a special laboratory and assembly of a staff that will be obsolete when the work is completed, it is both more economical and more expeditious to subcontract that portion of a large project to a laboratory where the facilities are already available. The most common arrangement is made between the corporation and the department head or director of an academic or research institution who agrees to perform the task and takes responsibility for assembling the necessary personnel and facilities. Research projects of this type are especially attractive to graduate schools in that they provide support and training for graduate students, serve as thesis topics, and utilize the talents of faculty and staff during the intersessions and summer holidays.

If the proposed activity is basic research that will provide knowledge of potential, rather than immediate, value, the spokesman or proposer should have an understanding or some appreciation of the company's long-range development plans and interests. A completed proposal should never be submitted without preliminary discussion and usually a great deal of it. The negotiations leading to a successful agreement between a corporation and an institution will be extensive and cover a wide range of policies and will require patience and flexibility on both sides.

The contract is the instrument most often used by commercial organizations for research projects. The award of research contracts is usually in the domain of the research and development arm of the corporation, headed by a vice-president or research director. Preliminary inquiries should never be directed simply to the main offices of the corporation or even to the research division. It is easy enough to find out who is in charge of research and address the communication to that individual. One director of research of a large corporation, speaking on this point, said, "It takes very little effort to find out the name of a vice-president or director of research. We try to reply to every communication we receive, but I don't feel any real obligation to answer those addressed to 'The _____ Corporation,' or to 'Director of Research.' " The best reference in such cases is *Standard & Poor's Register of Corporations, Directors and Executives*.

The introductory letter should describe the nature of the proposed project; state why the company should be interested in it; give the writer's qualifications to perform the activity; specify the approximate cost; and request a meeting to discuss the matter. The writer should be sufficiently familiar with the work of the company to describe the advantages that sponsorship of the project would yield. Before approaching a corporate research head, the following points should be considered:

1. Commercial organizations are profit-oriented and proposals to them should indicate clearly the ultimate financial advantage that may accrue. The advantages must be of sufficient magnitude to be attractive. No corporation is likely to give $50,000 to develop a process or a piece of equipment—no matter how clever the idea may be—if the most that can be realized by its use is in the neighborhood of $1,000 per year.
2. Corporations are most likely to subcontract to institutions located in the same community as one of their plants or main offices.
3. Proprietary rights are of paramount interest to business and

industrial organizations. Any questions regarding rights to patent or license research or development products or those relating to distribution of royalty income must be resolved early in the negotiation. The individual or institution performing the work must be prepared to accept the terms indicated by corporation policy.

4. Specifications as to timing, quality of product, and general guidelines for performance of corporation-supported activities are subject to whatever direction, scrutiny, or supervision the company may wish to exercise.

The American businessman is well behind his European counterpart in the establishment of organizations for the stated purpose of investing a share of corporate earnings in the improvement and development of scholarship, scientific research, cultural programs, and the creative arts. An important step was taken toward recognition of corporate responsibility in the arts fields in 1967 with the establishment of the Business Committee for the Arts. The formation of such an organization was suggested by David Rockefeller, chairman of the Chase Manhattan Bank and vice-chairman of the board of trustees of the Museum of Modern Art. C. Douglas Dillon, former secretary of the treasury, was the first chairman. Goldwin A. McLellan, former public affairs director of the Olin Corporation, was named president, a position he still holds.

During its early years the BCA did not bring about any dramatic increase in corporate support for the arts. In 1972 the retiring chairman, Robert O. Anderson, of the Atlantic-Richfield Corporation, stated that corporate support for the arts had increased by roughly 160 percent since 1965 (two years before the Committee was formed)—from $22 million to $56 million in 1971. The figures were later revised by the committee, which now reports an increase of 400 percent from 1965 to 1970—from $22 million to $110 million. Viewed as a percentage of pretax corporate earnings during that period, the totals are less than impressive, no matter which ones are used. In 1965 pretax profits were $77.8 billion; $74.0 billion in 1970; $85.1 billion in 1971; and $98.0 billion in 1972. In 1973 profits before taxes reached a whopping $126.6 billion, and the figure on corporate contributions to the arts rose to $144 million.[32]

Discrepancies on estimated annual support of the arts are the result of differences in the interpretation of what constitutes a philanthropic contribution. If deductible business expenses that benefit the arts are included, the figure is not the same as it is if only direct donations to artists or arts programs are taken into account. Just as corporations make "in-kind" donations of equipment and products that do not show up on their giving estimates, they also support the arts in ways other than through traditional philanthropy. The increasing use of contemporary art in the decor of corporate offices or building lobbies, for example, provides a large, new outlet for the work of modern artists and an opportunity for their work to be seen by a larger audience, while it serves to make the offices and buildings more interesting and attractive.

There are currently 113 corporate members of BCA, and their organizations support educational television programs—an exceedingly important contribution in view of declining federal support for central programming; finance opera productions in both urban and "grass roots" communities; help support museums; finance publication of arts information calendars and announcements; and contribute to the education of young performers, artists, and symphony conductors. The BCA has undoubtedly been a factor in bringing the need for this kind of corporate support to the attention of its members but it may be that the major contribution of the BCA is in serving as a model for similar organizations that might be formed to stimulate corporate support in other areas including the sciences and the humanities.

The BCA will advise an arts organization on an approach to businessmen, including its basic letter and prospectus; provide information to businessmen who consult them about an arts organization; and serve as a reference for arts organizations that provide BCA with appropriate information. It will not supply an organization with a list of names to contact or help with any actual fund-raising or act as a conduit for funds.

[32] Source: Reports of Business Committee on the Arts, Inc., and *Giving, USA.* 1974 Annual Report.

The address of the Business Committee for the Arts, Inc., is 1700 Broadway, New York, New York 10010.

Information on educational activities of business concerns may be requested from: Council for Financial Aid to Education, Inc., 680 Fifth Avenue, New York, New York 10017. Their publication, *Aid to Education: Programs of Some Leading Business Concerns*, 1974 edition, gives information that is useful for anyone planning to approach a corporation. The listing of the office or individual in the organization responsible for philanthropic activities is very useful. This publication has been priced at $7.00 in the past but the next edition, due in 1976, is expected to cost more.

The Council's *Handbook of Aid to Higher Education by Corporations, Foundations, and the Federal Government* is no longer being distributed but supplements to the original publication are available from time to time. Information on the supplements can be obtained directly from the Council.

Publications on corporate philanthropy that make useful reading on the subject are:

Blumberg, Phillip I. *Corporate Responsibility in a Changing Society: Essays on Corporate Social Responsibility*. Boston: Boston University School of Law, 1972.

Chagy, Gideon. *The New Patrons of the Arts*. New York: Harry Abrams, Inc., 1972.

Chagy, Gideon. *State of the Arts and Public Support*. New York: Ericksson, 1971.

Chamberlain, Neil W. *The Limits of Corporate Responsibility*. New York: Basic Books, Inc., 1973.

The Application

There are three distinct phases in the process of applying for grant funds: the Preliminary Approach or Preapplication Phase; Submission of the Proposal—Application Phase; and Decision-Making or Postapplication Phase.

Each phase, just as in human development, must be passed through because during each one facts are learned and experiences gained based on the previous phase and as preparation for the next one. Also, as in human development, if any phase is inadequately experienced or skipped, it may mean trouble ahead.

The Preapplication Phase consists of two simultaneous and synchronous procedures—consultation with officials of the institution that will administer the grant, and consultation with the prospective funding organization.

The Application Phase covers the preparation and submission of the formal proposal. Every granting organization has its own procedure or form for applications, but there are some general guides that apply to almost all of them or that can be adapted to meet the requirements.

The Postapplication Phase represents the period during which review and processing of the application occurs. This activity is under the control of the grant-making organization, but the applicant who understands the process will survive it more comfortably and respond more effectively if called upon to do so during that period.

The Application

WHAT TO DO BEFORE YOU APPLY—THE PREAPPLICATION PHASE

This is the "learning" stage and if it is handled adequately, the transition through the remaining phases will be greatly facilitated.

This phase begins when all potential funding sources have been identified. Only those organizations that have demonstrated by their recent grant-giving records an interest in the kind of activity to be proposed or those with newly announced programs in the field remain on the list. Organizations with special requirements that cannot be met in respect of geographic location, type of institutional affiliation, academic credentials, obligations for the future, etc., should have been deleted. Deadline dates for the remaining ones are checked to ensure sufficient time for preparation, consultation, and submission of a proposal that does justice to the idea. In estimating the time required, allow time for preapplication discussions. Appointments cannot always be made on short notice, and for some activities many meetings with representatives of the prospective funding agency and the site institution will be necessary.

New, up-to-date information should be requested directly from the funding organization. Program guidelines, application forms, and even the most recent printed information obtained from reference services, directories, journals, or annual reports, may be superseded by the time it comes to the applicant's attention.

Requests for current information, forms, and guidelines should be in writing. If the program announcement bears a recent date and forms and guidelines are attached, as occasionally happens, it may be unnecessary to write. But printed materials are seldom so clear or so complete that no additional questions need to be asked.

When all available information has been collected, it must be read thoroughly; the temptation is great to ignore the fine print, where critical information is sometimes given.

An outline or abstract of the proposed activity should then be prepared, if it has not already been done. This is a brief statement that tells the following: What is to be done, why it is worth doing, what will be the specific objective, who is to do it, what facilities it requires, how long it will take, and the approximate cost. This statement contains the basic information necessary for preliminary discussions with the appropriate officials at the site institution and at the prospective granting organization. The *curriculum vitae* of the principal investigator or project director (the applicant, usually) should be brought up to date.

Grant-making organizations prefer to make awards to institutions rather than individuals. This has been true of governmental agencies for a long time. Foundations have been more lenient. However, since the 1969 Tax Reform Act, foundations tend to insist that the funds be placed under the control of an institution for administration. The act holds grantors responsible to see that no funds dispensed by them are misused. Supervision of every grant places an administrative burden on foundations that is excessive for most of them, especially those with limited or no professional staff. It is easier to meet this legal requirement by making awards to institutions and holding them responsible for proper use and management of the funds. The researcher or scholar who conceived the idea or wishes to respond to a Request for Proposal and who will actually write the proposal must also serve as the "go-between" and carry on the negotiations between the institution and the funding agency throughout the application process.

Selecting the Appropriate Institution

Preapplication consultations begin at the institution that will provide facilities and services for the project and sign the final proposal as the formal "applicant." If there is an institutional grants office, the applicant will have visited it during the search for possible funding sources; it is in that office that discussion should begin. If there is no grants office, the chief executive, president, director, or chancellor may be the appropriate official or will direct the applicant to the appropriate office.

Consultation with the institutional representative has two main functions: first, to determine if the project is acceptable to the institution and if facilities can be made available for it; second, for clarification of institutional policies on such matters as reimbursement of institutional overhead costs; faculty and staff released time to work on funded projects; patents and copyrights; equipment and property acquisition and use; and other policies relevant to particular activities, such as protection of human subjects, care of laboratory animals, etc.

At the conclusion of the first discussion, the applicant should know the answers to the following questions.

1. Is the project feasible and acceptable to the institution?
2. Can space be made available for it?
3. Will facilities and services be available as necessary? This includes *general* services such as janitorial, utilities, elevator, copying, and telephone services; and any necessary *special* facilities, such as electron microscopes, computers, laboratory animal quarters, parking space, loading docks, etc.
4. What financial arrangements will be acceptable to the institution? What does the institution expect from the grantor? Which items should appear as separate elements in the

proposal budget, and which are covered by a formula-based overhead or indirect cost item? The formula may be a percentage of total direct costs or a percentage of personnel costs. (See section on Indirect (Overhead) Costs.)

5. What contribution is the institution willing to make to the project for which no reimbursement from grant funds is expected? Such contributions may be in the form of contributed staff or faculty time, use of specialized equipment, data processing services, or sharing of other costs.

6. What, if any, special provisions must you make for use of human subjects, experimental animals, or other activities requiring review by designated institutional committees?

The relation of the project director or principal investigator to the institution is a fundamental factor in the success or failure of a sponsored activity. Whether the institution is a college campus, a research laboratory, a drug treatment center, or a public playground, the extent of its involvement in the project must be fully clarified in the beginning. Each party to the agreement must know what is available and to what extent, what the administrative channels are for obtaining services and facilities, and how the rights and obligations agreed upon are to be exercised.

Most educational and research institutions encourage their staff and faculty to apply for support from outside sources and are willing and even eager to accept the responsibilities entailed in the negotiation and administration of support agreements. But even under ideal circumstances, difficulties can develop unless all the necessary information is exchanged in the preapplication period.

Some of the areas in which misunderstandings are most likely to arise are discussed in the next section on The Institution as Grantee.

There are a few other pitfalls; although less frequently the subject of conflict, they are relevant to the eligibility of the institution to receive a grant.

Suitability

The suitability of an institution rests upon two elements: It must be willing and able to make its facilities available; and it must be viewed by the granting organization as an acceptable grantee. For example, during the Vietnam War, a number of colleges and universities enacted policies opposed to the acceptance by them of Department of Defense contracts and barred military recruiters from the campus. Obviously, at these schools those faculty members wishing to do DOD research would not find the institution receptive. In response, some federal agencies now have policies forbidding the use of their funds for support of activities to be conducted at institutions that still bar visits by military recruiters. Clearly, under such conditions, the funding agency would find the institution unacceptable.

Civil Rights Act

Every applicant organization requesting federal support is required to conform with the provisions of the Civil Rights Act of 1964, which states that no person in the United States shall, on the ground of race, color, or national origin be excluded from participation in, be denied the benefits of, or be subjected to discrimination under any program or activity receiving federal financial assistance. Grantee institutions are required to file Assurance of Compliance according to the guidelines of each granting agency, and this can be done on a "blanket" basis covering all activities at the institution sponsored by a specific agency. If an institution has not filed an Assurance of Compliance with the pertinent agency, the award may be held up until this is done.

Affirmative Action

Some governmental funding programs require assurance that institutions have filed acceptable affirmative action plans. Unless these assurances are given, awards may be delayed or denied. State and local government agencies receiving funds under formula grants are required to develop and maintain a merit system of personnel administration, including an affirmative action plan to assure equal employment opportunity for women and minorities, and many of them pass along these requirements to organizations and individuals receiving support through formula grants.

Foundations and corporations are not always bound by the same regulations as governmental agencies which, after all, dispense funds from the public coffers. However, many educational, research, and other nonprofit institutions receive the major portion of their grant funds from governmental sources and have incorporated federal regulations covering some activities into their own bylaws, making them applicable to all other sponsored activities.

In most cases, for the individual applicant affiliated with an institution, the negotiation of institutional approvals is a routine matter. The "unaffiliated" researcher or scholar is in a rather different situation—he or she must find an institution willing and able to accept responsibility for administering the grant. The independent researcher, particularly in the social sciences and the humanities may not need extensive facilities—access to museums, libraries, or archives is often all that is required. Or in certain kinds of survey research, the "laboratory" is the community, the street, a park, or a public transportation vehicle. The less-than-full-time scholar or researcher finds projects of these kinds quite feasible but may be out of luck because grant-making organizations are often reluctant to make awards to individuals. Many professional women find themselves in this category during the years when they have young children. One institution has been set up especially to assist women who cannot manage a full-time institutional commitment but who want to continue study and research on a part-time basis. In Cambridge, Massachusetts, Lynn Slavitt runs a nonprofit organization, Research for Social Change, Inc., to assist women in preparing applications and finding funding sources, and provides administrative services, such as bookkeeping, health insurance, and other support services that a grantee needs. Research for Social Change maintains a friendly relationship with The Radcliffe Institute, one of the leaders in recognizing the special problems of the woman scholar. In March, 1974, the two groups jointly sponsored a conference on "Demystifying the Research Grant," where representatives from foundations and federal agencies discussed trends, philosophies, and technicalities of grant making. Other such meetings are planned for the future.

Other institutions that undertake administration of grants for unaffiliated applicants are, in many cases, oriented to one discipline or field of study, i.e., social research, economics, community welfare and development, etc. The applicant who arranges for sponsorship by such an institution relates to it in the same way a faculty or staff member interacts with his or her institution. In each situation, the applicant—the individual who conceives the idea and writes the proposal—acts as the liaison between the institution and the prospective granting organization during the preapplication phase.

THE INSTITUTION AS GRANTEE: INTERACTION OF THE INSTITUTION AND THE FUNDING ORGANIZATION

The institution providing the facilities will be closely identified with the project and the funding agency will look to that organization for compliance with its guidelines and regulations. The institution in turn will look to the principal investigator or project director to fulfill its requirements in such matters as use of facilities and personnel and appropriate compensation as agreed upon.

In order to deal fairly with the institution where the work will be done and to understand some of its demands, every applicant must be acquainted with certain basic facts about sponsored activities. Some of the major areas in which misunderstandings and misinformation can create problems are: Protection of Human Subjects; Indirect (Overhead) Costs; Patents and Copyrights; Laboratory Animals; Equipment Acquisition and Disposition; and Cost Sharing and Matching Funds.

PROTECTION OF HUMAN SUBJECTS

Developments in modern medical technology and recent revelations about their application to subjects and patients have brought about more precise and more stringent governmental regulations concerning the participation of human subjects in experimental studies.

Since 1973 the Department of Health, Education, and Welfare has been prohibited from supporting activities involving human subjects without assurance from the site institution that adequate safeguards have been established for the protection of the rights and welfare of the subjects. Other federal agencies with grant-making programs have followed the lead of HEW and accept evidence of compliance with HEW requirements as sufficient assurance for their purposes.

Institutions with a sizable volume of federally funded programs now feel obliged to extend the policy covering protection of human subjects to all activities regardless of sponsorship, and indeed this may soon be a statutory requirement. In July of 1974 the National Research Act was signed into law. It authorizes the establishment within HEW of an eleven-man commission to conduct a comprehensive study of the basic ethical principles underlying biomedical and behavioral research and to develop guidelines for conducting such research. The commission will function for two years but the act also provides for the establishment of a permanent National Advisory Council for the Protection of Subjects of Biomedical and Behavioral Research after the commission ceases to exist.

The first and most pressing assignment to the commission was to conduct a fetal research study and make recommendations concerning the nature, extent, and purposes of research involving living fetuses and consider alternative means for achieving such purposes. The commission has been given only four months to complete that study, and until then all research on living fetuses, unless such research is done for the purpose of assuring survival of such fetus, was ordered discontinued under any HEW-sponsored project within the United States or abroad.

Institutions providing facilities for research involving human subjects are required to establish an organizational review committee composed of not less than five members with varying backgrounds to ascertain that every proposal includes adequate measures for the protection of the rights and welfare of all subjects. Committees may not consist entirely of persons who are officers, employees, or otherwise affiliated with the institution, which means that at least one member must be from another institution or from the community. No committee member may participate in the review of a proposal in which he has an interest as either a researcher or a consultant.

In projects involving minors, prisoners, the institutionalized mentally ill, or pregnant women, the committee has additional responsibilities, being required in some instances to establish a consent committee. That committee oversees the actual processes by which individual subjects are selected and consents secured; monitors progress of the activity and the continued willingness of the subjects to participate; intervenes on behalf of subjects if conditions warrant; and performs any other duties deemed to be pertinent to the activity.

At first, HEW required that certification of approval by the organizational review committee be forwarded to the appropriate agency official not later than thirty days after submission of the application. In March, 1975, this was modified to allow a maximum grace period of ninety days. Grant applicants seeking funds to support research involving human subjects should submit the proposal to the organizational review committee in time for the review to be completed within the grace period. Reviews may require as much as a month to six weeks, depending upon the nature of the project and the promptness of the committee to act.

Human subjects committees are concerned with matters such as: exposure to stress, use of deception, anonymity and confidentiality, supervision of assistants, selection of subjects, inducements or payments to subjects, and the provisions made for privacy and consent. The committee must be assured that the subjects will be adequately protected in all these regards; that the risks to the individual are outweighed by the potential benefits to him or by the importance of the knowledge to be gained; and that informed consent is obtained.

Determining the degree of risk to which a subject may be exposed is not always easy. The federal regulations define a "subject at risk" as any individual who may be exposed to the possibility of injury, including physical, psychological, or social injury, as a consequence of participation as a subject in any research, development, or related activity which departs from the application of those established and accepted methods necessary to meet his needs or which increases the ordinary risks of daily life, including the recognized risks inherent in a chosen occupation or field of service.

Using this definition, one must assume that any human subject who participates in a project to any degree and for any purpose may be "at risk." It is hard to conceive of any social science study, for example, in which some "social injury" is not a possibility—the censure of one's neighbors can be injurious in some communities.

Obtaining informed consent means that the investigator is obligated to inform the subject or his responsible agent of those aspects of the activity that might reasonably be considered important factors in the subject's decision to enter the project; such a consent to participate must be in writing and the consent form used must have the approval of the organizational review committee. Some committees design their own consent forms. If no form is provided, two guides that may aid in preparing such forms are on pages 184 and 185, a long form and a short form. The seriousness of the risk and the requirements of the committee will determine the amount of detail and specificity the form contains.

Two important facts should be borne in mind regarding informed consent: (1) Consent by a subject to participate in a project in no way relieves the investigator from his basic responsibilities for safeguarding the rights and welfare of the subject; and (2) every consent form should contain a statement giving the subject the option to withdraw from the project at any time.

The Institute of Society, Ethics, and the Life Sciences, The Hastings Center, 623 Warburton Avenue, Hastings-on-Hudson, New York 10706, publishes an annual bibliography to provide introductory references in the field of biomedical ethics, a sample of the technical literature, and discussion of specific issues in biomedical ethics. The Center also publishes a report six times a year with short articles on bioethics, and three times a year, a publication containing longer papers on current concerns of Center scholars. Articles and information materials distributed by The Hastings Center are useful to anyone engaged in research involving human subjects.

General regulations regarding protection of human subjects were published in the May 30, 1974 *Federal Register*. Proposed guidelines for projects involving minors, fetuses, abortuses, pregnant women, prisoners, and the institutionalized mentally ill appeared in the August 23, 1974 *Federal Register* for comment after which the final version is to be published. Further changes in the policies will appear in the *Federal Register* before being codified in the federal regulations.

The Department of Health, Education, and Welfare has a publication entitled, *The Institutional Guide to HEW Policy on Protection of Human Subjects,* which may be ordered from the Superintendent of Documents, GPO, Washington, D. C. 20402. It is Publication No. (NIH) 1740-0326, and costs $.25.

INDIRECT (OVERHEAD) COSTS

Every sponsored activity has both direct and indirect costs. Direct costs are those readily identifiable with the project, such as salaries and fringe benefits, supplies, equipment, travel, publication costs, etc. Indirect or overhead costs are those incurred by the institution in providing support services which are shared by other activities. Examples of such costs are general administrative expenses; research administration expenses; operation and maintenance expenses; library expenses; and departmental administration expenses.

The idea of indirect costs is to reimburse the institution fairly for that portion of its services necessary to carry out the provisions of the grant, and which cannot be identified and funded as a separate element in the direct costs portion of the budget. Although the amount of the indirect costs may appear in the award document (and be added into the total of the *grant* or *contract*) the principal investigator or project director has no control over that portion of the award. The use of funds recovered by the institution in this manner is a matter entirely between the grantee institution and the funding agency.

The federal government authorizes the use of a predetermined fixed rate to cover indirect costs at educational and other tax-exempt, nonprofit institutions. Use of this fixed rate, referred to as the "negotiated indirect cost rate," simplifies administration of grants or contracts, facilitates the preparation of budgets, and permits more expeditious closeout after the work is completed.

Institutions that have even a modest volume of federal support usually have negotiated a fixed indirect cost rate that is acceptable and recognized by all federal granting services. Responsibility for negotiation and audits at most educational institutions has been

SUBJECT'S CONSENT STATEMENT (Long Form)

Name of Project Director
or Principal Investigator: _____
Title of Project: _____

   I hereby acknowledge that on _____, I was informed by
                              (Date)

_____ of the _____,
   (Principal Investigator)   (Institution)

of a project concerning or having to do with the following: (Describe briefly) _____
_____
_____

   I was told with respect to my participation in said project of the possible risks
involved, the procedures involved; possible alternative procedures; and the expected
benefits from my program; i.e., that: (State information given)
_____
_____
_____
_____

   I am fully aware of the nature and extent of my participation in said project and
possible risks involved or arising therefrom. I hereby agree, with full knowledge and
awareness of all of the foregoing, to participate in said project. I further acknowledge
that I have received a complete copy of this consent statement.

   I also understand that I may withdraw my participation in said project at any time
and that I may inspect a copy of the Institutional Assurance filed by the
_____ with the U.S. Department of Health, Education and
   (Name of Institution)

Welfare (or other federal agency).

Date: _____

Place _____
        (City and State)

                      _____
                     (Signature of Subject or Responsible Agent)

                      _____
                     (Printed Name of Subject or Agent)

                      _____
                   (Residence Address of Subject or Agent)

                      _____

SUBJECT'S CONSENT STATEMENT (Short Form)

Name of Project Director
or Principal Investigator: _____
Title of Project: _____
   I hereby acknowledge that on _____, I was informed by
                                   (Date)

_____ of the _____,
   (Principal Investigator)   (Institution)

of a project having to do with _____.
                                   (Insert Brief Description of Nature of Project)

   I was told of the possible risks involved; the procedures involved; possible alternative procedures; and the expected benefits from the program.

   I am fully aware of the nature and extent of my participation in said project and possible risks involved or arising therefrom. I hereby agree, will full knowledge and awareness of all of the foregoing to participate in said project. I further acknowledge that I have received a complete copy of this consent statement. I also understand that I may withdraw my participation in said project at any time and that I may inspect a copy of the Institutional Assurance filed by the _____
_____ with the
             (Name of Institution)

U.S. Department of Health, Education and Welfare (or other federal agency).

Date: _____
Place _____
         (City and State)

                                _____
                                 (Signature of Subject or Responsible Agent)

                                _____
                                 (Printed Name of Subject or Agent)

                                _____
                                 (Residence Address of Subject or Agent)

assigned to the Department of Health, Education, and Welfare (HEW). Beginning in January, 1974, the HEW comptroller decentralized the negotiation of indirect cost rates within the ten federal regional offices. Indirect cost rates, as well as research patient care rates, and state-wide and local-wide cost allocation plans with colleges and universities, state and local units of government, hospitals, and nonprofit institutions, are now performed by the office of the regional comptroller of the region in which the organization is located. Addresses and telephone numbers of each regional comptroller's office and the states for which they are responsible are listed in Appendix VII.

The fixed rate for indirect costs is usually expressed as a percentage of the salaries and wages shown in the direct costs portion of the budget; or it may be expressed as a percentage of the total of all direct costs.

Some organizations negotiate two rates: an "on-site" or "on-campus" rate and an "off-site" or "off-campus" rate. The latter (off-site or off-campus) rate is applied when it is necessary to utilize facilities not under the control of the grantee. In education projects, for example, it may be necessary to conduct a project away from the main campus for the convenience of the subjects, or a research investigation may require use of facilities or work areas of a type not available within the institution. In such cases, the direct costs section of the budget may include an item to cover space rental, which explains why the *off-site indirect cost recovery rate is lower than the on-site rate*. In situations where the activity is partly on- and partly off-site, the rate is determined by the site where the major portion is performed unless the grant is larger than $100,000. In that case, it is possible to apply the on-site rate for the work performed at the institution and the off-site rate for that portion performed elsewhere.

Examples:

The institutional rates are: "on-site, 50% of salaries and wages, excluding fringe benefits"; and "off-site, 25% of salaries and wages, excluding fringe benefits."

1.   100% of project performed on-site. Salaries and wages total $100,000, excluding fringe benefits. The budget line for

indirect costs would read:

> Indirect costs: 50% of salaries and wages excluding fringe benefits: $100,000 × 50% (on-site rate) $50,000

2. 100% of project performed off-site (same amount of salaries and wages). The direct costs portion of the budget could include space rental:

> Rental of space (3,000 ft² @ $5/ft² annually) January 1– December 31 _____ $15,000

The indirect cost entry would read:

> Indirect costs: 25% of salaries and wages excluding fringe benefits: $100,000 × 25% (off-site rate) $25,000

3. 50% of project performed on-site and 50% off-site. If it is necessary to rent space off-site, the cost appears as a space rental item in the direct costs section as shown above.

The indirect cost entry then reads:

> Indirect costs: *50% on-site.* 50% of salaries and wages excluding fringe benefits: $100,000 ÷ 2 × 50% $25,000

> 50% off-site. 25% of salaries and wages, excluding fringe benefits: $100,000. ÷ 2 × 25% _____ $12,500.

Total indirect costs: _____ $37,500

If the indirect cost rate is expressed as a percentage of total direct costs, the calculation procedure is the same, but the base figure used is that of *Total Direct Costs* instead of the total of *Salaries and Wages excluding fringe benefits.*

The determination as to whether an item is to be included in direct costs and listed individually or covered by the indirect cost allocation is dependent upon the way the institution is organized and the policies under which their research programs are conducted. The applicant must therefore have a clear understanding with the institution's authorizing official concerning the items that must appear as direct cost items and those which will be covered by the indirect cost recovery. Some institutions include personnel fringe benefit costs in the indirect cost allocation; others do not. At some places, provision of space implies that basic furniture and equipment, i.e., desks, file cabinets, typewriters, etc., will be furnished, but not always. Seemingly minor items can become serious problems for the investigator if he has not included them in the direct costs and finds that he must pay for them directly. It is wise to inquire specifically about such things as secretarial services, office supplies, Xeroxing, telephone, postage, fringe benefits, computer facilities, typewriters, calculators, dictating machines, and tape recorders, if a project will require these services or supplies.

It is worth noting that indirect costs are not allowed in certain federal programs, and the program guidelines will always state this when it is the case.

Indirect costs of instruction activities—for example, training grants—carry a standard indirect cost rate irrespective of the fixed institutional rate. Most training grant programs allow 8 percent of total direct costs for indirect cost recovery.

The National Science Foundation specifically excludes indirect costs on the following types of grants:

a. Grants awarded to individuals.
b. Grants awarded solely for travel, equipment, construction, facilities, or dissertation research.
c. Grants in which NSF support is exclusively in the form of fellowships, traineeships, or other fixed amounts such as cost-of-education allowances.
d. Grants involving special programs or unusual circumstances under which full indirect costs are considered inappropriate, such as grants for the sole purpose of enabling U.S. scientists to conduct research and/or teach in a foreign country.

Federal agencies do not usually include indirect costs in grants awarded for the support of a meeting or conference, except those requiring a long period of preparation and extensive facilities for organization, planning, and conference sessions.

The determination to allow or not to allow indirect or overhead costs on projects funded by state and local governments varies throughout the country—many federal programs are administered through block grants to the states and grants made from such funds through state authorities may or may not resemble the federal pattern. Many programs of the Office of Education are administered in this way; such programs are considered to be in support of or to enhance ongoing educational programs, and thus it is assumed that no burden is placed upon the institution, and no indirect costs are allowable. Consultation and agreement with the official or office administering city and state grants is essential to clear up the question of indirect costs in advance.

Many foundation board members do not fully understand the concept of indirect cost or institutional allowances, mainly because they are unaware of the burden that some funded activities can place on the facilities of the institution. Foundation program officials usually understand this and can be helpful in advising on the presentation of the budget in a way that is acceptable to the directors or other decision makers. Often it is only a question of terminology. A foundation that would balk at an item for "overhead" may accept "administrative costs" or "space and equipment rental" without a question. Most institutions include basic services such as telephone, office furniture, duplicating services, and supplies in the indirect cost package. But these items can be listed individually in budgets submitted to funding organizations when the concept of indirect or overhead cost is unacceptable.

Industrial corporations usually award grants or contracts to individuals for activities in which they have an interest—often it is in their view a way of subcontracting for the performance of certain work which they prefer not to do in their own laboratories or shops. Therefore they expect to pay the actual cost of the project, provided every item is clearly spelled out. They are not, in general, receptive to inclusion of items for general institutional overhead. Some corporation executives believe that disagreement on this point, and on the question of proprietary rights, especially patent and copyright matters, presents a serious obstacle to closer cooperation between educational and industrial organizations.

The question of indirect costs must be cleared up with the official who endorses grant applications for the grantee institution before the budget can be prepared, and preferably before entering into preliminary discussions with a potential grantor. If an application is being submitted to a federal agency, the institution's current negotiated indirect cost rate must be used. This changes from time to time as cost of doing business changes and new rates are negotiated. At some institutions, the matter of housing the proposed activity must be settled in order to determine whether the "on-site" or "off-site" rate is applicable.

Most educational and other nonprofit institutions that have negotiated an indirect cost rate with federal agencies recognize that dealing with private foundations or corporations is a different matter, but every institution has its own idea of what is reasonable. Therefore, the principal investigator must settle this point before going very far in negotiations with a funding organization and certainly before the final application is submitted to the institutional official for endorsement.

Detailed information on indirect cost rates and administrative requirements applicable to *grants and contracts issued by the federal government* will be found in the following documents:

Educational Institutions

> Federal Management Circular 73-8 (FMC 73-8), *Cost principles for educational institutions* (Formerly OMB A-21)
>
> Federal Management Circular 73-6 (FMC 73-6), *Coordinating indirect cost rates and audit at educational institutions* (Formerly OMB A-88)
>
> > Order from: General Services Administration
> > 18th and F Street, N.W.
> > Washington, D.C. 20405
> > Attn: Office of Federal Management Policy
>
> *Direct and Indirect Costs of Research at Colleges and Universities,* published by the Commission on Federal Relations, American Council on Education, One Dupont Circle, Washington, D.C. 20036 (Cost: $10.00 for 100 copies)
>
> *A Case for Full Cost Reimbursement,* from Studies in Management, Vol. 3, No. 8, March, 1974, publication of Committee on Governmental Relations, National Association of College and University Business Officers (NACUBO), One Dupont Circle, N.W., Washington, D.C. 20036

Indirect Costs of Research, published by Commission on Resource Allocation, The University of Michigan, Ann Arbor, Michigan 49027

State and Local Governments

Office of Management and Budget Circular A-102 (OMB A-102), *Uniform administrative requirements for grants-in-aid to state and local governments*

Office of Management and Budget Circular A-87 (OMB A-87), *Cost principles for grants-in-aid to state and local governments*

> Order from: Office of Management and Budget
> Executive Office of the President
> Washington, D.C. 20503

A counterpart to Circular A-102 to establish uniform requirements for grants-in-aid to colleges, universities, hospitals, and other nonprofit organizations is in process and will probably be issued as one of the FMC series, but until then, hospitals and nonprofit organizations can refer to the following:

Hospitals

Department of Health, Education, and Welfare publication OASC-3, as amended September 5, 1969 and September 24, 1970, *Principles for determining costs applicable to grants and contracts with hospitals*

> Order from: Superintendent of Documents
> U.S. Government Printing Office
> Washington, D.C. 20402

Nonprofit Organizations

Department of Health, Education and Welfare Publication OASC-5 (revised), dated August 1970, *Principles for determining costs applicable to awards to non-profit institutions*

> Order from: Superintendent of Documents
> U.S. Government Printing Office
> Washington, D.C. 20402

Commercial Organizations

Federal Procurement Regulations, Subpart 1-15.2, *Procedures for use in cost-reimbursement type supply and research contracts with commercial organizations*

Order from: Superintendent of Documents
U.S. Government Printing Office
Washington, D.C. 20402

PATENTS AND COPYRIGHTS

Although they are often discussed together, patents and copyrights really have only one thing in common, and that is the potential to produce royalty income. Agreement on distribution of income must be established in both cases before beginning a project that has the potential for producing patentable or copyrightable results.

The differences and similarities of patents and copyrights are clearly indicated in the chart on page 199, Patents and Copyrights—A Comparison of Major Differences, which was prepared by the Committee on Governmental Relations of the National Association of College and University Business Officers.

Patents

The patent system is one of the most effective methods of assuring that any useful product or process developed or improved by research or study is made available to the public on reasonable terms.

The industrial community with its concern for profits has been keenly cognizant of this and most corporations have developed very effective systems of protecting their laboratory results, evaluating their applicability for commercial use, and carrying through the process of patenting, licensing, and marketing the ultimate product.

But patent management is a highly skilled operation requiring the services of experts in a number of professional fields, and educational institutions often conclude that the volume of patentable results likely to emerge from their programs does not justify the expense involved in setting up an in-house patent management operation. Many colleges and universities that have articulated policies and procedures for handling patentable results use the services of a professional patent management organization for evaluation, patenting, and licensing activities.

If there is any possibility that a proposed project may produce a patentable product, the investigator should see that the award document includes the patent provisions applicable to that specific grant, and that the role of the institution *vis-à-vis* the funding agency and his own role *vis-à-vis* the institution are explicated in such a way as to prevent later misunderstandings.

What kinds of discoveries are patentable? The 1952 Patent Act sets forth the classes of discoveries eligible for patenting as "a new or useful process, machine, manufacture, or composition of matter, or any new and useful improvement thereof." The act allows the patenting of new varieties of asexually produced plants other than tuber-propagated plants or plants found in an uncultivated state. This is the *complete list* of subjects the law deems to be patentable. To make the question of what is or is not patentable even clearer, some subjects are specifically placed *outside the scope of patents*. They are: theories; ideas; plans of action; methods of doing business; discoveries of laws of nature or scientific principles; things immoral or injurious to health and the good of society; and works eligible for protection under the copyright laws.

In the United States a patent application may be filed within one year after the invention is published. In many foreign countries a patent cannot be obtained if there has been any publication prior to patent application. However, under an international convention, a patent application in the United States will preserve for one year the rights to file patent applications abroad even though there has been publication subsequent to the U.S. patent application but before foreign patent application.

Each industrial corporation has its own arrangements for handling proprietary rights. Most of them reserve to themselves the right to patent and license inventions resulting from work they support but share royalty income with the inventor or with the institution and the inventor. (Even so, commercial organizations are more generous with individual contractors and grantees than they are with their own employees, who usually get $1.00 a year for patentable inventions.) In the past, academic institutions have been so eager to get research contracts and subcontracts from industry that they have accepted this arrangement, but they are now beginning to assert their right to a share of the ownership of work done using campus facilities, including both patent and publication rights. This is understandably creating some conflicts between corporations and colleges and universities regarding cooperative research efforts. Universities and colleges are beginning to consult professionals before entering into contract arrangements with industrial concerns and negotiating agreements whereby, in some cases, the industry has the right of first refusal on a license (for a proper fee, of course), but not exclusive rights.

Foundations handle the matter of proprietary rights on an *ad hoc* basis, as a rule. The largest of them, The Ford Foundation, has no standard patent clause in its award documents and will include such a clause only after determining that it is appropriate. Most foundations that support activities likely to produce patentable results are generous in the arrangements for patenting and licensing.

The federal government generally encourages grantee institutions to make useful discoveries available for public use, often assigning patent and licensing privileges to academic and other nonprofit institutions. Some federal agencies such as the Departments of Defense, Interior and Transportation, NASA, and the Environmental Protection Agency have restrictive patent clauses. Federal grants and contracts with agencies that have restrictive policies often contain a "patent deferred clause," which simply means that the determination of rights in inventions will be deferred until such time as an invention has been identified and reported. NASA and DOD will sometimes waive their rights to industrial corporations to encourage the development of a product if it is considered to be in the national interest to do so. The National Science Foundation will also, under certain circumstances, permit industrial or commercial organizations to retain title to inventions developed with NSF support, provided they agree to make the product available to the public. The Department of Health, Education, and Welfare and the National Science Foundation will enter into separate institutional agreements with academic or nonprofit organizations which provide that all inventions made with support of grant or contract funds belong to the grantee subject to certain rights and limitations. The effect of these agreements is to assign to the institution, at the time of award, the right to patent any product that may result.

Momentum has been gathering recently in support of the establishment of consistent regulations covering the assignment of rights to inventions developed with federal funds. Under the chairmanship of Norman J. Latker, Patent Counsel, Department of Health, Education, and Welfare, a subcommittee of the Committee on Government Patent Policy is studying the feasibility of the idea. There is hope that at least the civilian (non-defense) agencies will be able to agree on a standard policy.

Of course, the entire national patent structure may soon change depending upon the outcome of current litigation. Public Citizen, Inc., one of Ralph Nader's organizations, was successful in enjoining General Services Administration from granting exclusive licenses on patents *already owned by the government* (Public Citizen v. Sampson). Public Citizen is now challenging the GSA procurement regulations based upon the presidential patent policy statement of August, 1971, permitting federal agencies, *at the time of award*, to grant principal rights in inventions to the performing organization under certain circumstances as is done, for example, under the HEW and NSF institutional agreements.

Public Citizen is supported in its position by the antitrust division of the Justice Department (thereby proving that patent policies can also make strange bedfellows). Early in 1973, the antitrust division of Justice prepared a policy opinion which held that it is unconstitutional for the government to grant exclusive title to inventions under programs that it finances, since the Constitution states that Congress shall have the "power to dispose of and make all needful rules and regulations respecting the territory or other property belonging to the United States." That opinion runs counter to policy statements of President Kennedy in 1963 and President Nixon in 1971, to Department of Defense policy since World War II, and to the basis for the institutional agreements used by HEW and NSF. Those who do not agree with the Justice Department and the Nader organization in this matter argue that without exclusive licensing rights, there is no incentive for organizations to undertake the expensive, lengthy, and hazardous procedure of transferring a technological idea or process from the laboratory to the market place. The risks are too great, the likelihood of the venture resulting in appropriate remuneration to the developer is too small, if discoveries are in the public domain.

When an institution has been assigned the rights to patenting and licensing of an invention, there are various ways it may go about exercising those rights. Some have established patent offices where the evaluation of the invention, filing of patent applications, and licensing is handled. Others have institution-affiliated foundations that handle patent matters. Both of these arrangements have the advantage of allowing the inventor to work closely with the unit promoting the invention. The disadvantage is that in-house arrangements are expensive and the volume is not great enough to justify it for many organizations.

A third alternative that is preferred by many is the use of one of the professional patent management organizations. This has many financial advantages because, for a minimum outlay, the institution has access to skilled and experienced evaluative, legal, marketing, and patent management expertise.

Research Corporation, 405 Lexington Avenue, New York, N.Y. 10017 is the oldest, best known, and most effective of the patent management organizations. It will enter into institutional agreements to provide evaluative, patenting, and licensing services on all discoveries submitted by an institution, on a royalty-sharing basis. They will also provide those services to institutions and individuals on a case-by-case basis under a royalty-sharing agreement. An individual researcher proposing to seek the services of any patent management organization should be certain that he has the clear right to negotiate with them. Some funding agencies—the Department of Health, Education, and Welfare is one—assign patent rights only to grantee institutions, not to individuals.

The Research Corporation plows back a portion of its royalty income into research through grant programs which support research in the natural sciences and human nutrition through the Research Corporation Foundation.

Another patent management organization is the Battelle Development Corporation in Columbus, Ohio, which was set up originally to exploit the Xerox invention. Battelle evaluates inventions from various sources, including independent inventors, industrial organizations, universities, and its own staff. It will also provide the support necessary to develop the invention to a stage where it may be licensed or sold to an organization that will produce and market it. The financial arrangements are similar to those of Research Corporation, but income to Battelle supports its own in-house research whereas Research Corporation supports an active grant-making program. Battelle's address is: 505 King Avenue, Columbus, Ohio 43201.

The Wisconsin Alumni Research Foundation, P.O. Box 2037, Madison, Wisconsin 53701 provides evaluation, patenting, and licensing services for institutions in the state of Wisconsin.

Most academic and nonprofit institutions have little or no awareness of the importance to them of patent management know-how. In order to narrow this gap in both knowledge and awareness, the Research Corporation has been awarded a grant by the National Science Foundation for an experimental seminar program to enhance patent awareness at educational institutions. Beginning in 1974, eight seminars will be held—two in the 1974–75 academic year and six in 1975–76. The seminars will be private, not open to the general public, but the plan is to make the instructional material available to other academic institutions through the NSF at the end of the programs. Planned sites for the seminars are: University of Washington, University of Michigan, Case-Western Reserve University, Princeton University, University of Maryland, University of Georgia, Virginia Polytechnic Institute, and Polytechnic Institute of New York.

If a project is carried on at an institution with no established policy or procedure for handling patentable research products, the investigator should know this at the earliest possible moment and be guided by it—that moment being at the time a formal proposal is submitted. If an application is submitted to an agency with which the grantee institution has an agreement to receive patent rights, the researcher should protect his individual rights by executing a formal agreement regarding distribution of royalties with the institution before a grant or contract is negotiated and accepted. The usual agreement calls for a division of royalty income between the institution and the inventor, with specific responsibilities assigned to each in the development and exploitation of the idea.

Everyone concerned should understand and agree to the existing policies, and it is equally imperative that the prescribed procedures be scrupulously followed. An indispensable first step is the written disclosure of any findings and their presentation for evaluation as to their patentability. This is the opening act that sets in motion the long process by which new technology is transferred from the laboratory to useful application. The next step is up to the organization holding the right to file for a patent or eligible to acquire the right.

If any necessary act in the chain of events is omitted, the results may be a disastrous loss or, as in the "Gator-Ade" case, merely a ludicrous and expensive melodrama with a satisfactory ending. "Gator-Ade" resulted from experiments conducted by a Florida university faculty member under a grant from the Department of Health, Education, and Welfare. Grant funds covered purchase of materials and equipment and payment to human subjects, in this case the university's football team. When the investigator was satisfied that he had developed a drink that was an effective "energizer," he filed a disclosure statement with the appropriate university office. After waiting a reasonable length of time during which the university took no action on the matter, the researcher set up a private foundation which, jointly with the Stokely-Van Camp Company, proceeded to apply for a patent and enter into a licensing agreement under which Stokely-Van Camp had exclusive production and marketing rights and shared income with the foundation. Since HEW had not assigned patent rights in this case and, under their existing policy, could have made such assignment only to the university, HEW and the university—in the only known case of its kind—brought suit against the foundation and the licensed manufacturer. The case was settled out of court, amicably, by an arrangement whereby the foundation (i.e., the inventor), the university, and Stokely-Van Camp share the income. This is just what probably would have happened if the university had exercised its institutional privilege when the disclosure statement was first submitted, and a wasteful legal contretemps could have been avoided.

Copyrights

Copyright royalties are monies paid by a publisher or distributor to an author for permission to reproduce and/or disseminate the

PATENTS AND COPYRIGHTS—A COMPARISON OF MAJOR DIFFERENCES

	Patents	Copyrights
Coverage	Processes, machines, products of manufacturing, compositions of matter, plants, and improvements on the above, and designs.	Books, periodicals, lectures, dramatic or dramatico-musical compositions, musical compositions, maps, works of art, drawings or plastic works of a scientific or technical character, computer programs, photographs, pictorial illustrations, labels, motion pictures and video tapes, audio recording.
Essential criteria	Must be novel, have utility and be nonobvious.	Need not be novel, only the original product of the creator.
When statutory rights established	When patient is granted by the Patent Office (usually about three years after application date).	When the work is published containing the proper copyright notice (Registration of the right follows).
How statutory rights established	By filing a formal disclosure of the invention (with allowable appended claims) in the Patent Office together with the prescribed fee.	By depositing a copy or copies of the work in the Copyright Office together with the prescribed fee.
Examination	Examined for the essential criteria (see above).	No examination (other than meeting registration formalities).
Outside professional service required	Filing and prosecution requires services of a registered patent attorney.	None-Registration may be done by author.
Cost	Generally in the $1,000 to $2,000 range.	$6 plus the cost of the deposit copies.
Term and renewability	17 years, not renewable.	28 years, renewable for an additional 28 years.*
Marking	Failure to place patent number on patented article does not invalidate the patent.	Failure to employ copyright notice on the original publication puts the work in the public domain.
Who may apply	Except in unusual circumstances, the inventor's signature must appear on the patent application.	Either the author or his assignee may copyright the work.

* Congressional Bill introduced in 1974 and expected to be enacted by 94th Congress in 1975 changes this to "life of the work's creator plus 50 years." Table reprinted with permission of the Committee on Governmental Relations, National Association of College and University Business Officers, One Dupont Circle, Suite 510, Washington, D. C. 20036.

author's work under copyright. A work is under copyright when it is published with a proper copyright notice and properly registered at the Copyright Office.

Copyrightable materials include writings, sound recording, films, drawings and other graphic representations, computer programs, and computer data bases, any or all of which may result from grant-supported activities.

Distribution of income from a work under copyright that is completed with grant assistance involves the author, the sponsor or agency that supports the work, the institution that provides the facilities, and the publisher or distributor.

Foundations usually do not demand or even expect to share in the income from publication of creative works which they support. A foundation may contract for books or reports to be published in the name of the foundation, but that is a different matter.

Corporations rarely support projects that produce copyrightable materials outside of their own organizations; if scientific results accomplished with corporation support are published, all that is expected usually is acknowledgment of the company's assistance, although, in some cases, restriction may be placed on publication of material that relates to or overlaps with other work going on in the corporate plants or laboratories.

As in the case of patents, each federal funding agency handles the question of copyright materials according to its own policies. The Office of Education of the Department of Health, Education, and Welfare established the public domain policy in 1965. The policy declared, in effect, that materials produced as a result of research activities supported by funds from the OE would be placed in the public domain. The range of materials included writings, recordings, pictures, drawings, graphic presentations, computer programs—virtually every kind of educational material imaginable. Other federal agencies have their own policies, however, and any project that might result in royalty-producing published materials should contain a clause specifying the policy to be followed.

Misunderstandings and disagreements over distribution of royalty income are most likely to develop between the principal investigator and the institution providing the facilities for the project. Many academic and research institutions have established policies setting forth the guidelines for handling of royalty income, based upon the degree to which institutional facilities were utilized. Therefore, any proposed activity with the potential to result in material that will be placed under copyright must be discussed in advance with the official authorized to approve the project for the institution. At that time, a clear understanding concerning distribution of royalty income should be discussed and the principal investigator should review in advance any agreements he may be asked to sign when funding for the work is assured. If there is any doubt that the institutional requirements in the matter will be acceptable to the investigator who will be responsible for the work, it should be discussed *before* the proposal is submitted to a granting organization.

In controversies over rights to published works that reach the courts, the reference most likely to be consulted is *Nimmer on Copyright* by Melville B. Nimmer (Matthew Bender & Co., Inc., Albany, 1963), a two-volume treatise on the law of literary, musical, and artistic property and on the protection of ideas.

Other useful references for patent and copyright matters are: *Copyright and Intellectual Property*, by Julius J. Marke. New York: Fund for the Advancement of Education, 1967. 111 pages.

Handbook of College and University Administration—Academic Volume. Asa S. Knowles (editor). New York: McGraw-Hill Book Company, 1970. Chapter 8—*Academic Inventions, Patents, and Licenses*, by Willard L. Marcy, Vice President—Patents, Research Corporation, New York, N. Y. and Albert S. Davis, Jr., Resident Counsel, Research Corporation, New York, N. Y. Chapter 9—*Copyright*, by Julius J. Marke, Law Librarian and Professor of Law, New York University, New York, N. Y.

Patents at Colleges and Universities, 1974, and *Copyrights at Colleges and Universities*, 1972, issued by the Committee on Governmental Relations, National Association of College and University Business Officers, One DuPont Circle, N.W., Suite 510, Washington, D. C. 20036.

University Research and Patent Policies, Practices and Procedures, by Archie M. Palmer, National Academy of Sciences—National Research Council Publication 999. May be ordered from Office of Patent Policy

Survey, National Academy of Sciences—National Research Council, 2101 Constitution Avenue, Washington, D. C. 20418.

Research and Invention, a quarterly newsletter on academic research and invention, published by Research Corporation, 405 Lexington Avenue, New York, N. Y. 10017.

Annual Report on Government Patent Policy, Combined December 1971 and December 1972, prepared by the Federal Council for Science and Technology in consultation with the Department of Justice. May be ordered from the Superintendent of Documents, U.S. Government Printing Office, Washington, D.C. 20402. Price: $1.75.

LABORATORY ANIMALS

Man is indebted to the laboratory research animal for the indispensable role it plays in medical, biological, and behavioral studies from which the human race eventually benefits. The scientific community has long been mindful of this obligation and recognizes its ethical responsibility to provide humane care and treatment for experimental animals.

Scientists have also learned that only properly cared for animals yield reliable research data and consider the cost of breeding and maintaining healthy animals as a good investment.

Two diametrically opposed groups—researchers who use animals in their studies and societies that militantly oppose such practices—can be jointly credited with bringing about legislative action to set standards for breeding, selling, housing, transporting, feeding, exercising, and keeping records of laboratory animals.

Since passage of the Animal Welfare Act of 1970—which amended previous laws—most institutions have been progressively upgrading their research facilities to comply with the law. The act provides for regulating the transportation, purchase, sale, housing, care, handling, and treatment of animals used in research, for exhibition, and for other purposes. It also provides for the protection of owners of animals from theft of their animals (to prevent the sale or use of stolen animals) and ensures that certain animals intended for use in research or for exhibition purposes or for use as pets are provided humane care and treatment. The Department of Agriculture has the responsibility for administering the law and requires that institutions using laboratory animals and maintaining animal facilities be registered by the USDA. Registration is obtained upon assurance that the institution provides adequate veterinary care, inspection, records and reports, and maintains appropriate facilities and operating standards.

Institutions maintaining, using, importing, or breeding laboratory animals for purposes of scientific research or investigation are eligible to apply for accreditation by the American Association for Accreditation of Laboratory Animal Care (AAALAC), 4 East Clinton Street, P.O. Box 13, Joliet, Illinois 60434. Full accreditation by AAALAC is accepted by the National Institutes of Health as assurance that the animal facilities meet the standards of the NIH policy on laboratory animals. Organizations registered with the USDA and meeting the requirement of the National Institutes of Health must establish an institutional committee responsible to set and administer standards for activities involving laboratory animals, including provisions for review and approval of proposals in which animals will be used.

Private organizations concerned about the use of animals in research can and do mount forceful campaigns in opposition to the use of certain animals in specific types of research. There has been increasing pressure to ban chemical, biological, and radiation research on dogs during the past few years, which resulted (in June, 1974) in an amendment to the DOD Appropriations Act, 1975, rigidly restricting use of dogs in certain kinds of research, and the possibility of further legislation remains.

The investigator who plans any study using animals must be prepared to assure the laboratory animal committee of the sponsoring institution that every aspect in which the animals will be involved will be conducted in accord with current legal requirements and local customs.

"Local customs" is not a minor factor. Private citizens who become aware of an experiment using animals by hearing dogs bark or smelling a pig sty, or by a sudden infestation of unfamiliar insects, can mount powerful opposition that must be dealt with. There are many cases on record where research projects have been stopped by the action of local people who objected to the effect of the study on their environment.

Proposals involving the use of animals should include full explanation of the (1) arrangements for breeding or acquisition of the animals; (2) supervisory and animal caretaking personnel; (3) facilities, i.e., physical plant where the animals will be maintained and used; and (4) design of the project or activity.

Arrangements for Breeding or Acquisition of Animals

The source of supply of animals has important implications, not only for assurance regarding their care and handling, but as supporting and explanatory data to justify the amounts in the budget for their acquisition.

Breeding facilities and even the method of transporting animals from the breeder to the laboratory must meet the criteria for consideration of the animals' welfare as well as meeting the needs of the study. Any special requirements must be explicitly understood by the supplier in conjunction with the request for a quoted price. Standard price lists are not sufficient if animals of a certain species, weight, age, or genetic strain will be required in *specific* quantities to be delivered on *exact* dates. Production schedules must be planned well in advance, and since many award notices are received a very short time before a project begins and are even retroactive in some cases, very close communication and coordination must be established between the researcher and the supplier, and very clear agreements must be reached on commitments, costs, etc., if figures included in the application budget are to be reliable.

If the investigator plans to breed his own animals, the fundamental considerations are expertise, cost, space, personnel, and facilities, including utilities and equipment. It is more difficult to estimate the cost of breeding animals than of purchasing them, since production is uncertain at best and can be affected by so many unexpected factors.

Experience is the best guide and the novice who plans to undertake his own breeding will do well to consult extensively with researchers who have had such experience and who can advise on costs, methods, production schedules, etc.

Supervisory and Caretaking Personnel

Projects or activities involving live, warm-blooded animals and the procurement of living animal tissues for biomedical activities must be performed by, or under the immediate supervision of, a scientist qualified in the scientific area under study.

Animal maintenance and care facilities should be under the direction of a veterinarian with specialized training or experience in laboratory animal medicine. It will be his responsibility to see that the supporting staff and animal handlers are adequately trained for their duties, and to maintain a sound personnel health program. Hazards such as possible transmission of diseases between animals and people are serious concerns for both the personnel and the animals. Even minor diseases that are not seriously hazardous to the animals may have an effect on the experiment that makes the results questionable.

The availability of qualified supervisory and caretaking personnel is a matter about which the researcher should be very certain before designing an experiment to be carried on at an institution.

Animal Laboratory Facilities

A well-designed, properly maintained physical plant is an essential element in good animal care. There must be sufficient space for animals and personnel. Specialized laboratories are required for needed activities such as surgery, intensive care, necropsy, radiography, and preparation of special diets; for the diagnosis, treatment, and control of laboratory animal diseases; and for quarantine. Space should be provided for the receiving and storage of food, bedding, supplies, and equipment. Personnel must have lockers, toilets, sinks, and showers. Equipment and personnel for washing and sterilizing equipment and supplies and for disposing of all waste and refuse must be provided.

If radioactive materials are to be used, the researcher, the director of the laboratory animal facility, and the institutional radiation safety officer are jointly responsible to see that the safety measures are appropriate for the level and type of radiation involved. When specific radioactive isotopes are to be used, expert advice must be sought.

Project Design

A study or activity proposing the use of animals should be designed and based on sufficient knowledge of the disease or problem under investigation to conclude that the significance of the anticipated results will justify its performance. The intent should be such as to yield fruitful results for the good of society.

The project should be conducted in a manner to ensure that the animals are not subjected to unnecessary suffering and injury; the scientist should be prepared to terminate a study whenever it seems certain that its continuation may result in unnecessary injury to the animals.

Animals must be anesthetized or otherwise rendered incapable of perceiving pain or discomfort necessitated by the research and must be maintained in that condition until the threat of pain has ended. In cases where anesthetization would defeat the purpose of the project, the principal investigator must specifically approve and supervise each case.

Postexperiment care of subject animals must be such as to minimize discomfort in accordance with acceptable practice in veterinary medicine.

When it is necessary to sacrifice a laboratory animal, the animal must be killed in a humane manner in such a way as to ensure immediate death in accordance with procedures approved by the institutional committee. No animal should be discarded until death is certain.

The primary reference on standards of laboratory animal care is the *Guide for the Care and Use of Laboratory Animals* (Fourth edition). Previous editions of the Guide were issued under the title *Guide for Laboratory Animal Facilities and Care*.

The Guide deals with the management, housing, care, and use of animals, including methods to provide for their proper maintenance under laboratory conditions. It contains recommendations on protection of the animal colony against occupational hazards and on animal anesthesia, surgery, postsurgical care, and euthanasia.

Prepared by the National Research Council and published by the U.S. Department of Health, Education, and Welfare, the Guide can be ordered from: The Superintendent of Documents, U.S. Government Printing Office, Washington, D.C. 20402, for $.55. The stock number is 1740-0343.

Also available from the GPO is a manual issued in January, 1974, entitled *Cost Analysis and Rate Setting Manual for Animal Resource Facilities*, prepared by the Division of Research Resources for the National Institutes of Health.

A useful guide for the researcher who uses mice is *The Laboratory Mouse: Selection and Management*, by M. L. Simmons and J. O. Brick, published in 1970 by Prentice-Hall, Inc., Englewood Cliffs, New Jersey.

The American Association for Laboratory Animal Science (AALAS) is an organization made up of individuals and institutions professionally concerned with the production, care, and use of laboratory animals. Its membership includes animal breeders, researchers, and veterinarians specializing in laboratory animal science. The Association provides a means for collection and exchange of information on all phases of laboratory animal care and management. Its Animal Technician Certification Board develops uniform standards for technician training by defining the qualifications, preparation, and approval of examinations for training programs and certifies successful candidates. The Association publishes the *AALAS Bulletin* and a bimonthly journal, *Laboratory Animal Science*. For information about the Association and its publications write to AALAS, 4 East Clinton Street, Box 10, Joliet, Illinois 60434.

Implementing rules and regulations of the Animal Welfare Act of 1970 are published in the *Code of Federal Regulations* (CFR), Title 9— Animals and Animal Products, Subchapter A—Laboratory Animal Welfare, parts 1, 2, and 3. Any and all amendments to the rules and regulations are periodically published in the *Federal Register* under the heading, Department of Agriculture Animal and Plant Health Inspection Service.

Copies of the rules and regulations can be obtained from the Federal Veterinarian in Charge, Animal and Plant Health Inspection Service, in the capital city of most states.

Researchers in the United States are also required to respect the wildlife laws of other countries by the Lacey Law passed in 1900 and amended many times. The implications of failure to comply with that law were rather dramatically demonstrated in the summer of 1974 when Dr. Charles G. Sibley, director of Yale's Peabody Museum, was fined $3,000 by the United States Fish and Wildlife Service for importing eggs of the peregrine falcon from Great Britain for research purposes. The investigation had international ramifications in which bird-egg collectors were fined in England and a Danish museum official was fined and discharged.

The Endangered Species Conservation Act of 1969 was established to prevent the importation of endangered species of fish or wildlife into the United States; to prevent the interstate shipment of reptiles, amphibians, and other wildlife taken contrary to state law; and for other purposes.

The implementing rules and regulations for this Act are published in the *Code of Federal Regulations* (CFR), Title 50—Wildlife and Fisheries, Chapter 1—Bureau of Sport Fisheries and Wildlife, Fish and Wildlife Service, Department of the Interior. Amendments are published in the *Federal Register*.

A current United States List of Endangered Fauna can be obtained by writing to the Office of Endangered Species, U.S. Department of Interior, Fish and Wildlife Service, Washington, D.C. 20240. (See Appendix VIII.)

A visit to the institution's laboratory animal facilities is mandatory before designing a project for which the use of such facilities is essential. The director or supervisor should be consulted on the availability of space, personnel, labs, etc., required for the study.

The chairman of the institutional committee on animal research should also be consulted to ensure that the idea and design meet the approval of the committee and will not hold up the endorsement of the official who must sign the proposal for the institution.

Any special requirements, such as space for isolating animals from the main colony, radiation sources, or special handling for specific pathogen-free or germ-free animals must be negotiated and committed before the application is submitted to potential funding organizations.

EQUIPMENT ACQUISITION AND DISPOSITION

Any project that involves the acquisition of one or more items of equipment costing as much as $200 each has the potential to create misunderstanding and disagreement between the researcher and the institution where the work is being done, unless the grant or contract clearly indicates where the title to equipment is to vest and unless there are clear guidelines regarding accountability and disposition of the equipment, especially if the principal investigator moves from one institution to another during the lifetime of the grant.

Grants or contracts from foundations or corporations seldom include funds for the acquisition of expensive equipment items. Industrial organizations usually make awards to educational and other nonprofit institutions for research on the basis that the institution has the facilities available. If it should be necessary to provide funds for expensive equipment, the corporation might prefer to make the investment in its own laboratories. Foundations rarely have any interest in the equipment once the project has been completed, and they frequently leave the matter to be resolved between the investigator and the institution or provide for its sale at the end of the project and return of the proceeds to the foundations.

Since the issuance of Federal Management Circular 73-7 in December, 1973, the policy of the federal government is to vest title to equipment purchased or fabricated under any type of research instrument at educational institutions in the institution without further obligation to the government. The funding agency may, however, under certain circumstances, reserve the right, at the time of the negotiation of the award, to transfer title to a third party eligible under existing statutes, if the equipment item costs more than $1,000.

This policy is viewed as a form of governmental contribution to the scientific capability of academic institutions and also as a means of relieving the government of the cost and administrative burden of accounting for, shipping, storing, and disposing of the equipment.

The researcher who proposes to seek funds for a project requiring the use of specialized or expensive items of equipment should make inquiries of the appropriate institutional personnel to ascertain if existing facilities include such equipment and if so whether it can be made available at the time it will be needed for the project. It is always a mistake to assume that the mere presence of the equipment implies that the problem is solved. The researcher, dean, professor, or technician who controls the equipment, supervises its maintenance, and schedules its use is the proper individual to consult. In many places specialized facilities such as equipment for electron spin resonance and nuclear magnetic resonance studies or for mass spectrometry, chromatography, amino acid analysis, and spectrophotometry, and high speed centriifuges or high powered electron microscopes are in such demand that their use is scheduled on a round-the-clock, 24-hour-a-day basis—and far in advance.

If the equipment is not available at the institution, it should be included in the budget. Some federal agencies assist their grantees and contractors to obtain equipment declared "excess" from other federal projects and, in this way, project directors are able to stretch their funds and enhance their research projects. The National Science Foundation has been the major agency obtaining excess property for use by its grantees. HEW and EPA used to do so but have discontinued the practice.

"Excess property" is property under the control of any federal agency that is not required for its needs and the discharge of its responsibilities, as determined by the head of the agency. Once the determination has been made that the agency no longer needs a piece of equipment, a report to that effect is filed with the General Services Administration, which tries to find another federal agency that might be able to use the item. After acquiring accountability for pieces of excess property in this manner, federal agencies sometimes give the property to grantees or contractors who use the equipment for federally sponsored research, at a cost of no more, usually, than the transportation to the research site. Colleges and universities have acquired excess property through Titles I and II of the Higher Education Facilities Act, under Title VI of the Higher Education Act, under the Vocational Education Act, and through a variety of federal research programs. In most cases, the federal government retains the title to excess property, but the Department of Interior and the National Science Foundation claim to have legislative authority to transfer title of excess property to grantees and contractors.

"Surplus property" is excess property offered by GSA to all other federal agencies and which no agency requests. It can then be donated for authorized purposes such as education, public health, civil defense, etc., or offered for sale to any nonfederal organization. There is not much possibility of acquiring an excellent item of equipment in this manner—most of the best pieces have been grabbed up by another agency as "excess property" and passed on to one of their staff members, grantees, or contractors.

There is a movement by federal authorities to streamline federal property utilization programs, and a recent GSA report recommended that the present excess property program be phased down by January 1, 1975 and discontinued by January 1, 1976. After that, all federal property that is now available through the excess property program would be declared "surplus property" and distributed through the federal surplus property program.

If this recommendation is implemented, federal agencies would no longer be able to assist their grantees or contractors in obtaining equipment by this means. As of this writing there is no legislation pending in Congress to implement the report, and grantees who require expensive items of equipment should make inquiries of the funding agency about the possibility of obtaining such equipment through the excess property program.

The guidelines of some grant and contract programs require individual prior approval for the purchase of certain equipment items, in which case the item must be individually listed in the budget and fully explained in the budget justification or narrative portion of the application, and *specific* approval must be granted by the agency in writing.

Any special restrictions concerning the acquisition or disposition of property should be written into the award document unless the program guidelines are sufficiently detailed. Each philanthropic organization, corporation, and body politic has its special requirements. State and municipal regulations are sometimes complicated by the intermingling of federal, state, and municipal funds for programs that must conform to the regulations of more than one governmental unit. Or sometimes the state is merely a "pass-through" for federal grants, in which case the operating policies must be clearly defined.

Equipment purchased by educational institutions for federally funded programs falls into three categories: (1) permanent equipment—those items with an acquisition cost of $200 or more and an expected life of one year or more—all such items must be provided for in the approved budget; (2) general purpose equipment—all items usable for activities of an institution other than research, i.e., office equipment and furnishings, air conditioning, motor vehicles, data processing equipment—specific approval must be obtained to use government funds for purchase of such equipment; (3) permanent research equipment—items costing $1,000 or more—specific approval must be given by the funding agency for acquisition of each item.

When the principal investigator on a grant transfers from one nonprofit institution to another and moves the project with him, the institution where title to the equipment is vested can decide whether he shall transfer the equipment. If the activity for which the equipment was purchased will not be continued at the original institution, and if the equipment is not needed at the institution which holds title (usually the original institution), and the cost of transfer is not excessive, and the project will continue at the new location, it can usually be transferred with the principal investigator. Depending upon the terms of the grant, of course, and the available funds, grant funds may be used to defray the cost of such transfers.

Guidelines governing the acquisition and disposition of property by educational institutions in the administration of federally funded projects are contained in:

Federal Management Circular 73-7 (FMC 73-7), Administration of College and University Research Grants, (formerly OMB A-101) Attachment A, *Standard policies and practices for administration of research projects at educational institutions in the United States.*

Federal Management Circular 73-8 (FMC 73-8), *Cost principles for educational institutions* (Formerly OMB A-21).

Order from: General Services Administration
18th and F Streets
Washington, D.C. 20405
Attn: Office of Federal Management Policy

Guidelines for State and Local Governments in the acquisition and disposition of property in connection with Federal projects are found in:

Office of Management and Budget Circular A-102 (OMB A-102), *Uniform administration requirements for grants-in-aid to state and local governments*

Office of Management and Budget Circular A-87 (OMB A-87), *Cost principles for grants-in-aid to state and local governments.*

Order from: Office of Management and Budget
Executive Office of the President
Washington, D.C. 20503

For commercial organizations:

Federal Procurement Regulations, *Procedures for use in cost-reimbursement type supply and research contracts with commercial organizations.*

Order from: Superintendent of Documents
U.S. Government Printing Office
Washington, D.C. 20402

COST SHARING AND MATCHING FUNDS

Cost sharing and/or matching fund grants are those given with the understanding that the recipient institution will participate in the financial support of the project. The rationale for this type of grant is that the institution will utilize its available resources more efficiently and exercise more prudent fiscal policies if it shares in the expenses of the activity.

For many federal programs, cost sharing or matching funds is a condition of eligibility imposed by the legislative appropriation making the funds available. Private foundations and industrial organizations seldom make a formal demand for a commitment on the part of the institution for a contribution to the cost of a project, although they often expect a portion of the total expense to be borne by the grantee institution.

Cost Sharing

Ever since 1966 the appropriations acts of the Congress have required cost sharing on research grants made by the Department of Health, Education, and Welfare. The same requirement extends to the independent agencies, such as The National Science Foundation, for grants resulting from proposals not specifically solicited by the agency, i.e., an "unsolicited proposal," as differentiated from an offer resulting from a Request for Proposal (RFP).

The idea of cost sharing is encouraged by federal management guidelines covering all federal support programs even for those that have no statutory requirement for it, for example, HEW research contracts. The level of cost sharing in those cases is wide open for agency determination; the guideline reads ". . . the amount of cost participation should reflect the mutual agreement of the parties, provided that it is consistent with any statutory requirements."[1]

Educational institutions and other nonprofit and not-for-profit organizations may be asked to contribute as little as "less than 1 percent" of some projects, and "at least 1 percent" is not unusual.

Cost participation by commercial or industrial organizations has a very wide range of acceptable levels with the federal government, from as little as 1 percent or less of the total project to more than 50 percent. Much depends upon the degree of national interest in the project and the agreement on title to or right to use inventions, patents, or technical information resulting from the project. There are two approaches to cost sharing on federal programs: (1) by institutional cost sharing agreements covering all grants and contracts subject to cost sharing awarded by an agency to a given organization; or (2) by separate cost sharing agreements for each research project.

Fixed institutional cost sharing rates are negotiated for Department of Health, Education, and Welfare programs by the Public

[1] Federal Management Circular 73-3: *Cost Sharing on Federal Research.*

Health Service, Office of Administrative Management, Division of Grants and Contracts, Cost and Audit Management Branch, 5600 Fishers Lane, Rockville, Maryland 20852.

Applications submitted from institutions with a fixed cost sharing rate do not show the rate or make any reference to cost sharing; the award document carries a statement that the grant is subject to an institutional agreement on cost sharing and gives the date of the agreement.

Agencies that enter into separate cost sharing agreements for each project may or may not require a detailed budget breakdown of the institutional contribution. To ensure compliance with the cost sharing policy of the National Science Foundation, a statement must appear on all applications that the organization will "cost share in accordance with current NSF policy." Current NSF policy is that grantees must share in the costs of a project on more than a "token participation" basis—"token" being defined as 1 per cent. If the statutes relevant to a program require more than that, it will be specifically stated in the NSF program announcement.

Some federal programs require that cost sharing amounts be itemized in the budget—the Air Force Office of Scientific Research is one, and this is also a requirement of some programs of the National Endowments for the Arts and the Humanities. The grantee's contribution must be listed and the basis for the calculation indicated. Faculty or staff time, for example, will be entered in the dollar amount represented by the portion of time spent on the project, based upon the appropriate annual or academic year salary.

Support that qualifies as cost sharing does not necessarily derive from the grantee institution only, but may come from any nonfederal source. The participation may be cash or in-kind contributions and may include charges for real and nonexpendable property or the value of goods and services directly benefitting the project for which the grant was made. *Cost sharing* usually implies donated *services* or *materials* and when it is required in matching portions is called a "soft match."

When the requirement is for *cash* gifts, the award is referred to as a *matching funds* grant, and called a "hard match," for obvious reasons.

Matching Funds

Some congressional allocations of funds are made with the specific condition that they be used only in matching gift programs. Unless the legislation stipulates that the matching portion must be in cash, the agency can and often does rule that colleges and universities may utilize resources and personnel effort as the "matching" portion. The Law Enforcement Assistance Agency requires matching funds in connection with *block grants* and *discretionary grant* programs, and their counsel has interpreted the legislative history of the funding to mean that 10 percent matching in cash is mandatory for all grantees, including colleges and universities. Other LEAA programs do not have this requirement. The National Endowments for the Arts and the Humanities and the National Science Foundation are federal agencies with matching fund programs.

A matching grant is an offer by the funding agency to support a proposed program by accepting gifts for a portion of the amount offered and by matching the gifts with a prestated portion of federal money.

Matching gifts must be from nonfederal sources other than the grantee institution. Individuals involved in a project or their close relatives also are not acceptable as donors of matching funds. A well-publicized example of a matching grant was one made in 1974 by the National Endowment for the Arts to the Metropolitan Opera Company of New York. The Arts Endowment agreed to match gifts to the Metropolitan up to $1 million, resulting in a total grant of $2 million. A national fund-raising campaign was launched to raise the $1 million in matching funds by donations from the general public.

A frequent misconception is that the availability of matching funds will ensure grant support. Applications for matching grants are subject to the same scrutiny and review as outright grants, and funds for such grants cannot exceed the total congressional appropriation to an agency specifically for that purpose.

The method of payment of gifts and administration of the total grant may vary among agencies. At the National Endowment, payment of the gift funds follows one of two possible arrangements: (1) gifts are sent directly to the agency by the donor or donors; or (2) the applicant institution may be designated as a collection agent for the accumulation of gifts to be applied to the grant. In either case, the funding agency administers the whole—the gifts plus the matching money—as a single grant in support of the project.

Matching grants specify the length of the period during which an offer of support will remain in effect and the granting agency will determine whether an extension of the period is warranted if the gift money has not been collected within the original period prescribed.

Agencies that require cost sharing or matching gifts include the specifics in the program guidelines.

The official authorized to endorse a proposal for an institution and to take responsibility for administering a grant or contract must be fully informed of the requirements and terms of applications submitted under cost sharing or matching conditions.

The institution that proposes to enter into a matching grant agreement should be fully cognizant of the responsibility devolving upon it to produce the matching portion of the grant and be prepared to take the necessary action to acquire it.

Applications for grants of either type should be submitted as the final formal step after a period of negotiation during which commitments and agreements have been reached among all organizations and individuals concerned. The institution's participation in the fund-matching activity should be agreed upon in unambiguous language, and preferably in writing.

No general guide to cost sharing or matching programs is sufficient; special instructions must be followed for each program. The Department of Health, Education, and Welfare has a guide to institutional agreements that contains much generally useful information. It is DHEW Publication No. (HSM) 73-24, *A Guide to Institutional Cost Sharing Agreements*, which can be ordered from: Public Health Service, Division of Grants and Contracts, 5600 Fishers Lane, Rockville, Maryland 20852.

The Federal Management Circular 73-3 (FMC 73-3), *Cost Sharing on Federal Research* (formerly OMB A-100) states the overall federal policies on the subject. Order it from:

General Services Administration
18 and F Streets, N. W.
Washington, D. C. 20405
Attn: Office of General Management Policy

How to Interact with the Funding Organization

The first approach to a foundation or a corporation should be in writing. Your letter should include a statement of the reason for writing to that particular organization and exactly what is being proposed. An abstract or summary of the project and the applicant's credentials may be attached. In place of the abstract a description of the proposed activity may be incorporated into the body of the letter. If it is at all feasible for the writer or a representative who can speak for the proposal to visit the funding organization, the letter should close with a request for an appointment.

Model letters or "canned" samples may be helpful but there is always the danger that you may not be alone and that others are using the same model. Moreover, it is difficult to follow a sample letter and retain the qualities of spontaneity and enthusiasm that go far in making an idea sound exciting. For those who feel that a model is absolutely necessary, some excellent examples can be found in *A Manual for Obtaining Foundation Grants,* by Louis A. Urgo and Robert J. Corcoran and *A Manual for Obtaining Government Grants*, by Louis A. Urgo.[2]

If letters are addressed to the director of a program or head of the appropriate office it indicates that the applicant has some knowledge of the structure of the funding organization—that he has "done his homework." It takes little research to confirm the name. If there is any question, call the organization's switchboard or, for corporations, look at the entry in *Standard and Poor's Register of Corporations, Directors and Executives,* which can be found in most reference libraries.

After a reasonable time—about two weeks—if an organization does not reply to a letter, a telephone follow-up will confirm that it was received and give the caller an opportunity to ask for an appointment.

Visiting a foundation or corporation office without an appointment is an invitation to rejection. It is improbable that the executive with even mid-level decision-making authority will be available, and in most cases it is a waste of time to talk with anyone else.

[2] Published by Robert J. Corcoran Company, Fund Raising Council, 40 Court Street, Boston, Massachusetts 02108.

As soon as an appointment has been made, preparation for it should begin. The abstract has been submitted; a full-blown draft proposal can now be written. Dr. Lindsey Churchill, formerly of the Russell Sage Foundation, reminds applicants: "They may say, 'Come in for an informal interview.' Don't believe it! There is no such thing as really informal scrutiny. You can be asked the most searching questions right from the first five minutes of the most preliminary talk and you better come up with the right answers. Don't go to a private foundation without your ideas well in order."

The best way to have your ideas in order is to put them down in writing. If asked, be prepared to leave a copy. It may be an opportunity that will not come again.

Many of the questions raised will concern matters that were discussed with the institutional representative. Those items that have to do with the financial arrangements are certain to be brought up.

"Foundations are getting as hardnosed as bankers," cautions Robert Mayer, assistant director of the New York Community Trust and former Ford Foundation executive. "It is logical to assume that, since you are considering approaching a foundation for a grant, you have a specific need—a shortfall of operating funds, a special project, a capital improvement required. Study your need carefully." A list of the questions an applicant should be prepared to discuss with a foundation official follows.

"Have you exhausted all possibilities to meet the need from your existing resources? . . . Are there other financial sources that could be tapped? . . . Have you examined the anticipated costs of your project in the most minute detail?" . . . And most importantly, "Is this trip really necessary? What benefits will accrue if this need is met? Who will benefit? How?"[3]

Edith Friedman, executive director of The Bruner Foundation, offers these suggestions for visiting foundations: "One, be business-like; two, be honest; three, know what you mean to do; four, ask questions; and finally, never, never argue with a foundation about

[3] Robert A. Mayer. "What Will a Foundation Look for When You Submit a Proposal?" *Library Journal* (July 1972).

the relevance of your proposed project to their program. . . . If they say it doesn't fit, it doesn't."[4]

The same general rules can also be applied to visiting corporations, with one addition. Corporations are profit-oriented organizations and they are interested in the potential of ideas for a dollars-and-cents return. This does not apply to company-sponsored foundations, which function just about like other foundations, nor does it apply to corporate departments established to handle philanthropic activities. It does pertain to the research and development divisions that might be approached for support of a project directly related to the corporation's production interests.

Federal funding agencies encourage consultation on applications either by telephone or by personal visits. For one thing, the Freedom of Information Act makes it mandatory that information be dispensed openly, but for another—cynicism about civil servants aside—many governmental representatives really care about the way appropriated funds are used. Often, they really want to support good programs and welcome the opportunity to discuss tentative proposals, especially if they know that an activity has the endorsement of a reputable institution and will be under the direction of a well-qualified scholar, researcher, or administrator. Some program directors require a preapplication to be submitted and approved before a final application is accepted.

A National Endowment for the Humanities Education Division brochure states in unmistakable language, "Those applicants who send in their applications close to the deadline date, without first having consulted the staff, are often at a competitive disadvantage when the applications are reviewed." The National Endowment is not alone. Staff members of many federal agencies will review preliminary proposals and advise the applicant on the outlook for possible funding. No staff member can deny an applicant the right to submit a proposal but it is foolish to ignore the advice of professionals who have shepherded hundreds or thousands of applications through reviewing committees, funding councils, and other decision-

[4] Institute on Funding for Colleges, Universities and Non-Profit Organizations, National Graduate University, Washington, D.C., September 25–26, 1973, Special Session on Foundations.

making groups, and can estimate with great accuracy the odds on your proposal's success.

The open-door policy of most federal offices should not be interpreted as an invitation to "shopping expeditions." The visitor should have a specific idea, preferably in at least outline or abstract form, to discuss. And although it is possible, it is unwise to visit without an appointment. Administrators of governmental programs travel extensively in connection with their duties and even when they are present may be too busy to give drop-in visitors a fair hearing.

Appointments to visit governmental representatives can usually be made by telephone. Making an appointment in advance allows time for material to be mailed to and read by the representative with whom the project is to be discussed.

Preparation for visits to government offices is very much the same as for foundations. But greater attention must be given to the questions, "What benefits will accrue if this need is met? Who will benefit? How?" If the purpose of a proposed activity falls within the interest and purview of the program for which funds have been appropriated, the final decision rests mainly on the degree to which it promises to benefit some element of society.

After your discussions with a representative of a granting organization, you should leave knowing the answers to the following questions:

1. Is the organization sufficiently interested in the project to suggest that a formal proposal be submitted?
2. What level of support is reasonable to request? Is long-term funding for an extensive project possible? Or seed money for planning and preparation to seek funding from other sources? What is the acceptable funding level for a one-year period? For the total project?
3. What categories of support does the program authorize? Personnel costs, including fringe benefits; equipment; supplies; fees to subjects; travel and per diem; conference costs; institutional overhead—any type of cost likely to be incurred in carrying out the project should be discussed. The grantee institution must have this information before accepting responsibility for the funds; otherwise, it could turn out to

cost the institution as much as or more than the funding agency contributed. Some projects are not acceptable unless their costs are fully reimbursed; in other cases, a sharing arrangement is acceptable.

4. What aspects of the draft proposal should be strengthened or emphasized? A program director or agency representative may be completely sold on an idea from the outset, but he will have to sell it to the committees or boards that make the final decisions, and it may run into stiff competition. The experienced agency official usually knows what the committees or boards are most interested in and, perhaps more importantly, he knows what may prejudice them against a project. If suggestions are offered, they should be taken. If they are too radical or threaten the integrity of the plan, the applicant always has the option to withdraw.

5. What, if any, special requirements or restrictions will the applicant and the institution have to agree to? Policies should be clarified on: purchase and disposition of equipment with grant funds; assignment of patent rights; distribution of royalties from published material; financial and auditing procedures; reporting requirements; personnel or travel policies.

6. When is the final, formal proposal to be submitted? The dates are sometimes stated as "postmark date," but in other cases the "deadline date" means the application must be in the office of the granting organization on that date.

No matter how the visit to a funding agency turns out, it is a good idea to write a letter following up or confirming the conclusions. If a formal proposal is to be submitted, the date agreed upon for its arrival should be restated and the commitment to meet the date confirmed. But, even if the visit was a disaster from the applicant's point of view, a letter should be sent expressing appreciation for the opportunity to discuss the proposal and hoping for better success next time. This will close the matter on an amiable note and may pave the way for another approach with the next idea.

The applicant is now ready to return to the office of the institutional official who will ultimately sign the formal proposal and accept responsibility for the funds, if awarded. Answers to questions that arose in the first meeting concerning the granting organization can now be answered. If there appear to be no serious conflicts, the final proposal can then be written.

The Application

WRITING THE PROPOSAL— THE APPLICATION PHASE

The only aspect of the entire grant-getting process totally under your control is writing your proposal. Fashions in grants come and go as in everything else. What organizations clamored to support yesterday goes begging today because of national and international crises, natural disasters, or political vicissitudes. There is nothing the grant seeker can do to change that. But no matter what the political or social climate, or what the current "glamor" field may be, every applicant has it in his power to prepare and submit a first class proposal.

The indispensable ingredient of a good proposal is a good idea. There is no substitute for it. Dr. Raymond B. Fosdick, former president of The Rockefeller Foundation, warns, "There is a common fallacy—and even some foundation executives may not be immune from it—that money can create ideas, and that a great deal of money can create better ideas. . . . The difficulty is the lack of men with fertile spirit and imagination . . . with flaming ideas demanding expression."[5]

The most beautifully prepared application will not turn a pedestrian idea into an inspired one, but the best idea in the world, inadequately described or unimaginatively presented, can be misinterpreted or even overlooked. On this point, one foundation official commented, "Foundation executives and program officers must distinguish between projects that are plausible and articulately described but lack substance, and those that have some real or potential merit but are presented so poorly that it is easy to miss their worth."

Figures on the number of applications rejected for poor or inadequate presentation are almost impossible to unearth; it is too difficult to pin down the reasons for disapproval, and often more than one deficiency is involved. In a recent analysis of over 700 disapproved applications to the Public Health Service, Louis E. Masterman found three major reasons for rejection: Eighteen percent failed because of the nature of the project, 38 percent because of the competency of the applicant (and Masterman carefully noted that it was not that the applicants were incompetent but that they failed to convince the reviewers of their competence), while a miscellaneous group of 5 percent was rejected for a variety of other reasons. The remaining 39 percent were disapproved because of inadequate planning and *carelessly prepared applications*.[6]

The situation has not changed much since 1959 when Dr. Earnest M. Allen surveyed 605 PHS applications. Reporting in *Science*, Allen listed four categories in which applications were found to be deficient: the Problem, the Approach, the Man (*sic*), and Other. He found that 58 percent had shortcomings in their choice of a problem—lack of originality or sufficient significance; 73 percent were inadequate in the approach—design poorly thought out, controls inadequately conceived or described; in 55 percent of the applications the qualifications of the investigator (the "Man") did not *appear* to be adequate as they were presented. In many cases, it seemed to be a matter of poor presentation rather than lack of experience or training. The final,

---

[5] Raymond B. Fosdick. *Chronicle of a Generation*. New York: The Foundation Center.
[6] Louis E. Masterman. *The Mechanics of Writing Successful Federal Grant Applications*. St. Louis, Missouri, Institute of Psychiatry, University of Missouri, School of Medicine.

miscellaneous category included such things as unrealistic requirements for equipment or personnel, unfavorable institutional setting, etc.[7]

Dr. George N. Eaves, executive secretary of the NIH Molecular Biology Study Section, finds that failure may frequently be related to many of the ambiguities and inaccuracies associated with poor scientific writing. As an example he cites an application that was disapproved because the proposed experiments were based on apparent misconceptions of the current status of the field and on misinterpretation of the pertinent literature. Also, the principal investigator did not appear to have the necessary background and experience to conduct such difficult studies. Then he asks: How much of the misinterpretation was truly that and how much was related to the author's careless use of words in conveying his interpretation? Did the principal investigator appear not to have the necessary background for the proposed investigations merely because he failed to devote sufficient attention to the "biographical sketch"? Was the investigator overly modest or had he left too much to the imagination?[8]

One reviewer for a government grant program returned from an evaluation session shaken and mystified. "We really had to scrape the bottom of the barrel to come up with enough recommendations and even then we were unable to approve as many as there were funds to support. Fifty percent of the applications had to be thrown out—they were hopeless."

An agency program director commented sadly, "The strange thing is that some of them won't let you help them. They borrow an out-of-date guideline brochure from a college down the road, dig up the wrong application form somewhere, and mail in a proposal just under the deadline. There is no time for discussion or revisions. I have on occasion telephoned such an applicant and suggested that we send him the current guidelines with the appropriate forms and that he rewrite the proposal for the next competition. Instead of being grateful for the help, he thinks he is being given the brush-off and insists on his *right* to have the proposal considered in the current

[7] E. M. Allen. *Science*, Vol. 132 (1960), p. 1532.
[8] G. N. Eaves. "Who Reads Your Project-Grant Applications to the National Institutes of Health?" *Federation Proc.* 31 (January-February 1972): 1.

round. What can you do? It's like watching a sinking ship—all you can do is stand there and salute."

Both public and private funds for support of research and graduate education have decreased in recent years even as inflation steadily erodes the buying power of those that are available. The decline in available funds has proceeded in exactly opposite synchrony with the nation's annual production of trained scholars and scientists. During the decade of the sixties, the number of Ph.D.'s awarded annually tripled from 10,000 in 1960 to 30,000 in 1969.[9]

Although not all grant applicants are holders of doctoral degrees or even graduate students, the proportion is very high, and whatever the reason, the number of applications has risen to new heights since 1970. The Research Division of the National Endowment of the Humanities, for example, reports a tripling of applications between 1970 and 1974.

One might logically expect that the intensified competition has brought about an improvement in the quality of the applications, but that apparently is not the case. Dr. George Eaves asserts flatly that, "As the number of applications has increased the overall care with which the applications have been written has diminished."[10]

As the number of applications increases, so does the work of the reviewers, forcing each reviewer to spend less time in attempting to understand and evaluate each proposal. The practice of making site visits or inviting applicants to furnish additional clarifying material to the committee is much less likely to be followed than in the past. There just isn't enough time. Thus, for most applicants the written proposal serves as the major or only medium through which the case in favor of an award is argued. It is clearly worth the investment in time and effort to prepare an impressive case.

What makes a good proposal? Should it be long or short, wordy or concise? What about the budget? Should it be calculated down to the penny or include some "fat"? Are committees influenced by

[9] U.S., Office of Education. *Doctors' Degrees Conferred by All U.S. Institutions: by State, Academic Field, Sex and Institution, 1960–61 through 1969–70.* Washington, D.C.: U.S. Government Printing Office, 1972.

[10] G. N. Eaves. "The Project-Grant Application of the National Institutes of Health." *Federation Proc.* 32 (May 1973): 5.

famous names in the personnel section? Is the prestige of the endorsing institution a factor? Should the details of a highly technical research project be included and will the reviewers understand it if they are? And some have asked, why do it at all? Is a proposal really necessary?

While the last question may be largely rhetorical, it is one that must be answered occasionally. The obvious reason and one that applies to all grant sources is that the formal written application is the only effective way whereby a large number of qualified individuals can compete for limited funds. Another, perhaps less obvious reason, relates to the use of public funds, the major source of grant support. The worthiness of projects to receive public funds must be determined by a system that is open and fair and which brings expert judgment into the decision-making processes. The basis for such a system and for obtaining competent judgment is the formal application.

There are probably as many answers to all the other questions as there are funding agencies and people on their staffs and boards. No one is without bias, and every individual program director, council member, or reviewer reacts favorably or unfavorably to certain particular items in an application and to the way they are handled. There are, however, identifiable hallmarks that separate the excellent proposal from the merely passable one and the acceptable from the hopeless.

One of the early warning signs that a proposal is in good hands is the applicant's sensitivity to timing. Funding organizations are more hospitable to the prospective applicant who approaches them well in advance of the deadline date for submission of a proposal. It attests to his ability to plan carefully and augurs well for the execution of the proposed activity.

Some grant-making agencies will accept proposals at any time and the submission date is governed by the date the funds are needed. The vital factor in determining how far ahead to submit a proposal for which no deadline date has been established is the time required for review and decision. Foundations and corporations usually complete the reviewing process faster than governmental agencies, and this point should be discussed in the preapplication meeting. (See section on What to Do Before You Apply—The Preapplication Phase.) The National Science Foundation suggests that applications submitted for no-deadline programs be received approximately six months before the funds are needed. It takes about six months to one year between submission of an application to a federal agency and notification of the award. Delays of various kinds can extend the period up to as much as two years!

An unmistakable feature of the superior proposal is evidence that the writer understands its function. Grant applicants are sometimes exhorted to use methods developed in the commercial world and expressed in terms such as salesmanship, packaging, the customer, and so on, but this is a distortion. A proposal is not a sales pitch.

The function of a proposal is to convince those who control the distribution of funds and judge the worth of a project that:

1.   A proposed activity is within the scope of the established objectives of the funding agency's program or stated purposes.
2.   The action to be taken is valuable because it will solve an immediate problem or elicit fundamental information, or because it will extend existing knowledge and assist in the eventual solution of a problem.
3.   The proposer is well acquainted with the "state-of-the-art"; that he knows what has already been done, is qualified to perform the described activity, and has access to the necessary facilities.
4.   The importance of the anticipated results sufficiently justifies the time to be spent on it and the money it will cost.

The presentation of these points takes many forms and the length may vary from a two- or three-page letter to documents of several hundred pages, with attachments. If some reviewers are impressed by bulk, many are not. Dr. Manning Pattillo, foundation executive and former president of The Foundation Center, comments, "In the majority of cases the essential facts can be stated in three or four pages. If it takes much more space than that to outline the proposal, probably it has not been thought through sufficiently."

And Dr. Pattillo adds, "No fancy bindings, gold lettering or other decorations."[11]

The best guide as to the length of a proposal comes from the granting organization itself. In other words, give them what they want. Guidelines usually indicate the expected length, or the preapplication consultation will yield a clue. The type of activity is the chief determinant. A research proposal may require extensive documentation of related research activities, design and sampling procedures, instrumentation, or collection and interpretation of data. A performing arts company's request for an operating subsidy may require documentation of past, present, and future financial transactions and obligations. The proposal of a sculptor to create a suitable work to be placed in the town square, or of a novelist to write a new book, can be summarized in a few sentences, but information on the applicant's credentials may take many pages, with attachments.

Nearly all government agencies have standard application forms that must be used but some do not, and very few foundations provide the applicant with more than a statement of the information required. The federal government has been promising for some time to produce a standard application form for all federal agencies but has not come up with one yet. The NSF and NIH are experimenting with a common form (NSF currently has no standard form) but it is uncertain whether even two agencies can design a standard form that meets the needs of both.

Application forms are sometimes lengthy and complicated, but completing them is simply a matter of filling in the blanks and is not difficult except, perhaps, for the narrative portions. The description of the project is completely in the hands of the writer, and this is far and away the most important part of the application and requires the most care.

The main drawback to using a proposal form is its lack of flexibility. Some projects just do not seem to fit into the format and great liberty must be taken in the placement of some elements of information. (Does it go under 2b. or 4c.? In Section I or III?) Also, the space allowed may be inadequate for the detail an applicant wishes to

---

[11] Manning M. Pattillo. "Preparing the Foundation Proposal." In F. Emerson Andrews, ed., *Foundations: 20 Viewpoints*, New York: Russell Sage Foundation, 1965.

include, requiring the addition of carryover pages, which slows up the reading and reviewing process.

Whether a form is provided or only the sketchiest of instructions given, every well-written request for support contains these essential elements:

1. An idea and a clearly thought out plan of action to accomplish something important.
2. Project or program description in concise, straightforward language with a minimum of technical jargon.
3. Statement of the purpose and importance of the work, the ends to be achieved, and the specific results to be obtained.
4. Name or names of those who will carry out the activity, and their qualifications for doing it.
5. Where the work will be done.
6. Why the organization to which it is directed should support it.
7. How much time it will take; if it is a successive project, incremental time periods for each step are estimated and the dependency of each further step on the results of the previous one indicated.
8. The cost, by specific elements.

In quite brief applications, the essential information may be abbreviated and some of the elements combined under one heading. In lengthy proposals, the information may be organized into the following components:

1. Cover page, or covering letter.
2. Summary or abstract describing the essence of the project.
3. Narrative description of the proposed activity.
4. Detailed budget with appended justification for any expenditures not fully explained in the narrative.
5. Credentials of the applicant and all professional staff to be involved in the project (*curriculum vitae*, publication lists, and recent reviews, if applicable).
6. Certifications, as required, attesting to compliance with Civil Rights, Protection of Human Subjects, agreement on assignment of patent rights, or commitments regarding

cost-sharing, matching funds, or use of grant funds (see sections on these matters in The Institution as Grantee: Interaction of the Institution and the Funding Organization).

7.   Official endorsements of the institution providing the facilities and accepting responsibility for administration of the funds.

THE COVER PAGE

The cover page is the place to include information that does not fit into any other part of the proposal; for example, the name of the fiscal agent to whom the funds are sent, the applicant's Social Security number, the institution's Internal Revenue Service identification number, or any other specialized information required for a specific proposal.

The covering page serves as an identification tag; it should contain all the information necessary to guide the document into the proper processing channels. Many large organizations have central receiving divisions or departments where applications are logged in and routed to the appropriate office. An application arriving without an "identification tag" is at the mercy of the receiving personnel who may be highly skilled but lack the knowledge or the time to accurately identify the subject matter of many proposals. Misrouted proposals will be delayed and the time loss can be disadvantageous or even fatal.

A far-fetched but true illustration of what can happen in the routing process concerns a personal letter sent to a newly-appointed foundation executive by a friend who thought it would be amusing to write the letter in the form of a request for a grant. The communication was sent from Canada, where the writer was spending some lonely weeks during which his major source of entertainment was going to see American films. The subject chosen for his "application" was, therefore, "Influence of American Film Making on Canadian Society." Since he had plenty of time on his hands, he did a thorough and fanciful job of proposal writing, including an abstract, a description of the research plan, and his credentials. A very detailed budget itemized the costs involved in the research—attending films, transportation and parking fees, admission, tips to ushers, popcorn, candy, soft drinks, etc. The addressee was not in the foundation's division that dealt with sociological implications of film making and thus the "proposal" wound up in the reviewing machinery of another program. Only a timely follow-up by the writer, who became apprehensive when he did not receive an immediate reply applauding his humorous communication, prevented his receiving a letter of rejection from the foundation! The addressee managed to rescue it just in time.

Every cover page should contain the following basic information plus any other specialized information required by the circumstances of the program or the funding organization.

1. Name and address of the organization to which the proposal is addressed. Applications to federal agencies should include the name of any other federal agencies to which the proposal is being submitted.

2. Subject of the proposal and the type of support requested, e.g., grant, contract, or fellowship; for training, research, or conference.

3. Name of the applicant, i.e., the individual preparing the proposal, the project director or principal investigator, address, telephone number, and Social Security number.

4. Name of the institution endorsing the proposal and accepting the responsibility for administration of the grant if awarded, the address of the institution, and the Internal Revenue Service identification number or certification as to the nonprofit or not-for-profit status, if applicable. Applications to governmental agencies include the congressional district in which the institution is located, and for HEW proposals, the Identity Number.

5. Name, address, telephone number, and title of the official authorizing the institutional endorsement. This is the official who will represent the institution in negotiations with the funding agency.

6. Name, address, telephone number, and title of the institutional fiscal agent to whom the grant funds will be paid.

7. Project period—beginning and terminating dates. A statement that it is a new, renewal, or continuation application.
8. Amount of the request. This figure may be broken down into direct and indirect costs. If the project is for more than a one-year period, the cost for the first year should be given, as well as the total cost.
9. Signatures of the principal investigator, the institutional representative, and any others required by the funding organization.
10. Date the application is submitted.

Although the cover page is the first part of the proposal anyone sees, it is the last to be prepared. It cannot be completed until the entire application has been written and is ready for the necessary signatures.

The guides on pages 236 and 237 are suggested for preparing a cover sheet when no standard application form is used or when the form does not include a cover page. Cover Page Guide A is for foundations and corporations. Cover Page Guide B is for governmental agencies.

The Abstract

The abstract or summary is a condensation of the project containing all the key points necessary to give the reviewers an overview of what is being proposed in 100 to 300 words. Some application forms place it on the cover page, in which case it is an additional aid in routing the proposal to the appropriate review committee. The abstract is used by some funding agencies to provide information to the Smithsonian Science Information Exchange (SSIE), an indexed register of ongoing scientific research projects which serves as a primary information clearing house on research activities in the United States. Sometimes the abstract is used also for the exchange and coordination of application information between federal funding agencies.

Abstracts should be written concisely and clearly. If the project deals with a highly specialized topic, technical terms that appear in the body of the proposal should appear in the abstract and be under-

COVER PAGE GUIDE A

For Applications to FOUNDATIONS AND CORPORATIONS

Type of Support Requested: _____
(Grant, Contract, Fellowship, Scholarship)

1. Submitted to: _____
   (Name of Funding Organization)
   Address with Zip Code: _____
   _____

2. Proposed Project:
   Title: _____
   From: _____ To: _____
   (Beginning Date of Project)   (Completion Date of Project)
   Amount Requested: _____ _____
   (Total)   (First 12 months)

3. Submitted by: _____
   (Name of Applicant Organization)
   Address with Zip Code: _____
   _____

   Type of Institution: _ A. Profit _____ Not-for-Profit _____ Commercial _____
                         B. Federal _____ State _____ Local _____ Other _____

4. Principal Investigator or _____
   Project Director (or Both): _____
   Address with Zip Code: _____
   _____
   _____ _____
   (Social Security No.)   (Telephone with Area Code)

5. Human Subjects Involved: No _____

                             Yes _____   Approved: _____
                                                           (Date)
                                      Pending Approval: _____
                                                           (Expected Date)

6. Project Site: _____
   (Name of Institution Providing Facilities)
   _____
   Address (Where Project Will Be Done)
   _____
                                                (Zip Code)

7. Fiscal Agent: _____
   (Individual to Whom Funds Should Be Sent)
   _____
   (Address with Zip Code)
   _____
                                         (Telephone with Area Code)

8. Endorsements:

   Principal Investigator   _____   _____
                            (Signature)   (Typed/Printed Name)
   Approving Institutional
      Official   _____   _____
                            (Signature)   (Typed/Printed Name)
   Other Approving Official _____   _____
                            (Signature)   (Typed/Printed Name)

9. Date Submitted: _____

COVER PAGE GUIDE B
for Applications to GOVERNMENTAL AGENCIES

Type of Support Requested: _____
(Grant, Contract, Fellowship, Scholarship)

1. Submitted to: _____
    (Name of Funding Organization)

    Address with Zip Code: _____

    _____

2. Proposed Project:

    Title _____

    From: _____ To: _____
    (Beginning Date of Project)   (Completion Date)

    Amount Requested: _____ _____
    (Total)   (First 12 Months)

    _____ _____
    (Overhead or Indirect Costs - Total)   (Overhead or Indirect Costs- First 12 Months)

3. Submitted by: _____
    (Name of Applicant Organization)

    Address with Zip Code: _____

    _____

    Type of Institution: A. Profit _____ Not-for-Profit _____ Commercial _____

    B. Federal _____ State _____ Local _____ Other _____

    IRS Identification Number: _____ Congressional District _____

    Identity No. _____ Civil Rights Compliance Filed _____
    (Date)

4. Principal Investigator or _____

    Project Director (or Both): _____

    Address with Zip Code: _____

    _____

    _____ _____
    (Social Security No.)   (Telephone with Area Code)

5. Human Subjects Involved: No _____

    Yes _____   Approved: _____
    Date

    Pending Approval: _____
    (Expected Date)

6. Indicate if proposal has been or will be submitted in whole or in part to other possible
    sponsors, including other governmental agencies, and name the agencies: _____

    _____

7. Project Site: _____
    (Name of Institution Providing Facilities)

    _____
    Address (Where Project Will Be Done)

8. Fiscal Agent: _____
    (Name, Title, and Organization of Official Responsible for Administering Funds)

    _____
    (Address with Zip Code)

    _____ _____
    (Telephone with Area Code)

9. Endorsements

    Principal Investigator   _____   _____
    (Signature)   (Typed/Printed Name)

    Approving Institutional   _____   _____
        Official   (Signature)   (Typed/Printed Name)

    Other Approving Official _____   _____
    (Signature)   (Typed/Printed Name)

10. Date Submitted: _____

lined and explained. This is very important for those applications referred to national councils or boards of directors for final approval. Members of such groups usually read the reviewers' recommendations and often read the abstract; they seldom read the entire proposal.

The abstract is a summary of the entire proposal and cannot be written until all other portions have been completed except the cover page.

THE PROJECT DESCRIPTION

This is the main body of the proposal, the section on which the decision will turn. Here the basic idea is expressed, the philosophy or premise underlying it is explained, the methods for developing it are described, and its ultimate purpose is asserted and defended.

By the time this part of the application is ready to be written, the proposal has been through a refining process. Its salient points have been summarized to serve as the basis for preapplication discussions; a tentative or draft description of the project may have been written. The weaknesses and strengths of the proposal have been exposed to the criticism of representatives of the institution where the work will be done, and of one or more funding agencies, and perhaps that of one or two colleagues.

The writer's enthusiasm for the project should be at its highest peak, an excellent state of mind for the preparation of this portion of the application. The information must be well thought out, the procedures explained thoroughly, the necessary data precisely presented, but through it all the message to the reader must be: "This is a good idea; it will yield worthwhile results; it is in good hands."

More than anything else, the format used in writing the project description depends upon the type of activity. If a standard application form is to be used, the guidelines for filling it in prescribe the information to be included, in what order, and usually in what detail. Organizations that do not use printed forms often have standard guidelines to be followed and if so, they should be read carefully before writing the project description.

Whether there is a form or not, whether there are guidelines or not, the preapplication consultations will have given the applicant many clues as to what the organization will be looking for. And the description should emphasize those points closest to the interests and objectives of the funding agency. The potential funder must have been selected on the basis that the proposal fits into its overall objectives; it is foolish and usually fruitless to attempt to artificially adapt the purpose and significance of a planned activity to the stated or implied purposes of a granting organization.

No outline or format will be suitable for all types of activities and there are a number of excellent guides to writing proposals of a specific kind (see page 268). Some general points should be covered in the Description of the Project portion of all proposals. With additions and modifications, the following list can be applied to many, perhaps most, types of applications.

Introduction

This section includes the statement of what is to be done—its significance and overall purpose; the background of the project—what has been or is being done both generally and specifically in the same or related fields; the rationale or philosophy behind the proposed activity—explanation and justification for unique or innovative approaches.

The introduction will be far more detailed in research applications than in other types, especially the references to other work, reflecting a thorough knowledge of the literature and current research pertaining to the subject field.

One of the more comprehensive tools to ensure that an applicant has knowledge of prior work in the physical and life sciences is the *Science Citation Index*® (SCI®). This index utilizes a unique system, citation indexing, which organizes scientific and technical articles by the articles which they cite in common. If the applicant is aware of some of the key older papers pertinent to the proposed research, he can be led from the entries to those papers to all more recent papers in the same subject area. This is of utmost important in ensuring that the proposed research is not a duplication of previously published work.

The SCI is completely multidisciplinary, covering over 100 fields of science and technology from 2,400 world wide journals. Cumulatively, its annual issues cover better than 90 percent of the published scientific journal literature of the past 300 years. SCI is available at most U. S. libraries of colleges and universities, some major public libraries, most large government-sponsored scientific libraries, and virtually every medical school library in the United States.

A comparable publication, the *Social Sciences Citation Index*®, started in 1973, (and which covers the worldwide journal literature from all the forty or more social sciences), contains about half a million source articles in the 1970–1975 editions, and references to over 2.5 million earlier publications relevant to the social sciences. It is also found in the principal research libraries enumerated earlier, in four-year college libraries, and in many large municipal and state libraries.

The *Research Grants Index*, a listing of grants and contracts sponsored by the Public Health Service, is printed each fiscal year and contains relevant bibliographies on each grant listed. This Index may be ordered from the Superintendent of Documents, GPO, or from the PHS.

The National Library of Medicine through its MEDLINE programs compiles and disseminates information and bibliographic material on biomedical science research. It is dispensed through on-line computer terminals in medical schools and many hospitals. The *Science Citation Index* and the *Social Sciences Citation Index* are also available for on-line searching through the SDC ORBIT and Lockheed DIALOG systems, respectively.

The National Technical Information Service (NTIS) collects and disseminates technical report information generated by government-funded research. NTIS currently offers computer-generated custom bibliographic service of more than 250,000 abstracts of federally sponsored technical reports published since 1964. NTIS also has available for distribution a bibliography, prepared by the National Science Foundation, of translations of significant research literature from unfamiliar languages, such as Chinese, Japanese, Russian, and other East European languages. For information write: National Technical Information Service, Department of Commerce, Springfield, Virginia 22151.

Another central source of current information about ongoing scientific research is the Smithsonian Institution's Science Information Exchange (SSIE), an index of more than 100,000 descriptions of research in progress, which can be ordered by subject. The brochure listing available subjects may be ordered from: Science Information Exchange, Inc., Room 300, Madison National Bank Building, 1730 M Street, N.W., Washington, D. C. 20036.

The repertoire of every granting official is replete with stories about applications to conduct research, develop instruments, or perform other activities that have already been done or that are nearing completion in another laboratory or geographic location. There are even stories about those going on in the applicant's own institution—so the need to ensure that one's research is unique and represents new areas of investigation is self-evident.

The rationale for an innovative idea may require extensive explanation in connection with a demonstration project to test the feasibility of a theory or approach as, for example, a unique approach to education of the handicapped or to addiction therapy. For certain research projects in which new approaches are proposed, detailed and persuasive presentation may be necessary.

Objectives

This is where the specific objectives are stated and their relation to the overall purpose explained. If a publication is expected to result from the work, a new invention, a new method, the discovery of heretofore unknown basic knowledge, confirmation of a theory, or the performance of a new symphonic work, these are specific objectives.

Methods of Procedure

State the plan or design of the project in step-by-step sequence including time estimates, techniques or methodology to be used, instrumentation required, use of subjects and control groups, collection and analysis of data, evaluation methods, interpretation of results. Any special provisions that must be made for transportation to other sites, conferences, acquisition of unusual items of equipment or services, or any possibly hazardous aspects of the project should be discussed.

As with others, this portion will be far more detailed for a research project than for other proposals. If animal subjects are to be used, give information on the source of supply, means of transportation, and exact descriptions of the animals, including specific requirements as to age, weight, etc. If human subjects are used, details should be given of the group from which the samples will be drawn and of sampling methods to be employed; provisions for protection of the rights and welfare of the subjects must be described.

Professional jargon should be avoided but if some terms are unavoidable, they must be explained. Many reviewers, almost without exception in federal agencies, are professionals in the fields of the proposals referred to them, but boards of directors or national council members who may have final approval of an application frequently are not.

Significance

The applicant obviously has a preconception of what the eventual result of a project will be and hopes it will "succeed" in achieving its objectives. The significance, however, can often be stated in two ways: If the idea works, it has a certain significance; if it doesn't, it has another that may be equally important. A study undertaken to uncover new knowledge has intrinsic value, and its significance may be, at the moment, exactly that. An attempt to test the feasibility of a theory may be significant if it turns out to be either workable or unworkable; the significance of the creation of a work of art may be in providing an opportunity for the development of a young artist, or for community beautification.

Facilities Available

The space, equipment, environmental factors, or specific population required for the project may be implicit from the procedural methods already described, but they must be specified and assurance given that they can be provided. If the institution where the work is to be done is making facilities available, the basis for the agreement concerning their use must be stated, i.e., what is being contributed, what is included in indirect costs, what must be reimbursed from grant funds.

If facilities at institutions other than the project site are to be used, an official statement authorizing their use should be attached.

The principal investigator's credentials will be presented to the funding agency in the form of a resumé, or *curriculum vitae* and bibliography, but no documentation will speak louder on behalf of the application and the applicant's competence to carry it out than a complete, clear, detailed, carefully prepared description of the project.

THE BUDGET

In his *Preface to Fables, Ancient and Modern,* John Dryden wrote, " 'Tis with a poet, as with a man who designs to build, and is very exact, as he supposes, in casting up the cost beforehand; but, generally speaking, he is mistaken in his account, and reckons short of the expense he first intended."

'Tis with grants applicants as with poets and builders, they often reckon short.

And there *are* those who reckon long. This is referred to as "fat" in the budget and is thought by some to be the only safe course. In a highly publicized controversy over the budget and its documentation submitted to the New York State Council on the Arts for a grant to the American Ballet Theater, Sherwin M. Goldman, president of the Ballet Theater Foundation admitted that he "manipulated the figures." The *New York Times* story on the matter quotes Goldman: "The object of grantsmanship is to manipulate your figures so as to qualify for the most outside assistance. . . . I do manipulate figures all the time. It's my job."[12]

---

[12] *The New York Times*, June 20, 1974.

Well, that's one opinion. The subliminal message in the story is that those who accept this principle must be prepared to end up justifying their approach to investigators, auditors, and the press, and even for the possibility of returning grant funds after they have been awarded! Unless one is willing to face such eventualities, the wisest course is to assume that estimates of cost and supporting documentation should be as realistic and as accurate as possible.

Program directors, agency heads, review committees, and even foundation board members want precise information when they make an award to an individual or an organization.

Few people will argue with this. The difficulty is that applicants (like the poet and the builder) cannot see far enough ahead to make accurate estimates. The inexperienced proposal writer invariably overlooks some essential item resulting in confusion, misunderstandings, and, not infrequently, acrimonious encounters with the granting agency or with officials at the institutions where the work is being performed.

Expertise in budget preparation, as in other things, is learned by experience but also, as in other things, nobody starts out with experience. And experience is not always transferable—costs vary in different localities, institutional policies vary remarkably. The experienced applicant dealing with a new institution may need as much guidance as the totally inexperienced one.

The overall level of costs, the total amount requested in the budget, is determined by the needs of the project and the limitations set by the granting organization. During preapplication meetings with representatives of the potential funding organization and the site institution, questions concerning the level and type of support likely to be approved are among the major points discussed. If there is disagreement on the needs of the project or a requirement for partial support to come from other sources, agreement must be reached on these points before submission of the formal application. Some program guidelines stipulate the categories of cost that will be approved and set an upper limit on the total amount that may be requested.

When it comes to making up the budget, a great deal of information about it has been accumulated. The official representative of the site institution has indicated what institutional facilities and services can be provided—with or without reimbursement from grant funds; specific items that may or may not be included in the direct costs have been cleared with the granting organization; if matching funds from other sources are required, they have been obtained or assured.

The grants officer or institutional official who will sign the proposal should also be consulted on the details of the budget. Assistance in budget preparation is one of the services usually provided by grants offices, and the staff is able to advise on preparation of budgets for all types of activities. Those with experience in dealing with many granting organizations can offer helpful suggestions based on the particular requirements or idiosyncracies of some. Grants office personnel are also familiar with institutional policies that apply to grants budgeting, such as wage and salary rates, fringe benefit coverage and calculations, indirect cost rates, etc.

If there is no grants office, colleagues in the same department or the same field are a good source of information on costs such as fees to subjects, local transportation, space rental, availability of non-professional staff and rates of pay, student assistants, etc. Experienced colleagues can also advise on time estimates—a critical factor in estimating the cost of some projects.

Pay scales and fringe benefit rates can be obtained from the personnel or payroll office. On college and university campuses, part-time employees may be recruited through the student financial aid office, a good place to inquire about availability of personnel and pay rates.

Cost of equipment must always be checked with the vendor. Price fluctuations are so frequent that catalogs are out of date by the time they come off the press.

Transportation costs also fluctuate wildly and must be checked for currency. In planning travel abroad, the time of year a trip is made will affect the cost because of the seasonal rate changes.

Any costs for which the estimates cannot be obtained otherwise should be discussed directly with the individual in charge of the facility or the service. This is critical for use of specialized and large-scale facilities such as animal care laboratories, high energy accelerators, ultracentrifuges, electron spin resonance and nuclear magnetic resonance facilities, recording studios, radiation laboratories, computers, etc., both for estimates of costs and for prescheduling the use of the service.

The amount of detail required in the budget depends entirely upon what the granting agency wants. Generally speaking, foundations require less detail than governmental agencies.

If a standard application form is used, the budget page indicates exactly what categories of cost may be included, where they are to be entered, and what calculations are to be shown. If no budget page is provided, the needs of the project determine what categories to use. Cost factors involved in a construction project will bear little resemblance to those of a capitation grant for training para-medics; budgets prepared for operating expense subsidies will be quite different from those for research grants. Forms are nearly always provided for fellowship and scholarship applications.

Direct costs incurred by grant activities fall within some or all of the following categories:

1. Personnel: salaries and wages; fringe benefits; consultant and contract services.
2. Expendable supplies.
3. Equipment: purchase and rental.
4. Travel: foreign, domestic, and local.
5. Communications: telephone installation and service and toll calls; messenger, cable, and telegraph service.
6. Publications: brochures, reports, page charges, reprints of articles.
7. Other costs: all items not included in the other categories.

DIRECT COSTS

Personnel

Keep in mind that professional and nonprofessional personnel costs for most projects can be divided into three elements: salaries and wages; fringe benefits; and consultants and other services purchased on a contract basis.

a. Salaries and Wages

This includes all personnel who will be spending full or part time on the project in an employee status. The name (if known), title of position, amount of time to be spent on the project, rate of pay, and total amount to be paid are shown for each individual. The Project Director, for example, may expect to spend full time on a one-year grant at a salary of $20,000 per year. The entry would read:

M. J. Doe, Project Director, 100% time for 12 months
   at $20,000/year _____ $20,000

The salary rate for those spending part time on the project must be the same as the current salary of the individual. If it is necessary to establish a salary for the grant position, it must be commensurate with salaries paid at the grantee institution for staff or faculty with equivalent training and experience.

Part-time personnel are listed by name, if available, exact salaries, percentage of time to be spent, and total to be paid, in this manner:

R. J. Roe, Research Assistant, 50% time for 12 months
   at $10,000/year ($10,000 × 50%) _____ $5,000

or

50% time for 6 months at $10,000/year ($10,000 × 25%) $2,500

The fringe benefits and indirect costs would be divided proportionately. This is shown in the budget guides on later pages.

If the names are not available, entries for personnel may read:

Research Assistants, to be appointed (2) at $10,000/
   year, 50% time for 6 months ($10,000 × 25% × 2) $5,000

For large projects, it is a good idea to break down the salaries and wages section into professional and nonprofessional to reflect at a glance the type of effort required. The nonprofessional category includes administrative and clerical staff, craftsmen, and other personnel performing duties other than those directly contributing to the research or programmatic activity.

Some institutions share the cost of a project by releasing personnel to participate in the activity on a contributory basis. If, for example, the Principal Investigator or Project Director will be released from institutional duties in order to spend full time on the grant activity, and the institution agrees to provide half of the cost, the entry would read:

	Requested from Grantor	Institutional Contribution
Professor M. J. Doe, Principal Investigator, 100% time for 12 months at $20,000 (50% Institutional Contribution) __	$10,000	$10,000

If Professor Doe will spend 30 percent of the academic year on the grant project, and the institution agrees to contribute 10 percent, the entry would appear like this:

	Granting Agency	Institutional Contribution
Professor M. J. Doe, Principal Investigator, 30% of Academic Year, Annual Salary $20,000 (10% Institutional Contribution) _____	$4,000	$2,000

At colleges and universities the question of summer salary is handled according to the policies of the institution and in compliance with procedures acceptable to the granting organization. Many academic salaries are referred to as "academic year" salaries; the academic year in most places is nine months. In computing summer salaries for grant purposes, the monthly rate is one-ninth of the annual rate. Many colleges and universities will not permit faculty to commit more than two-ninths time, or two months, during the summer.

If Professor Doe spends two months during the summer on the project, and the institution's academic year is nine months, the summer entry would be:

	Granting Agency	Institutional Contribution
Professor M. J. Doe, Principal Investigator, 2 summer months, salary $20,000 academic year (2/9 × $20,000) __	$4,444	——

b. Fringe Benefits

All personnel in both professional and nonprofessional categories must be accounted for in fringe benefits calculations. Some institutions have agreements with governmental agencies to use a composite rate for calculation of fringe benefits. If the total salaries and wages for both professional and nonprofessional personnel add up to $40,000, and the composite rate for fringe benefits is 20 percent, the line would read:

Fringe Benefits

$40,000 × 20% _____ $8,000

The institutional agreement may be to use one rate for professional and another for nonprofessional employees and then the entry might read:

Fringe Benefits

Professional Personnel, $30,000 × 20% _____	$6,000
Nonprofessional Personnel, $10,000 × 15% _____	1,500
Total Fringe Benefits _____	$7,500

If the funding agency requires that fringe benefits be itemized, the cost of each type of coverage is listed. Statutory benefit rates vary from state to state and exact figures must be obtained from the grantee institution's payroll office. Employees are covered by some or all of the following benefits: workmen's compensation, state disability insurance, unemployment compensation, Social Security, hospital, medical, dental, and retirement benefits. Fringe benefits that are itemized may be stated in this form, although the categories and amounts will vary among institutions and according to geographic location:

State Unemployment Insurance,
   3.6% of first $4,200 of each salary
   (3.6% × $12,600) ------------------------------- $ 454
FICA (Social Security),
   6% of first $12,500 of each employee's salary
   (6% × $32,500) ------------------------------- 1,950
Health Insurance,
   10% of total salaries (10% × $40,000) ------------ 4,000

Budget guides on pages 255–263 show details of fringe benefit calculations.

c. Consultants and Contract Services

Consultant and other services obtained on a contract basis are shown separately and not included in the fringe benefit calculations. Fees for consultants and all other services must be approved by the funding agency and should be commensurate with those paid by the grantee institution for similar services.

One of the questions frequently asked concerns the listing of famous names in the personnel section of the grant application. Does it help? Will it influence the reviewers? Reviewers are, after all, human (no matter what rejected applicants sometimes think), and faced with a mountainous pile of applications to be reviewed in a short time, it is not unlikely that the appearance of the name of a well-known authority in a field will make an impression. Knowing this, it has become the practice at some institutions to involve their most illustrious staff and faculty in as many sponsored activities as possible. The result has been that many of the "big names" are spread quite thin and can give very little time to any one project. Reviewers are not oblivious to this, and the more sophisticated ones have learned to look for evidence that the eminent scholar or researcher will really participate in a proposed project and to what extent. It is, therefore, not advisable to use famous names to "decorate" a proposal; they should appear only if the individual will really make a contribution to the work being proposed.

Expendable Supplies

This is sometimes referred to as "consumable" supplies and includes those items and materials that will be used up in the course of the project. They may be listed under one general heading or by specific category. The most common categories are chemicals, office supplies, glassware, and animals. The presentation varies with the granting agency, but the estimated amounts that will be needed, unit costs, and total cost of each category are almost always required.

Equipment: Purchase and Rental

Items in this section will be those that are expected to have a usable life beyond the termination of the grant. (See section on Equipment Acquisition and Disposition.) Most granting organizations will not authorize purchase of equipment except those items specifically included and approved in the grant budget. Therefore, each item of office, research, or general purpose equipment needed for a project must be entered unless it is available at no cost to the grant through the site institution or another source.

Equipment may be purchased outright or leased. The policy on disposition of purchased equipment should be established at the time of the award.

Equipment items to be rented should be listed with exact length of time they will be needed, rental cost per month, hour, etc., and the total expected cost.

Travel: Foreign, Domestic, and Local

The three kinds of travel should appear in separate categories. Each domestic and foreign trip should be itemized, and the purpose, mode of transportation, length of time for the travel, and total cost shown in each case. If private car is to be used, give mileage allowance in effect at site institution. Travel to meetings and conferences should include name of the conference, sponsoring organization, and, if the traveler will be on the program, a statement about the form of participation, i.e., chairman of a session, speaker, etc. Per diem rates should be the same as those in effect at the site institution unless the granting organization stipulates another rate.

For local travel, indicate purpose and mode of travel. For example: "Bus and taxi fare for subjects to visit the laboratory, 100 round trip bus fares @ $1.00 each and 50 round trip taxicab fares @ $3.00 each."

Communications

Telephone charges are incurred by nearly every sponsored activity. When a project is housed "on-site," i.e., within the main institutional complex, installation costs and basic service are usually covered by the institution, with only toll calls being charged against the grant. If the project is "off-site," telephone installation, basic service charges, and an estimate for toll calls are all included in the budget.

Other types of communication, such as cable, messenger, or telegraph, will be needed for some activities and their cost will vary with the needs of the project.

Publications

If it is anticipated that research results or a final report will be printed in a professional journal, provision must be made for page charges and the cost of reprints, if there is no other source for covering such costs. The objective of some grant projects is the production of published materials and, in some cases, art work, graphics, photography, etc., should be taken into account.

If the publication is expected to produce royalty income, an understanding about the distribution of royalties should be reached with the granting organization and the site institution at the time of the award.

Other Costs

Miscellaneous items that are unique to the project or do not fit into any other category are entered as Other Costs. Examples of such costs are computer time, postage, library acquisitions, fees to subjects, duplicating, cost of rental space, and minor alterations.

Estimates of the unit cost and number of units should be given when appropriate, as in subject fees, duplicating, etc., or hourly rates and time estimates for machine or computer services paid for on a time-use basis.

If the project will not be housed in the main building complex of an institution, cost of space rental may be entered here. Accompanying costs, e.g., janitorial service, utilities, etc., are also taken into account. Rental entries include number of square feet and cost per foot on an annual basis. Minor alterations of space are sometimes permitted, such as moving partitions or cutting through a doorway, but these items must be negotiated item by item. Some guidelines specifically disallow such costs. Justification for alteration costs must be based on the need of the activity and be clearly explained.

INDIRECT COSTS

Indirect costs are calculated according to an established formula agreed upon between the granting organization and the grantee institution, or in accordance with the policy of the granting organization. The most commonly used formulas of federal granting agencies are:

a. A percentage of the total cost of salaries and wages, excluding fringe benefits.
b. A percentage of the total direct costs.

These are expressed as: "Such-and-such % S&W" (meaning __% of salaries and wages, excluding fringe benefits) or "Such-and-such % TDC" (meaning __% of total direct cost).

When institutions negotiate an indirect cost rate with federal agencies, two rates may be assigned. One is for activities sponsored by the institution and housed in the main institutional complex—it is called the "on-site" rate. The other is for activities for which the institution takes administrative responsibility but which are housed outside the main institutional building complex and this is referred to as the "off-site" rate. Since rental of space is usually included in budgets for those projects housed off-site and the grantee institution is not providing space, utilities, and building services, the "off-site" rate is lower than the "on-site."

In dealing with foundations and corporations, overhead or indirect cost allowances must be negotiated individually for each award. (See section on Indirect (Overhead) Costs.)

Agreement between the granting organization and the grantee institution on the handling of the indirect costs is settled in the preapplication phase and this budget item should never come as a surprise to the grant-making organization.

The budget guides on the following pages indicate how certain items of cost may be shown. They are not model budgets for an imaginary proposal and cannot serve as samples for any research or other project. Each item is an example of one kind of cost that might be incurred in many different kinds of sponsored activities. The calculations are shown to indicate how cost estimates are arrived at.

Budget Guide A reflects budget entries on the assumption that:

1.   The institution is providing space and facilities and the on-site indirect cost negotiated rate is being applied.
2.   The institution is making a contribution to the direct costs of the project.
3.   A composite fringe benefit rate has been established.

Budget Guide B reflects budget entries on the assumption that:

1.   The institution is providing administrative, accounting, purchasing, and personnel services only; the project is housed in rented space outside the main building complex of the institution; the off-site indirect cost negotiated rate is being applied.
2.   The institution is making no contribution to direct costs; and
3.   fringe benefits are itemized.

BUDGET GUIDE A
On Site Project—Institution Shares in Direct Costs— Composite Fringe Benefit Rate

DIRECT COSTS	Requested from Grantor	Institutional Contribution
I. PERSONNEL		
A. Salaries and Wages		
1. Professional Staff		
a. Prof. A. M. Doe, Principal Investigator Academic Year Salary, $20,000 (1) 40% of time during academic year ($20,000 x 40%)	$ 4,000	$ 4,000
(2) 100% of 1 Summer Month (1/9 x $20,000)	2,222	
b. B. N. Roe, Research Assistant at $12,000/yr. 50% of time for 12 months ($12,000 x 50%)	6,000	
c. C. O. Moe, Student Research Assistant at $2,000/academic year (approx. 15 hr/week during academic year)	2,000	_____
Total Professional Staff	$14,222	$ 4,000
2. Nonprofessional Staff		
a. D. P. Smith, Secretary, at $10,000/yr. 100% of time for 12 months	5,000	5,000
b. To be appointed, Clerk-Typist at $7,200/yr. 50% of time for 12 months ($7,200 x 50%)	3,600	_____
Total Nonprofessional Staff	$ 8,600	$ 5,000
Total Salaries and Wages (IA)	$22,822	$ 9,000
B. Fringe Benefits		
1. Professional Staff at 25% ($18,222 x 25%)	$ 3,556	$ 1,000
2. Nonprofessional Staff at 20% ($13,600 x 20%)	1,720	1,000
Total Fringe Benefits (IB)	$ 5,276	$ 2,000

	Requested from Grantor	Institutional Contribution
C. Consultant and Contract Services		
1. Dr. E. Q. Jones, Medical Sociologist, State Medical College 20 days at $100/day	$ 2,000	
2. F. R. Brown, free-lance writer, to write brochure narrative	3,000	
3. Systems Analyst	2,000	
Total Consultant and Contract Services (IC)	$ 7,000	
TOTAL PERSONNEL (IA, IB, & IC)	$35,098	$11,000
II. EXPENDABLE SUPPLIES		
A. Office Supplies (Stationery, duplicating and typing supplies, etc.)	$ 150	150
B. Glassware [test tubes, flasks, disposable petri dishes (plastic), etc.]	2,000	1,000
C. Chemicals (Including microbiological supplies)	1,000	500
D. Animals 100 newborn guinea pigs per week for 20 weeks at $2/each (100 x 20 x $2)	4,000	
TOTAL EXPENDABLE SUPPLIES (IIA, IIB, IIC, & IID)	$ 7,150	$ 1,650
III. EQUIPMENT		
A. Purchase of Equipment		
1. (2) Tape Recorders at $250	$ 500	
2. (1) Dictating Machine	400	
3. (1) Transcribing Machine		$ 400
4. Camera, with attachments	250	
Total Purchase of Equipment (IIIA)	$ 1,150	$ 400
B. Rental of Equipment		
1. Film Projector at $40/month for 10 months	$ 400	
2. Xerox Machine, $135/month for 12 months		$ 1,620
Total Rental of Equipment (IIIB)	$ 400	$ 1,620
TOTAL EQUIPMENT (IIIA & IIIB)	$ 1,550	$ 2,020

	Requested from Grantor	Institutional Contribution

IV.   TRAVEL

A. Foreign Travel

1. One trip to Cambridge, England for
conference on Community Mental Health,
August 6-10, 1976, Professor A. M. Doe
Air fare, round trip, tourist class $400
Per diem, 6 days at $40/day   240
                                 $640 $ 640

2. One trip to Rome, Italy for consultation
with Professor G. Pavia, University of
Rome, Professor A. M. Doe
Air fare, round trip, tourist class $500
Per diem, 4 days at $35/day   140
                                 $640   640

   Total Foreign Travel (IVA) $ 1,280

B. Domestic Travel

1. Travel by consultant, Dr. E. Q. Jones,
from New York City, 2 trips
Air fare, round trip, tourist class
$150   (2 x $150) $ 300
Per diem, 20 days at $35/day   700
                               $1,000 $ 1,000

2. Travel by Professor A. M. Doe for Interviews
one trip to Rochester, New York and
one trip to Chicago, Illinois
Air fare, round trip, tourist class,
   Rochester $170
   Chicago   150 $ 320
Per diem, 10 days at $35/day   350
                               $ 670 $ 670

   Total Domestic Travel (IVB) $ 1,670

C. Local Travel

1. Professional staff: 200 miles/month
at 15¢/mi for 10 months
(200 x 15¢ x 10) $ 300

2. Subjects, public transportation between
home and institution, by bus and taxicab   500

   Total Local Travel (IVC) $ 800

   TOTAL TRAVEL (IVA, IVB, & IVC) $ 3,750

V.   COMMUNICATIONS

A. Telephone:
   Installation and monthly service $ 600
   Toll charges: $100/month for 12 months
      ($100 x 12) $ 1,200

	Requested from Grantor	Institutional Contribution
B. Messenger Service and Telegrams	300	
TOTAL COMMUNICATIONS (VA & VB)	$ 1,500	$ 600
VI. PUBLICATIONS		
A. Graphic Arts: layout and design of brochure, design of stationery	$ 1,500	$ 1,000
B. Printing brochure	3,000	
C. Page costs for publication of report in professional journal, 10 pages at $60/page	600	
D. Reprints of journal article	200	
TOTAL PUBLICATIONS (VIA, VIB, VIC, & VID)	$ 5,300	$ 1,000
VII. OTHER DIRECT COSTS		
A. Computer Time, 6 hours at $200/hour	$ 800	$ 400
B. Postage, $100/month x 12 months	1,200	
C. Library acquisitions: books, journal subscriptions	500	
D. Fees to subjects: 50 subjects for 3 sessions at $10 (50 x 3 x $10)	1,500	
E. Duplicating: 2,000 pages/month at 5¢/page for 12 months (2,000 x 12 x 5¢)	600	600
TOTAL OTHER DIRECT COSTS (VIIA, VIIB, VIIC, VIID, & VIIE)	$ 4,600	$ 1,000
TOTAL DIRECT COSTS (I, II, III, IV, V, VI, & VII)	$58,948	$17,270
INDIRECT COSTS		
50% of Salaries and Wages, excluding fringe benefits ($31,822 x 50%) On-Site Rate Granting Agency, $22,822 x 50%	$11,411	
Institutional Contribution $9,000 x 50%		$ 4,500
GRAND TOTAL	$70,359	$21,770
Institutional Sharing	21,770	
Project Total	$92,129	
Percentage contributed by Institution	23.6%	

BUDGET GUIDE B
Off-Site Project—No Institutional Sharing of Direct Costs—Fringe Benefits Itemized

	Amount Requested
DIRECT COSTS	
I. PERSONNEL	
A. Salaries and Wages	
1. Professional Staff	
a. Professor A. M. Doe, Principal Investigator Academic Year Salary, $20,000 (1) 40% of time during academic year ($20,000 x 40%)	$ 8,000
(2) 100% of 1 Summer Month (1/9 x $20,000)	2,222
b. B. N. Roe, Research Assistant at $12,000/yr. 50% of time for 12 months ($12,000 x 50%)	6,000
c. C. O. Moe, Student Research Assistant at $2,000/academic year (approx. 15 hr/week during academic year)	2,000
Total Professional Staff	$18,222
2. Nonprofessional Staff	
a. D. P. Smith, Secretary, at $10,000/yr. 100% of time for 12 months	$10,000
b. To be appointed, Clerk-Typist at $7,200/yr. 50% of time for 12 months ($7,200 x 50%)	3,600
Total Nonprofessional Staff	13,600
Total Salaries and Wages (IA)	$31,822

Amount
Requested

B. Fringe Benefits

   a. FICA (Social Security)
       5.85% of first $12,500 of each employee's
          salary   ($23,822 x 5.85%) $ 1,394

   b. State Unemployment Insurance
       3.5% of first $5,000 of each salary
                       ($17,822 x 3.5%)   624

   c. Health Insurance and Hospitalization
       $25/month for each employee
                       (40.6 months x $25)*   1,015

   d. Retirement
       15% of Professional Salaries
                  ($18,222 x 15% = $2,733)
       12% of Nonprofessional Salaries
                  ($13,600 x 12% = $1,632)   4,365

       Total Fringe Benefits (IB) $ 7,398

       *Professor Doe's academic year released time
        omitted from FICA and unemployment calculations;
        prorated for health insurance and retirement;
        student assistant calculation based on
        part-time basis.

C. Consultant and Contract Services

   1. Dr. E. Q. Jones, Medical Sociologist,
          State Medical College
          20 days at $100/day $ 2,000

   2. F. R. Brown, free-lance writer, to
          write brochure narrative   3,000

   3. Systems Analyst   2,000

       Total Consultant and Contract Services (IC) $ 7,000

       TOTAL PERSONNEL (IA, IB, & IC) $46,220

| | | Amount
Requested |
|---|---|---|

II. EXPENDABLE SUPPLIES

A. Office Supplies
(Stationery, duplicating and typing
supplies, etc.) $ 300

B. Glassware
[test tubes, flasks, disposable petri
dishes (plastic), etc.]   3,000

C. Chemicals
(Including microbiological supplies)   1,500

D. Animals
100 newborn guinea pigs per week for
20 weeks at $2/each   (100 x 20 x $2)   4,000

TOTAL EXPENDABLE SUPPLIES (IIA, IIB, IIC, & IID) $ 8,800

III. EQUIPMENT

A. Purchase of Equipment

1. (2) Tape Recorders at $250 $ 500

2. (1) Dictating Machine   400

3. (1) Transcribing Machine   400

4. Camera, with attachments   250

Total Purchase of Equipment (IIIA) $ 1,550

B. Rental of Equipment

1. Film Projector at $40/month for 10 months $ 400

2. Xerox Machine, $135/month for 12 months   1,620

Total Rental of Equipment (IIIB) $ 2,020

TOTAL EQUIPMENT (IIIA.& IIIB) $ 3,570

		Amount Requested
IV. TRAVEL		

A. Foreign Travel

1. One trip to Cambridge, England for
    conference on Community Mental Health
    August 6-10, 1976, Professor A. M. Doe
    Air fare, round trip, tourist class $ 400
    Per diem, 6 days at $40/day   240
                                          $ 640 $ 640

2. One trip to Rome, Italy for consultation
    with Professor G. Pavia, University of
    Rome, Professor A. M. Doe
    Air fare, round trip, tourist class $ 500
    Per diem, 4 days at $35/day   140
                                          $ 640   640

    Total Foreign Travel (IVA) $ 1,280

B. Domestic Travel

1. Travel by consultant, Dr. E. Q. Jones
    from New York City, 2 trips
    Air fare, round trip, toursit class
    $150   (2 x $150) $ 300
    Per diem, 20 days at $35/day   700
                                          $1,000 $ 1,000

2. Travel by Professor A. M. Doe for Interviews
    one trip to Rochester, New York and
    one trip to Chicago, Illinois
    Air fare, round trip, tourist class,
       Rochester $170
       Chicago   150 $ 320
    Per diem, 10 days at $35/day   350
                                          $ 670   670

    Total Domestic Travel (IVB) $ 1,670

C. Local Travel

1. Professional staff: 200 miles/month at
    15¢/mi. for 10 months (200 x15¢ x 10) $ 300

2. Subjects, public transportation between
    home and institution, by bus and taxicab   500

    Total Local Travel (IVC) $ 800

    TOTAL TRAVEL (IVA, IVB, & IVC) $ 3,750

			Amount Requested
V.	COMMUNICATIONS		

	A. Telephone:
	  Installation and monthly service $ 600
	  Toll charges: $100/month for 12
	    months ($100 x 12) 1,200
		$ 1,800	

	B. Messenger Service and Telegrams	300	
	TOTAL COMMUNICATIONS (VA & VB)		$ 2,100
VI.	PUBLICATIONS		
	A. Graphic Arts: layout and design of brochure; design of stationery	$ 2,500	
	B. Printing brochure	3,000	

	C. Page costs for publication of results
	  in professional journal,
	  10 pages at $60/page
		600	

	D. Reprints of journal article	200	
	TOTAL PUBLICATIONS (VIA, VIB, VIC, & VID)		$ 6,300
VII.	OTHER DIRECT COSTS		
	A. Computer Time, 6 hours at $200/hour	$ 1,200	
	B. Postage, $100/month x 12 months	1,200	
	C. Library acquisitions: books, journal subscriptions	500	
	D. Fees to subjects: 50 subjects for 3 sessions each at $10 (50 x 3 x $10)	1,500	
	E. Duplicating: 1,000 pages/month at 10¢/page for 12 months (1,000 x 12 x 10¢)	1,200	

	F. Rental of Space, 2,000 sq. ft. at $8/sq.ft.
	  per year, utilities and janitorial service
	  included, for 12 months (2,000 x $8)
		16,000	

	TOTAL OTHER DIRECT COSTS (VIIA, VIIB, VIIC, VIID, VIIE, & VIIF)		$ 21,600
	TOTAL DIRECT COSTS (I, II, III, IV, V, VI & VII)		$ 92,340
INDIRECT COSTS			
25% of Salaries and Wages, excluding fringe benefits ($31,822 x 25%) Off-Site Rate			$ 7,956
	GRAND TOTAL		$100,296

BUDGET JUSTIFICATION

Any item in the budget that appears to be the least bit unusual or that might raise questions or force the reviewers to return to the description of the project to clear up a point should be explained at the end of the budget. Each item should be annotated to correspond to the budget entry to make it easy to identify.

Unusual costs in any one category, such as very large amounts for consumable supplies or expensive equipment or computer costs, are examples of costs that frequently raise questions. Travel, especially foreign travel or frequent long trips, should be meticulously explained. Large numbers of experimental animals, heavy costs for fees to human subjects, purchase of national survey results, and any large subcontract cost items should be individually justified in terms of the program needs and the need made clear in the Description of the Project. Other examples are unusual amounts of expensive chemicals, isotopes, and any proposed building alteration costs.

If the project description has been well written, and the budget takes into account all the necessary costs, it will be obvious to the reader or reviewer why certain items are included. But in long and detailed proposals, the Budget Justification notes will indicate which portions of the project certain budget items relate to and will speed up the review process, which will win at least the gratitude of the reviewer.

CREDENTIALS OF THE PROFESSIONAL STAFF

In the survey of rejected applications conducted by Dr. E. M. Allen, cited earlier, 55% of all the disapproved applications ranked low on "qualifications of the principal investigator." Analysis of those applications, and the analyses of Louis E. Masterman and Dr. G. N. Eaves ten years later, indicate that, in many cases, the seemingly insufficient experience and capability of the investigator is due mostly to the inadequate presentation of his credentials.

A certain amount of basic data are necessary, but the bulk of the biographical material should deal with the professional training, experience, and achievements of the principal investigator (or the individual who will be responsible for the fulfillment of the proposed activity) and all other professional personnel who will be involved. Previous accomplishments in fields directly related to the project described in the application should be emphasized. Reviewers should not be inundated with material, but relevant published materials of very recent work may be attached, or in the case of literary or performing artists, current reviews of recent work.

The materials should be presented as concisely as possible; only in unusual circumstances should a biographical sketch exceed three pages.

Basic information includes full name, address, telephone number, institutional affiliation and address, and in some cases, date of birth. In the majority of applications, biographies need not include marital status, name of spouse, number and names of children, or religious affiliation. For certain fellowships that include allowances for dependents, the family information is essential. Citizenship or visa status must be given if either is an eligibility requirement.

Professional education and training is indicated by listing all degrees, including name of the awarding institution and dates earned.

Professional experience is listed in reverse chronological order, with current position first, and includes all employment. Only significant unremunerated employment should be listed. Previous or currently held grants should also be shown if they are relevant to the current application or if work on another grant will go on simultaneously with the one being applied for. It is a good idea to include information about any grants awarded during the past five years from any source, with title, period of the award, and total funds received, as well as any currently pending applications. If an application is being sent to more than one governmental agency, each agency should be told which others are receiving it, and the duplication should be explained.

Biographical sketches to any agency should include for each professional staff member a chronological list of all or the most representative, or the most representative and recent, publications. In preparing the list, publications should be selected that have special relevance to the subject of the grant being applied for. Each publication reference should be complete, with full title and the journal references, as it would appear in a paper.

The beginning investigator who has no publications should include the title of his doctoral thesis and the names of his mentors for the doctoral research and for any postdoctoral research experience.

Commenting on bibliographies, Dr. George Eaves noted, "Probably as a result of the concept that equates accomplishment with quantity of publication, many investigators submit bibliographies which they clearly hope will be impressive, artificially lengthened by the inclusion of elaborate references to manuscripts 'in preparation' or 'to be submitted for publication.' When such manuscripts are only contemplated, which is frequently the case, it is a distinct disadvantage to the applicant investigator for him to list them, since it is predictable that he will be requested to submit copies of these manuscripts in support of his proposal.

"If the manuscripts have indeed been completed, even in draft form, a copy should be included with the application; if the manuscript would be relevant if completed, but is not yet written, the data can and should be incorporated into the text in the section entitled, 'Background.' "[13]

CERTIFICATIONS

Most certifications that accompany applications are the responsibility of the institution—for example, assurance of compliance with the Civil Rights Act of 1964; assurance of compliance with regulations regarding protection of the rights and welfare of human subjects; and, if animals are to be used, a written statement that the institution will evaluate, on a continuing basis, its animal facilities with regard to the care, use, and treatment of such animals. If the application is for a matching fund grant, the availability of the matching portion or plans for obtaining it should be documented.

At the end of the description of the proposed project, the Department of Health, Education, and Welfare requires this assurance state-

[13] G. N. Eaves. "Who Reads Your Project-Grant Application to the National Institutes of Health?" *Federation Proc.* 31 (January-February): 1.

ment from the principal investigator: "The undersigned agrees to accept responsibility for the scientific and technical conduct of the research project and for provision of required progress reports if a grant is awarded as the result of this application."

Negotiation for submission of the necessary certifications is handled with the appropriate institutional official well in advance of the final submission to that office for endorsement of the application.

INSTITUTIONAL ENDORSEMENT

As soon as the proposal writer has completed the document and affixed his signature, it should be submitted to the appropriate institutional official or officials for signing *before* reproducing the application in the necessary number of copies; otherwise, the copies will not contain the signatures, or all endorsers will have to sign multiple copies.

The official endorsement implies that the facilities of the institution normally provided to staff and/or faculty will be made available to the principal investigator or project director for the conduct of the proposed activity. This includes all services and facilities covered in the negotiation of the institutional indirect cost rate as well as the institutional contributions indicated in the budget and any other services normally provided by academic, research, or similar institutions.

For applications that have been thoroughly discussed in advance of the proposal-writing phase, this is a minor procedure. If agreement on one or more significant points has not been reached in advance, the delay could be so long that the application is disqualified from competition by failing to arrive on the deadline date.

Some institutions take responsibility for mailing applications and the proposal writer's job is done at the point the document is submitted for signatures. If the applicant receives it back from the authorizing official for mailing, the final steps are to make certain that all copies are complete and that the required number of copies is mailed in time to arrive on the deadline date or in time to be postmarked as required.

Guides to Writing Grant Proposals

Brodsky, Jean, ed. 1973. *The Proposal Writer's Swipe File*. Twelve professionally written grant proposals—prototypes of approaches, styles, and structures. Taft Products, Inc., 1000 Vermont Avenue, N.W., Washington, D.C. 20005.

Dermer, Joseph. 1972. *How to Write Successful Foundation Presentations*. Public Service Materials Center, 104 East 40th Street, New York, New York 10016.

Jacquette, F. Lee and Barbara I. Jacquette. 1973. "What Makes a Good Proposal?" *Foundation News* 14 (January-February): 18–21.

Krathwohl, David R. 1966. *How to Prepare a Research Proposal*. Syracuse University Bookstore, 303 University Place, Syracuse, New York 13210. $1.00 per copy.

MacIntyre, Michael. 1971. *How to Write a Proposal*. Education, Training and Research Sciences Corp., Washington, D.C. (A Subsidiary of Volt Information Sciences, Inc., New York, New York)

Masterman, Louis E. 1973. *The Mechanics of Writing Successful Federal Grant Applications*. Missouri Institute of Psychiatry, University of Missouri School of Medicine.

Mayer, Robert A. 1972. "What Will a Foundation Look for When you Submit a Grant Proposal?" *Library Journal* (July).

Pattillo, Manning M. 1965. "Preparing the Foundation Proposal." In F. Emerson Andrews, ed., *Foundations: 20 Viewpoints*. Russell Sage Foundation, New York, New York.

The Research Foundation of the State University of New York. 1973. *The Application Procedure*. Box 7126, Albany, New York 12224.

Urgo, Louis A. 1972. *A Manual for Obtaining Government Grants*. Robert J. Corcoran Company, 40 Court Street, Boston, Massachusetts 02108.

Urgo, Louis A. and Robert J. Corcoran. 1971. *A Manual for Obtaining Foundation Grants*. Robert J. Corcoran Company, 40 Court Street, Boston, Massachusetts 02108.

The Application

HOW GRANTS ARE AWARDED—THE POSTAPPLICATION PHASE

The Postapplication Phase should be the easiest part of the application process but in reality it is the most difficult of all for some applicants; it is the phase during which the initiative is entirely in the hands of the funding organization, and all the applicant can do is stand and wait. The urge to "do something" during this period is irresistible for some and they rush about telephoning friends who might be influential, checking on date, time, and place of review committee meetings, or bombarding the program officer with questions about the status of the application and the possibilities of its being approved. No one knows for certain whether this does or does not help because no study has been done—at least no well-publicized one—to indicate that such activities affect the outcome of a proposal one way or another. Not that it matters very much; individuals who are disposed to take action during a waiting period will not be deterred by statistical evidence that it doesn't help, because it helps *them.* They are constitutionally unable to await the results of any pending decision in which they have a stake. But it is useful to understand exactly what the process is and especially to know the estimated time lag between the date a proposal is submitted and the date an announcement of awards can be expected.

Most announced competitions that set a deadline date for submission of applications also state the date when awards will be announced and this appreciably alleviates the uncertainty, but for programs that have no established date for submission of applications or announcement of results the waiting period can be harrowing.

The means by which decisions are reached in governmental agencies are specific and upon request will be described to any applicant. Foundations and corporations, not being bound by the Freedom of Information Act, and not being answerable to a voting constituency, are neither as specific about the process nor as free with information.

FOUNDATIONS

A former foundation program officer, when asked to comment on how decisions on applications are reached, lamented, "It was one of the most bizarre experiences of my entire life to see this work. You can, believe me, go to a number of foundations and you will find staff members who don't know how decisions are made—and this is true of every foundation I have ever heard about. Generally, the president or chief executive will listen to any staff member, the newest or the youngest, and take his recommendation seriously. He often considers himself as a first among equals and not superior to any staff member, with the result that decisions frequently 'emerge' in the Quaker sense."

The climate created by that process is one in which the entire staff feels constrained to achieve the purposes and goals set by the board of directors but are given no precise guidelines for accomplishing what the board has in mind. The chief executive operates without specific guidance, as a rule, and the staff, endowed with the inestimable power to accept or reject proposals at the very first stage, performs its "gate-keeper" or first-level screening role with even less precise instructions.

Everyone is looking over both shoulders in turn—over one to see if the board is satisfied and over the other to see how his performance stacks up with that of his colleagues. The ability to continue having one's recommendations accepted depends heavily on how one's colleagues view the proposals that have been introduced and advocated in the past. A staff member who pushes through too many "losers" may wind up as a loser himself, whereas the one who achieves a reputation for picking winners may acquire an aura of omnipotence.

Thus the enthusiasm with which a staff member endorses or recommends approval of a project is in direct proportion to his belief that it will turn out to be one of those activities to which he can point with pride when the final report is in. If the program director is lukewarm about the idea, clearly he will not create amongst his colleagues and superiors that confidence that may be needed if it meets opposition or strong competition. Once the staff member has persuaded his colleagues and the chief executive to approve a proposal the battle is essentially won. Compromises may have to be made on scope or on certain budget items, but these are seldom critical.

The role played by foundation boards of directors in the grant-making process varies with the size, composition, and type of foundation. Small foundations with no professional staff often do not have regular board meetings and decisions are made on all matters by one member, the chairman of the board, or sometimes another member. In middle-sized and large foundations with professional staffs, the board establishes overall purposes and policies, leaving the details of program formulation and operating procedures to be worked out by the foundation officers and staff. This procedure was endorsed by John D. Rockefeller, Sr., who felt it was improper to intervene in the philanthropies he endowed. He was once quoted as saying, "I have not had the hardihood even to suggest how people, so much more experienced and wise in those things than I, should work out the details even of those plans with which I have the honor to be associated." Even those board members who do participate actively in the grant-making process sometimes maintain a public appearance of nonparticipation because they do not want every social occasion or chance meeting with individuals in the course of their daily lives to become grant-negotiation conferences.

The Peterson Commission estimated that "in nearly two-fifths of the foundations, board members play so small a role in foundation grant making as to border on the invisible. A donor or another single individual dominates many of these foundation."[14]

The report of foundations themselves to the Peterson Commission on the role of their boards shows that in 30 percent the board played "hardly any role at all" in grant making; 9 percent gave formal approval on recommendations with reversal of recommendations extremely rare; 5 percent reviewed recommendations on most applications within program area of the foundation; 12 percent approved or rejected all applications within program area; and 44 percent made the decision to approve or reject.

Some indication is given of the degree to which foundation boards participate in the grant-making process by the frequency with which they meet. The Peterson Commission found that 6 percent hold monthly meetings; 43 percent meet quarterly or semiannually; 35 percent meet annually or less often; 9 percent meet "whenever necessary" and 9 percent never meet at all![15]

The correlation between the number of foundations meeting semiannually or more often (49 percent) and the number that approve or reject all applications (44 percent) seems logical. Boards that meet less often than every six months cannot reserve decision making to themselves and operate a significant grant-making program.

Foundations that operate through a full-time professional staff give broad authority to the chief administrative officer, that is, the executive director, the executive secretary, or the president, in determining the kinds of activities that fall within the scope of the foundation's purposes and objectives, and for discriminating between the applications that best meet the criteria of the foundation and those

[14] See *Foundations, Private Giving and Public Policy: Report and Recommendations of the Commission on Foundations and Private Philanthropy.* Peter G. Peterson, Chairman. Chicago: University of Chicago Press, 1970, p. 88.
[15] See Peterson Report, p. 89, *op. cit.*

that must be rejected. The usual procedure is that the chief executive presents his recommendations for awards at regular board meetings and they are given what amounts to "rubber stamp" approval with reversal of the recommendations being very rare. Even so, award announcements are usually made only after formal board endorsement in organizations where regular board meetings are held and where all recommendations are presented for board approval.

A foundation program director sometimes will make a site visit to see exactly what facilities are available and to talk with the principal investigator, the responsible institutional official, or others who will be affiliated with the project. This is done to get a better assessment of the institution's interest in the project or to ascertain that adequate facilities are actually available or merely to get a better understanding of the proposed activity. Arrangements for site visits are made directly with the principal investigator or project director and it is up to him to see that any other appropriate personnel are available for discussions with the visitor and that facilities are available for observation if requested. The visit should be handled like any other official consultation, allowing the foundation official to set the pace and providing whatever information, observations, or discussions he may request. In most situations, it is neither necessary nor desirable to "wine and dine" site visitors. If they are treated courteously and given the information they require, that usually suffices.

The time lag between foundation submissions and awards ranges from a week up to several months. Decisions are usually made in one to six months, and the work can begin almost immediately, because funds are sent to the fiscal agent very soon after the announcements are made.

Once the award is made, many foundations pay little or no attention to the project until the end, when a final report is expected. The size of the project has a great deal to do with the amount of monitoring that takes place, however.

CORPORATIONS

Corporations that make grants directly and not through company foundations vary the decision process according to the type of activity being funded and the level of the grant or contract. Philanthropic programs, such as charitable gifts or fellowships and scholarships are handled through one of the corporate executive offices, usually the public relations or community relations offices. The mechanism of operation follows regular corporate operational procedures with the executive in charge being given authority up to a certain level, after which approval is made by a higher executive, a committee, or the board of directors. In many cases, the attitude of the program administrator or executive is decisive. If a proposal meets with his approval, it may be accepted immediately or recommended for support to higher authority; if he does not approve it, that is the end.

In the case of research grants or contracts submitted to the executive in charge of the research arm of a company or large corporation, the decision may be made by the vice president for research or director of research. If he is not receptive to an idea in the first place, the matter can go no further.

The time required for decision on direct grants by corporations can be very short because the decision is often in the hands of one or only a few people. A great deal depends upon the size of the request, the nature of the activity, and the knowledge held by the corporation concerning the applicant institution. If there has been a previous association that worked out satisfactorily, the timing can be greatly reduced. Otherwise, the corporation will want to investigate thoroughly the dependability, facilities, and competence of the institution and the personnel to be involved. Proprietary matters are very important to commercial organizations and these questions take time to negotiate satisfactorily.

Some companies and company funds take the view that once the grant-making process has established the eligibility and competence of an institution or individual to receive an award, they should not interfere or intrude. But others set up controls to insure conformity with certain stipulations and, recently, to ensure that the requirements of the 1969 Tax Reform Act are being complied with. They may make periodic visits to see that auditing practices are adequate and to attend seminars or meetings held as part of the project or its operation. One company fund describes its procedure this way: "Most of our grants are given on an annual basis and are not renewed until an informal report has been received concerning the matter in which the funds have been spent. For every grant which our foundation makes to a college or a department within a university, there is a representative of the corporation who is responsible for maintaining a close relationship with the institution or department. He visits the campus at least once a year and usually twice or more, to discuss problems and to get to know the faculty. In this way, we manage to keep abreast of the situation. Reports of these visits are submitted to the Department of University Relations. We believe this practice is essential to monitoring our grants."[16]

GOVERNMENT

All applications for governmental support undergo review by staff members of the funding agency and by at least one review group selected for special knowledge in the field. In some cases, the final decision is made by a council or committee based upon the recommendations of reviewers, the program director, and the agency head; in other cases, it is the agency head who makes the final decision, based upon the recommendation of the advisory groups.

The Public Health Service of HEW has since its earliest days insisted that all grant applications in support of biomedical research be subject to review by highly respected representatives of the scientific community. This is sometimes called the "peer review system" and has been under attack by those who are impatient with the progress being made in conquering killer diseases such as cancer and heart and lung diseases. Bills have been introduced in the U.S. Senate that would establish a panel to monitor the research activities of NIH and ADAMHA and report directly to the president. This was countered by a proposal of the HEW secretary for the establishment of a presidential commission to study the appropriate role for the

[16] Source: *The Impact of the Tax Reform Act of 1969 on Company Foundations.* John H. Watson III, Conference Board Report No. 595. The Conference Board, Inc., 845 Third Avenue, New York, N.Y. 10022.

federal government in biomedical research and make a recommendation to the president.

The peer review system received another severe blow in September, 1974, when the U.S. Court of Appeals ruled that applications for research grants submitted to the federal government should be open to inspection by anyone who asks. The ruling was the result of an action brought by the Washington Research Project, Inc., involving eleven applications for grants from NIMH, all of which had been approved and funded. Lawyers for the NIH suggest, therefore, that the ruling applies only to *approved* applications but the litigant claims that it covers all grant applications as soon as they are submitted. Since biomedical sciences is a fiercely competitive field, many researchers view the implications of this ruling with horror. Aside from the possibility that it could lead to plagiarism of research ideas, it could also affect the way grant proposals are written. Scientists might become wary of putting in details now considered essential for a proper evaluation of a proposed project, leaving the reviewers little to go on except the reputation of the applicant. Although the peer review system seems to be surviving at the moment, its future is far from secure.

The review process for the NIH and other Public Health Service agencies begins when applications are received by the NIH Division of Research Grants in Bethesda, Maryland. Each application is read by a scientist and assigned to the appropriate institute, or in case of overlaps in interests, to two institutes. Simultaneously, the application is assigned to the appropriate study section for scientific appraisal. (See list of study sections pp. 50–51.) If there is no study section with the composition to handle the subject of the proposal, an *ad hoc* study section may be formed from among NIH consultants knowledgeable in the field.

Each study section is served by an executive secretary who is responsible for coordinating and reporting the review of each application assigned to his advisory group. The executive secretary determines which two or more members of his study section are best qualified to evaluate each proposal and sends the proposal to those members by mail. Each reviewer prepares a detailed written critique of the proposals assigned to him and returns them to the executive secretary in advance of the meeting of the full study section. Six to eight weeks before the formal study section meetings, which are held three times a year, all members receive copies of all proposals to be reviewed, usually fifty to one hundred, which each member is expected to read. Thus, each member may read ten to twenty applications in detail and prepare a critique of each one and read all the others. Site visits, if they are to be made, will take place between the proposal readings and the formal meeting of the study section.

The study section executive secretary is the intermediary between the applicant and the reviewers, and if additional information or explanations are needed, the request is made through the executive secretary. If the applicant wishes to provide any additional material or communicate any information to the study section, that, too, must go through the executive secretary.

At the formal study section meeting, each application is reported on by the assigned reviewers who prepared the detailed critique, after which other members may make comments or ask questions. A majority vote of the study section determines whether an application is approved, disapproved, or deferred for later consideration. Each approved application is given a numerical score, which is used to establish the priority rating transmitted to the National Advisory Council for each application. Applicants are not informed of the study sections' decisions and the priority rankings are considered as confidential; therefore, applicants are urged not to ask the executive secretary about the status of an application prior to the Council meeting. Any information at that point is premature.

Study section review is based solely on scientific merit. Council review takes into account a broad area of considerations including the needs of the NIH and the missions of the individual institutes, the total pattern of research in nonprofit institutions, the need for initiation of research in new areas, the degree of relevance of the proposed research to the agency mission, and other matters. Councils do not change the priority scores of the study section but may recommend that an approved application be placed in a category to be funded or in one not to be funded based on program relevance. Thus the needs of the Institute are taken into account, but the priority score still guides the final decision.

After Council review, the professional staff in each institute takes over and matches the recommendations of the reviewers with the available funds. When it is not possible to fund all approved applications, a not unusual occurrence, the priority ranking of each proposal is critical. The professional staff member in charge of the program notifies applicants of the final decision and all questions concerning the application from then on should be directed to the program director, including requests for information regarding the decision. Notification is usually made within a few weeks after the Council meeting.

Unsuccessful applicants may ask why an application was not approved and the comments of the reviewers will be sent to him (anonymously). It is always wise to ask about disapprovals for two reasons: (1) it serves as a guide in preparation of future applications; and (2) it may develop that the application would be acceptable with certain revisions and can be resubmitted for a later competition.

NIH study sections meet three times a year, eight to ten weeks after the deadline for submission of applications. Council meetings may be one to three months following that. Consequently, the shortest time for the complete procedure is three to four months and it is usually longer. The safest course is to plan a project to start at least a year after the application is submitted and hope to have the decision within six to nine months.

The review of research proposals being considered at NIH for funding by the contract mechanism differs from the review of grant applications. To begin with, the procedure for acceptance of applications for contract research allows for a certain degree of preapplication screening. When the availability of Requests for Proposals is announced, potential contractors submit basic information attesting to their eligibility and competence in order to receive the Request for Proposal (RFP). The RFP contains specific instructions for preparation of the application, or to be more exact, the "contract offer."

Offers are submitted directly to the contracting officer who prepared the RFP by the established deadline date. They are first subjected to a review for technical evaluation. This review is conducted by one or more panels in the scientific or technical discipline associated with the contract requirements. Reviewers may be government and/or nongovernment personnel, depending upon the particular expertise needed.

Proposals found acceptable from the technical point of view are then reviewed from the standpoint of the elements of cost. The financial review, in addition to assessing the overall reasonableness of costs reflected in a proposal, may also disclose desirable shifts in emphasis that will affect the overall funding, such as changes in manpower loading or changes in material estimates.

The contracting officer then enters into negotiations with all offerors whose proposals are within an acceptable technical and financial range for the project. In some cases, especially for large contracts—those that will be $100,000 or more—the negotiation will be done by means of a site visit. For smaller contracts, negotiations will be conducted by telephone. During such discussions the proposer has an opportunity to present his position with respect to any aspects of the contract requirements.

After the discussions or site visits, the contracting officer will make the decision based upon the offer that seems to hold the greatest technical advantages to the government, cost and other factors considered.

Unsolicited proposals may also be the basis of a contract award, but the proportion of contracts awarded through this mechanism is very small. Unsolicited proposals should be sent directly to the contracting officer of the NIH component primarily interested in the subject matter of the proposal.

An unsolicited proposal may be the basis for a sole-source award based on an original idea that establishes the preeminent qualifications of the offeror. Or, an unsolicited proposal may result in the issuance of a competitive solicitation asking for other proposals dealing with the same subject.

More than one award may be made under the same RFP. Successful offerors are notified as soon as the decision is made, and written notice is sent to unsuccessful offerors that their proposals were not accepted.

The contract offer seldom or never comes as a surprise. In the negotiations dealing with cost factors or other points, it soon becomes clear that the contracting officer is viewing the proposal with favor. In some cases a revised budget, which determines the award total, is worked out in detail and agreed upon in such discussions.

As with grant applicants, contract offerors may receive, upon request, an explanation or evaluation of the considerations that resulted in the failure of a proposal to be accepted. This can be a useful learning experience, providing excellent counsel and guidance for future proposals.

The decision-making process for contracts used to take less time than for grants, and occasionally it still does, but it is best to be prepared for a wait of several months.

The NIH process has been described in detail because such a large proportion of applications for governmental support are received by that agency.

Independent government agencies also have review systems that involve more than one type of evaluation and more than one panel.

The National Science Foundation (NSF) programs (like the NIH ones) are administered by highly qualified professionals in the fields for which they are responsible. Staff review of applications is the major selection device; however, the program personnel at NSF are assisted in the evaluation process by other scientists selected especially for their knowledge of the proposal subject.

There is no deadline for submission of applications to the NSF and it is suggested that they be sent in at least six months before the funds are needed. One can usually expect a response within that period of time.

The National Endowments, both Arts and Humanities, also rely heavily upon the knowledge and judgment of their professional staff, especially in the preliminary draft stage. Applicants often fail to realize that consultation with an Endowment staff member is the first "screening." If the program officer feels that the proposal hasn't got a chance, he will make his judgment clear. Although no one will deny an applicant the right to send in a formal application, the preliminary evaluations of program personnel usually turn out to be upheld by the review panels. By the time a formal proposal has been submitted, one step in the evaluation process has been passed through. The next step is review by an outside panel, which varies in size and composition with each program. The evaluations of the panels, which are organized into priority rankings, are presented to the appropriate committee on the National Council, along with the applications, for their review and comment. The Committee votes to award, reject, modify, or defer. These decisions are brought before the entire National Council where they are voted again. The final decision is then made by the Endowment chairman, who takes into account all the previous evaluations based on the priorities as he views them, and notifies the applicant of the decision.

Many of the Endowment programs have deadline dates for submission of applications, but some do not. The review and decision-making process usually takes a total of about six months but can be longer.

The Site Visit

Projects involving large sums of money or long-range support are frequently "site visited." Opinions vary on the value of such visits. If the facilities of an institution are well known, if the principal investigator is sufficiently prominent, and if the agency has previously supported projects in the same location and involving the same personnel, it may seem unnecessary to take up the time of the panel and the applicant institution for such a visit. But in some cases visits are absolutely necessary if the reviewers are to do justice to the proposal.

Site visits are required by statute for certain types of projects and cannot be omitted. But even in situations where a visit seems to be superfluous, it frequently turns out to be a rich source of additional information upon which a final evaluation can be based. For example, a project may depend heavily upon the cooperation of an individual or a group in another discipline, laboratory, or department and the panel will want to be assured that the portion of the project so dependent can be reliably performed. Sometimes it is question of the extent to which an institution will participate in and contribute to a project. Whatever the figures stipulated in the budget might indicate, there are many informal, nonspecific ways in which the administration of an institution can encourage and support an activity or do just the opposite.

Site visits are usually arranged directly with the principal investigator by the executive secretary (at NIH) or other staff or panel members authorized to negotiate with the applicant. At the time such arrangements are made, the subjects to be discussed, facilities to be observed, or personnel to be interviewed will be specified. It is then up to the principal investigator to see that whatever meetings or observations the panel requests can be provided. It is wise to have the institutional official who signed the application available, but in some cases the panel will not ask that he be included in the meeting. All the principal investigator has to do is carry out the requests of the panel, and usually such visits are short—rarely more than one day and often only half a day.

"Wining and dining" governmental visitors is not only unnecessary, it is illegal. In fact, representatives of federal agencies traveling at government expense should not permit the host institution to provide them with lunch. This is occasionally embarrassing when inexperienced applicants insist upon making the site visitors "guests" in the normal sense of the word and offer them lunch as a normal gesture of courtesy. The site visitors should be viewed as any other colleague who happens to be performing a day's work in the applicant's institution instead of his own.

The tendency to read meanings into statements or comments of site visitors is irresistible and everybody does it, but restraint is advisable. The final decision is based on a number of considerations of which the site visit is only one and most of which the applicant can in no way control or influence.

Impatient applicants often manage to find out that an award has been assured at the decision-making level long before they receive the formal notification. It is never safe to begin work on a project, however, until the award document is actually in hand. Most grantee institutions will not permit the activation of a project, ordering supplies and equipment, employing personnel, etc., until the formal notice has been received. This sometimes generates great frustration on the part of the investigator who is anxious to get started, but many slips can occur between the committee or program director's decision to make an award and the final transmission of the notification, and it is always advisable to get it in writing.

Aside from the information that a grant has been made, formal award notices usually include guidelines for the administration of the grant. This material explains what the funding organization expects in the way of record keeping, reports, and any special stipulations pertinent to each specific award. This information should be read thoroughly and followed to the letter throughout the lifetime of the grant.

HEW has established a Grant Appeals Board to settle *postaward* disputes in connection with the *administration* of grant programs. The public Health Service set up procedures for informal review of decisions of its officials and resolution of disputes with grantees in order to preclude submission of cases to the HEW Appeals Board before PHS has had an opportunity to review the matter. Guidelines for resolution of postaward controversy between grantee institutions and Public Health Service agencies have been published in the PHS *Grants Administration Manual* and in the NIH *Manual*.

"Grantsmanship"

The wide-ranging variety of purposes for which grants are given is exceeded only by the variety of ingenious schemes that have been devised for obtaining them. Grant seekers have preempted the prerogative traditionally reserved for lovers and warriors—all's fair. And the applicant who succeeds by the use of methods that are somewhat devious is often envied by colleagues and dubbed a "sly fox" or "wily witch" more in a spirit of admiration than of censure. If the cause is noble, the proposal sound, and the applicant eminently qualified and sincere in his intent, any device for obtaining the necessary financial backing seems justifiable. But in the long run some practices are self-defeating. Granting organizations have all they can do to discriminate between the merits of the proposals submitted to them without having to simultaneously fortify themselves against the techniques of their presentation and advocacy. The principle of open competition may, in fact, have suffered due to the sophistication that has been brought to the grant-getting art (craft?) sometimes referred to as "grantsmanship." The use of political or personal influence to circumvent review committees or co-opt decision makers on behalf of a less than outstanding proposal, or other tactics such as artificially relating a proposal to program priorities, have made many granting organizations exceedingly cautious. At some of them—foundations, particularly—it is almost impossible to make an appointment to discuss a proposal without a personal referral. This attitude has given some organizations a reputation of being unapproachable but it is a normal response to past experience in many cases. Very few grant makers have not at one time or another been taken in by a high-powered, professionally engineered campaign in favor of a worthless proposal, or by a charming, articulate, impressively credentialed scholar who promised much and produced nothing. The consequence is that some program directors have begun to operate very much like project directors. They design the project, choose the institution, assemble the personnel, and *then* announce that an award has been made! In response to the question, "What proportion of your funds is awarded on the basis of unsolicited proposals?" one foundation executive replied succinctly, "Very little." He explained that they know what kind of things they are going to support and the staff, being professionals in their fields, know who the competent people are and where the work can best be done. Therefore, they often make arrangements for activities to be carried out at institutions and by people known to them. In this way, they insulate themselves from the salesmanship tactics with which some proposals are promoted. Of course, they may also close the door to valuable ideas and approaches by individuals beyond the circle of the organization and its established friends, but they are obviously willing to take that risk. This procedure is also followed very often by industrial and commercial organizations; they prefer to deal with people they know and they are less willing even than foundations to take a chance on an unknown applicant.

Government agencies that dispense public funds are more regulated in the methods they use for selection of grantees, but those that use the RFP to invite proposals for work done under contract can exercise a great deal of discrimination in disseminating information about availability of contracts.

People who administer grant-making programs are as ready to laugh at themselves as anybody else, but flippant, tongue-in-cheek (we hope) advice to applicants such as that given in a recent article probably does little to reassure funding organizations that they aren't being systematically duped. In the list of things "to do" and "not to do" were the following: (1) Keep creativity at a minimum—grantmaking organizations do not really want new ideas; what they *really* want is new language for old ideas. (2) Have a list of notables handy to sprinkle through the proposal in accordance with the topic and the objective. (Notables were divided into academic notables; local, establishment, liberal, white notables; local, minority-group notables; and educational or political notables.) The idea is that use of their names will ingratiate the applicant with the notable and at the same time impress the reviewers of the proposal. (3) Never apply for under $40,000. This is because people who deal in vast sums of money, particularly at the federal agencies, cannot really comprehend smaller sums and "it takes just about as much trouble to apply for $10,000 as to apply for $100,000."

Articles of this type are well-meaning; their purpose is to improve the process by means of the humorous approach, and there is often enough truth in them to validate the satire. But they serve more as a consolation to grant seekers who have tried and failed than as a real aid to those who are just starting out. And they do little or nothing to promote real understanding between unfunded researchers and scholars and those organizations that are in position to help them.

The three most common methods used for promoting a proposal by those who feel that something beyond the normal application and review procedure must be brought into the process are: (1) use of middlemen; (2) use of political and personal influence; and (3) artificial attempts to link the purpose of the proposed activity to the organization's stated aims.

Use of Middlemen. The professionally prepared proposal has become so commonplace that it does not take much imagination to envision a time when all applications that land on any given program director's desk will read exactly alike. Proposal writers—some of whom refer to themselves unabashedly as "bull slingers"—take the applicant's research or program plan and fashion it into a document that the writer believes will be effective and result in an award. As a rule, proposal writers know nothing about the subject field or the staff and facilities a project will require and, except for those who are affiliated with the applicant institution, have no understanding of the commitments that can be stated or implied in regard to institutional participation in the project. The main things the professional writer offers the applicant are organization of the material into an acceptable form and a certain kind of jargon. A service that organizes the material, prepares it in final form, and sees that all the accompanying information and documents are included can be useful to the busy applicant who has no staff assistant to help with those details. But the narrative, the part of the application that describes the objectives, the design, the methods, the rationale—that portion that tells what is to be done, why it is worth doing, and why the funding organization should support it—can be written only by the individual who conceived the idea and who will be responsible for carrying it out. Even if he is not a skilled writer, and even if some editorial assistance is required, the real flavor of the idea will lose some of its freshness unless it is conveyed by the originator. If the applicant is enthusiastic, confident that the proposed activity is sound and worthwhile, and convinced that he can do it, it will come through best in his own words. If he lacks enthusiasm and conviction, it will be difficult for the professional writer to convey it and misleading for him to try.

Another kind of middleman is the consultant who advises applicants and sometimes institutions on funding sources. Most consultants in the grants field are located in Washington, D. C. and also may be called lobbyists or institutional representatives. The services they promise and sometimes deliver are even more varied than the names they are called. The ethical ones, and there are many, make no exaggerated claims they cannot demonstrate and do not try to sell a client information he can just as well find out by himself. Some assist in following legislation through Congress, often a formidable undertaking; they may consult with congressional legislative staff concerning bills for programs that will lead to appropriations; some of them assist agency staff members in preparing guidelines. Thus, they often operate in two directions; they keep the client informed and at the same time pass along to the appropriate legislators information on the interests of their constituents. Washington consultants keep up with the changing staff patterns in government agencies and know when significant reorganizations occur affecting key programs. They may assist in arranging meetings with the appropriate agency officials and representatives of a university or nonprofit institution seeking a large grant for an extensive program.

Some consultants will assist in proposal preparation, submit applications, and follow up on the status of an application through-out the review and processing stages, but it is questionable whether this kind of service is worth what it costs. Many agency officials prefer to deal directly with the individual who will carry out the work and some will actually refuse to deal with anyone else. The introduc-tion of a middleman into the negotiations may sometimes lead to confusion, misunderstandings, and delays.

Some universities and other institutions have established offices in Washington and in their state capitals where the staff is available as an information clearing house or to assist in other ways. But even they can do very little for the individual grant seeker. A governmental representative who is asked to suggest possible funding sources for a proposal will look into the same published documents, the same guides, catalogs, and current periodicals that are available to the requester. He may be able to pick up the telephone and get direct information, but since the advent of direct dialing even this is not a tremendous service to offer a client. One Washington institutional representative commented, "The brilliant, secret funding sources or the big political forces promised by some middlemen is a myth made up by Washington representatives years ago to impress the people back home."

The myth of the man in Washington who could get his clients grants probably grew out of the stories that are circulated, some of them true, of negotiations that involve up to millions of dollars—stories like the ones that emerged in the Watergate scandal with references to cabinet members and lobbyists at cocktail parties; ques-tionable initials on questionable memoranda; and red wigs and laun-dered money and telephone calls from isolated booths on dark, rainy nights. All that sounds much more exciting than writing out an application, adding a publications list and a *curriculum vitae*, and getting off twenty copies of the darned thing by the deadline date. But the latter process is, on balance, preferable. While not everyone who follows that procedure gets an award, nobody has yet been sent to jail for doing it.

Use of Political and Personal Influence. A can't-fail method of get-ting a foundation grant, often passed along to the inexperienced grant seeker, is "Write the best proposal you are capable of, include all the reasons the work should be done, and detail your credentials in glowing terms. Then sign it with the name of the mother of the foundation's board chairman." Like most such stories, there is enough truth in it to keep it alive. But the whole truth is that no general rule about the use of influence applies to all foundations. Some small ones make grants only to friends of the donor family or to applicants referred by friends. In the larger ones, it may be helpful to know one of the officers or it may actually hurt. One experienced grant applicant, when he was reminded that he knew the president of a large foundation and might appeal to him for assistance, shook his head and replied, "Oh, he couldn't help me. He's too high up. Now, if I only knew someone at the program level, that would help." When John D. Rockefeller III was asked in a television interview how he felt about people approaching him on social occasions to discuss foundation support, he said it was a good way to keep in touch with things. But when the program director of a large foundation (not Rockefeller) was asked if she agreed with that statement, she replied, "Not many people speak to Mr. Rockefeller. It is foundation staff at my level who have to curtail their social life because people cannot resist trying to do business on any and every occasion." It was clear that any effort to gain influence with that foundation official by other than standard procedures would probably backfire. The only safe rule to follow in dealing with foundations is the one *they* use in dealing with *applicants*: Proceed with caution.

Many people believe that political and personal influence are absolutely indispensable in dealing with government organizations. One federal agency program director, when asked about political pressure, had this to say: "We have a kind of gentlemen's agreement with many senators and congressmen. If they are asked by a constituent to intercede on behalf of a proposal, they write me a letter, copy to the constituent, urging me to give the proposal full consideration. We reply, saying we have noted the request and that the subject proposal will receive our most careful attention. The congressman sends a copy of our letter to the constituent, and he is off the hook. We place the proposal in the same pile as all the others and that is the end of it. I have never received a complaint from a senator or a representative following our decision on a proposal that was handled in this manner, and I am sure they were not all funded."

Cases can no doubt be cited in which political influence was a factor, but it stands to reason that the whole system of review and decision would become meaningless if pressure from legislators became a significant factor.

Having a friend on a review committee may be more useful than having a friend in Congress, but most review committees—for example, the NIH Study Sections—are composed of eminently qualified, widely respected people, many of whom would be deeply offended by any suggestion that they favor the application of a friend or a colleague or even "go easy" on a review. If the reviewer knows the applicant's work and has high regard for it, solicitation of his approval is not necessary. If he knows the applicant and does not respect his work, it probably will not help.

Artificial Attempts to Link the Proposal to the Organization's Program. The "shoppers'" approach—finding out where the money is and writing a proposal that fits—is one of the more common devices used to get grant funds. All grant-making organizations voice disapproval of this approach but they often condone it or even encourage it. The transfer of information from the policy to the operational level in many agencies or organizations frequently leads to misunderstandings or even more frequently simply leaves a great deal to the interpretation of the staff. This fact, added to the poor administration that exists in some grant-making organizations, tempts applicants to test whether the screening apparatus can really detect the tenuous or nonexistent link between the proposal being submitted and the stated aims of the program.

Applicants who are given misinformation, or no information, when they try to determine the program interests of an organization sometimes interpret such behavior as an implicit invitation to stretch the facts a bit in order to make the proposal more acceptable. One scholar, whose work is in sixteenth-century literature, telephoned a foundation to ask about support for a proposed volume on the English literary renaissance. The staff member to whom he directed his inquiry wanted to know only one thing from him. "Are you an underdeveloped country?" she asked. In recalling the story, the scholar admitted that for a brief instant he wondered if he might qualify as an "underdeveloped country" but decided not to try.

If the applicant deliberately distorts his project to make it appear to be relevant to what the framers of the program had in mind, and succeeds in getting a grant, the truth usually comes to light only when the final reports are in. And since disclosure of the deception at that point serves little purpose and, in fact, might embarrass the granting organization as much as the grantee, it often appears to be a practice that can be followed with impunity. The culprit, however, rarely gets away with it completely. Officials in the grants business—like people in other fields of work—congregate at clubs, restaurants, professional meetings, conferences, and the like. And although they are not likely to boast of their mistakes or willingly admit being taken in by a shrewd operator, information does get passed around, and the "operator" often finds, when he approaches a new organization, that his reputation has preceded him. The temptation to use such devices grows stronger as the competition for funds grows keener, but the rewards, if any, are all short term.

Stalking the wild grant dollar requires some of the same qualities needed for other big game hunting—knowledge, preparation, skill, courage, patience, endurance, and limitless energy. Nobody—or very nearly nobody—has a grant forced upon him. Everybody has to go through the same mill—seeking out potential sources, making preliminary inquiries, and writing an application. Persistence often wins. It is sometimes a good idea to go ahead and apply even when the situation seems hopeless. This is especially true of federal funding sources. Administrators of government programs must always be prepared for an unexpected windfall of funds, and the most expert among them never gets caught without a backlog of meritorious applications. Many an applicant has succeeded because his proposal was there on the desk of the program manager when funds had to be dispensed in a hurry.

Persistence also pays off in dealing with foundations. The winning attitude is perfectly illustrated by the applicant who asked a colleague to review his foundation proposal before submission. The colleague returned it with the unequivocal judgment that, "No foundation in its right mind would give you money for that!" The applicant replied, cheerfully, "All right. I'll try the others!"

Appendix I

TYPES OF GRANTS

Block (or Bloc)—made usually to states or local communities for broad purposes as authorized by legislation. Recipients have great flexibility in
distribution of such funds as long as the basic purposes are fulfilled.

Capitation—grant made to an institution for training purposes, amount of
award based on enrolment.

Categorical—similar to Block grants, except funds must be expended within
specific categories.

Conference—a grant awarded to support the costs of meetings, symposia, or
special seminars.

Consortium—a grant made to one institution in support of a project being
carried out through a cooperative arrangement between or among the
grantee institution and one or more participating institutions.

Construction—a grant made to provide support for building, expanding, and
modernizing facilities.

Continuing Education—a grant made to provide support for additional training or education or to update training in specific fields.

Demonstration—a grant made to establish or demonstrate the feasibility of a
theory or an approach.

Discretionary or Project—a grant made in support of an individual project in
accordance with legislation which permits the grantor agency to exercise

judgment in selecting the project, the grantee, and the amount of the award.

Formula—a grant in which funds are provided to specified grantees on the basis of a specific formula, prescribed in legislation or regulation, rather than on the basis of an individual project review. The formula is usually based on such factors as population, enrolment, per capita income, or a specific need. The Capitation grant is one kind of formula grant; and Block grants are usually made on the basis of a formula.

Planning—a grant made to support planning, developing, designing, and establishing the means for performing research or accomplishing other approved objectives.

Project—See Discretionary or Project.

Research—a grant made in support of investigation or experimentation aimed at the discovery and interpretation of facts, revision of accepted theories in the light of new facts, or the application of such new or revised theories.

Service—a grant made to support costs for the purpose of organizing, establishing, providing, or expanding the delivery of services, e.g., health or mental health services, to a specified community or area. This may also be in the form of a Block grant.

Staffing—a grant made to an institution to provide support for salaries of professional and technical personnel and their inservice training. See also Capitation grant.

Study and Development—a grant awarded to study and develop innovative and experimental programs leading to the establishment of a permanent component.

Training—a grant awarded to an organization to support costs of training students, personnel, or prospective employees in research or in the techniques or practices pertinent to a particular area of concern.

Appendix II

U.S. FEDERAL AGENCY ACRONYMS

ADAMHA · Alcohol, Drug Abuse, and Mental Health Administration
ADAP   Airport Development Aid Program
AFDC   Aid to Families with Dependent Children
AFOSR   Air Force Office of Scientific Research
AID   Agency for International Development
AMS   Agricultural Marketing Service
AOP   Apprentice Outreach Program
APTD   Aid to the Permanently and Totally Disabled
ARC   Appalachian Regional Commission
ARS   Agricultural Research Service
ASCS   Agricultural Stabilization and Conservation Service
ASPR   Armed Service Procurement Regulation
AVTE   Adult, Vocational, and Technical Education

BAVTE   Bureau of Adult, Vocational, and Technical Education
BEH   Bureau of Education for the Handicapped
BEOG   See BOG
BEPD   Bureau of Educational Personnel Development
BIA   Bureau of Indian Affairs
BLS   Bureau of Labor Statistics
BOG   Basic Educational Opportunity Grants

CAB	Civil Aeronautics Board
CDC	Center for Disease Control
CFDA	Catalog of Federal Domestic Assistance
CFR	Code of Federal Regulations
CHP	Comprehensive Health Planning
CHS	Community Health Service
COP	Career Opportunities Program
CPI	Consumer Price Index
CRS	Community Relations Service
CSC	Civil Service Commission
CSRS	Cooperative State Research Service
DOD	Department of Defense
DOT	Department of Transportation
EEOC	Equal Employment Opportunity Commission
EPA	Environmental Protection Agency
EPDA	Education Professions Development Act
ERC	Energy Resources Council
ERDA	Energy Research and Development Administration
ERS	Economic Research Service
ESEA	Elementary and Secondary Education Act
FAA	Federal Aviation Administration
FCC	Federal Communications Commission
FCS	Farmer Cooperative Service
FDA	Food and Drug Administration
FEA	Federal Energy Administration
FHA	Farmers Home Administration
FMTA	Federal Mass Transportation Administration
FTC	Federal Trade Commission
FY	Fiscal Year
GAO	General Accounting Office
GPO	Government Printing Office
GSA	General Services Administration
HEW	Department of Health, Education, and Welfare
HIP	Hospital Improvement
HIST	Hospital In-Service Training
HMO	Health Maintenance Organization

HPSL	Health Professions Student Loans
HRA	Health Resources Administration
HSA	Health Services Administration
HSGT	High Speed Ground Transportation
HUD	Department of Housing and Urban Development

IREX	International Research and Exchange Board
IRS	Internal Revenue Service

LEAA	Law Enforcement Assistance Administration
LEEP	Law Enforcement Education Program

MA	Manpower Administration
MDTA	Manpower Development and Training Act

NASA	National Aeronautics and Space Administration
NBS	National Bureau of Standards
NCI	National Cancer Institute
NCJISS	National Criminal Justice Information and Statistics Service
NEA	National Endowment for the Arts
NEH	National Endowment for the Humanities
NHLI	National Health and Lung Institute
NIA	National Institute on Aging
NIAAA	National Institute on Alcohol Abuse and Alcoholism
NHTSA	National Highway Transportation Safety Administration
NIAID	National Institute of Allergy and Infectious Diseases
NICHD	National Institute of Child Health and Human Development
NIDA	National Institute of Drug Abuse
NIDR	National Institute of Dental Research
NIE	National Institute of Education
NIEHS	National Institute of Environmental Health Sciences
NIGMS	National Institute of General Medical Services
NIH	National Institutes of Health
NIMH	National Institute of Mental Health
NINCDS	National Institute of Neurological and Communicative Disorders and Stroke
NLM	National Library of Medicine
NLRB	National Labor Relations Board
NMFS	National Marine Fisheries Service
NOAA	National Oceanic and Atmospheric Administration
NPS	National Park Service
NRC	Nuclear Regulatory Commission

NSF	National Science Foundation
NWS	National Weather Service
OAWP	Office of Air and Water Programs
OCD	Office of Child Development
OCR	Office of Coal Research
OE	Office of Education
OEO	Office of Economic Opportunity
OEP	Office of Emergency Preparedness
OHD	Office of Human Development
OMB	Office of Management and Budget
OMBE	Office of Minority Business Enterprise
OME	Office of Minerals Exploration
ONR	Office of Naval Research
ONRR	Office of Nuclear Regulatory Research
OWRR	Office of Water Resources Research
PHA	Public Housing Authority
PHS	Public Health Service
RANN	Research Applied to National Needs
RCDA	Research Career Development Awards
REA	Rural Electrification Administration
SBA	Small Business Administration
SBIC	Small Business Investment Company
SCS	Soil Conservation Service
SEC	Securities and Exchange Commission
SEOG	Supplementary Educational Opportunity Grants
SRS	Social and Rehabilitation Service
SSA	Social Security Administration
SSIE	Smithsonian Science Information Exchange
STRI	Smithsonian Tropical Research Institute
TVA	Tennessee Valley Authority
USDA	United States Department of Agriculture
VA	Veterans Administration
VRA	Vocational Rehabilitation Act
YOC	Youth Opportunity Center

Appendix III

HEW REGIONAL OFFICES

REGION I: Connecticut, Maine, Massachusetts, New Hampshire, Rhode Island, Vermont.

John F. Kennedy Federal Building
Government Center
Boston, Massachusetts 02203

REGION II: New Jersey, New York, Puerto Rico, Virgin Islands

26 Federal Plaza, Room 1005
New York, New York 10007

REGION III: Delaware, Maryland, Pennsylvania, Virginia, West Virginia, Washington, D. C.

P. O. Box 13716
Philadelphia, Pennsylvania 19101

REGION IV: Alabama, Florida, Georgia, Kentucky, Mississippi, North Carolina, South Carolina, Tennessee

50-Seventh Street, N.E.
Room 404
Atlanta, Georgia 30323

REGION V: Illinois, Indiana, Minnesota, Michigan, Ohio, Wisconsin

300 South Wacker Drive, 34th Floor
Chicago, Illinois 60606

REGION VI: Arkansas, Louisiana, New Mexico, Oklahoma, Texas

1114 Commerce Street
Dallas, Texas 75202

REGION VII: Iowa, Kansas, Missouri, Nebraska

601 East 12th Street
Kansas City, Missouri 64106

REGION VIII: Colorado, Montana, North Dakota, South Dakota, Utah,
                   Wyoming

9017 Federal Office Building
19th and Stout Streets
Denver, Colorado 80202

REGION IX: Arizona, California, Guam, Hawaii, Nevada, American
                   Samoa, Trust Territory of the Pacific Islands

50 Fulton Street
San Francisco, California 94102

REGION X: Alaska, Idaho, Oregon, Washington

Arcade Plaza Building
1321 Second Avenue
Seattle, Washington 98101

Appendix IV

PUBLIC HEALTH SERVICE PROGRAMS

For detailed information write to the addresses indicated below in care of National Institutes of Health, Public Health Service, Bethesda, Maryland 20014.

PROGRAM	ADDRESS
Academic Career Development Award in Digestive Diseases and/ or Nutrition	National Institute of Arthritis, Metabolism, and Digestive Diseases
Aging Research Centers	National Institute on Aging
Allergic Disease Centers	National Institute of Allergy and Infectious Diseases
Allied Health Professions Grants	Division of Allied Health Manpower, Bureau of Health Manpower Education
Anesthesiology Research Grants	National Institute of General Medical Sciences
Animal Resources Grants	Division of Research Resources

PROGRAM	ADDRESS
Artificial Kidney-Chronic Uremia Program	National Institute of Arthritis, Metabolism, and Digestive Diseases
Biomedical Publication Grants	National Library of Medicine
Biomedical Sciences Support Grants	Division of Research Resources
Biotechnology Resources	Division of Research Resources
Cancer Core Enrichment Program	National Cancer Institute
Cancer Centers	National Cancer Institute
Cancer Research and Training Facilities Construction Program	National Cancer Institute
Capitation Grants (Nursing)	Division of Nursing, BHME
Capitation Grants (Health Professions)	Division of Physician and Health Professions Education, BHME
Clinical Cancer Training Program	National Cancer Institute
Clinical Investigator Awards in Digestive Diseases and/or Nutrition	National Institute of Arthritis, Metabolism, and Digestive Diseases
Comprehensive Centers for Sickle Cell Disease	National Heart and Lung Institute
Contracts	Office of Grants and Contracts, Office of the Director
Construction Grants	Division of Physician and Health Professions Education, BHME
Construction Grants: Medical Library	Division of Physician and Health Professions Education, BHME
Construction Grants: National Cancer Program	National Cancer Institute
Construction Grants for Schools of Nursing	Division of Nursing, BHME
Cooperative Clinical Cancer Program	National Cancer Institute
Cuban Refugee Program	Division of Physician and Health Professions Education, BHME
Dental Health Programs	Division of Dental Health, BHME
Dental Research Center Grants	National Institute of Dental Research
Diagnostic Radiology Research Centers	National Institute of General Medical Sciences

Program	Address
Facilities:	
Cancer Research	National Cancer Institute
Health Professions Education	Division of Physician and Health Professions Education, BHME
Medical Library Construction	Division of Physician and Health Professions Education, BHME
Fellowships:	
Dental Health	Division of Dental Health, BHME
Health Information Specialists	National Library of Medicine
Nursing Research	Division of Nursing, BHME
Research	Division of Research Grants
General Clinical Research Center Grants	Division of Research Resources
General Research Support Grants	Division of Research Resources
Health Information Specialists (training)	National Library of Medicine
Health Manpower Education Initiative Awards	Division of Physician and Health Professions Education, BHME
Health Professions Education Facilities Grants	Division of Physician and Health Professions Education, BHME
Health Professions Educational Improvement Grants	Division of Physician and Health Professions Education, BHME
Heart and Lung Specialized Centers of Research (SCOR)	National Heart and Lung Institute
Human Genetics Research Centers	National Institute of General Medical Sciences
International Centers for Medical Research and Training	National Institute of Allergy and Infectious Diseases
International Postdoctoral Fellowships	Fogarty International Center
Medical Library Construction Grants	Division of Physician and Health Professions Education, BHME
Medical Library Resources	National Library of Medicine
Mental Retardation Centers	National Institute of Child Health and Human Development

PROGRAM	ADDRESS
Minority Access to Research Careers (MARC)	National Institute of General Medical Sciences
Minority Schools Biomedical Support Grants	Division of Research Resources
National Caries Program	National Institute of Dental Research
National Organ Site Cancer Program	National Cancer Institute
Neurological and Communicative Disorders and Stroke Clinical Research Centers and Outpatient Research Units	National Institute of Neurological and Communicative Disorders and Stroke
Neurological and Communicative Disorders and Stroke Teacher-Investigator Special Traineeship Awards	National Institute of Neurological and Communicative Disorders and Stroke
Nursing Programs	Division of Nursing, BHME
Pharmacology-Toxicology Research Centers	National Institute of General Medical Sciences
Population Research Centers	National Institute of Child Health and Human Development
Public Health Programs	Division of Allied Health Manpower, BHME
Pulmonary Academic Awards	National Heart and Lung Institute
Radiation Therapy Clinical Research Centers	National Cancer Institute
Regional Medical Library Program	National Library of Medicine
Research Career Development Awards	Division of Research Grants
Research Contracts	Office of Grants and Contracts, Office of the Director
Research, Development, and Demonstration Grants	National Library of Medicine
Research Fellowships	Division of Research Grants
Research Programs—Project Grants	Division of Research Grants
Research Project Grants	Division of Research Grants
Research Project Grants (Nursing)	Division of Nursing, BHME
Research Resources	Division of Research Resources

PROGRAM	ADDRESS
Research Training Grants	Division of Research Grants
Special Dental Research Awards	National Institute of Dental Research
Special Project Grants (Health Professions)	Division of Physician and Health Professions Education, BHME
Special Scientific Projects (Medical Libraries)	National Library of Medicine
Student Loans and Scholarships	Division of Nursing, and Division of Physician and Health Professions Education, BHME

Training Grants:

Allied Health Personnel	Division of Allied Health Manpower, BHME
Clinical Cancer Training	National Cancer Institute
Dental Health	Division of Dental Health, BHME
Expended Auxiliary Management (Dental)	Division of Dental Health, BHME
Family Medicine	Division of Physician and Health Professions Education, BHME
Health Information Specialists	National Library of Medicine
Health Professions Teaching Personnel	Division of Physician and Health Professions Education, BHME
Nurse Scientist (graduate)	Division of Nursing, BHME
Professional Nurse Traineeships	Division of Nursing, BHME
Public Health (graduate)	Division of Allied Health Manpower, BHME
Public Health (Professional Public Health Personnel)	Division of Allied Health Manpower, BHME
Research	Division of Research Grants
Trauma Research Centers	National Institute of General Medical Services
United States-Japan Cooperative Medical Sciences Program	National Institute of Allergy and Infectious Diseases
Vision Research Centers	National Eye Institute
Vision Research: Outpatient Centers	National Eye Institute

Appendix V

FEDERAL INFORMATION CENTERS AND TELEPHONE TIELINES

GENERAL SERVICES ADMINISTRATION

State/City	Telephone*	Address	Toll-Free Tieline
ALABAMA			
Birmingham	322-8591		Atlanta, Ga.
Mobile	438-1421		New Orleans, La.
ARIZONA			
Tucson	622-1511		Phoenix, Ariz.
Phoenix	602-261-3313	Federal Building 230 N. 1st Avenue 85025	
ARKANSAS			
Little Rock	378-6177		Memphis, Tenn.

* The tieline numbers are toll-free only in the specified city.

State/City	Telephone*	Address	Toll-Free Tieline
CALIFORNIA			
Los Angeles __	213-688-3800	Federal Building 300 N. Los Angeles St. 90012	
Sacramento ____	916-449-3344	Federal Building U.S. Courthouse 650 Capitol Mall 95814	
San Diego ____	714-293-6030	202 C Street 92101	
San Francisco __	415-556-6600	Federal Building U.S. Courthouse 450 Golden Gate Avenue 94102	
San Jose _____	275-7422	_____	San Francisco, Calif.
COLORADO			
Colorado Springs __	471-9491	_____	Denver, Colo.
Denver _____	303-837-3602	Federal Building U.S. Courthouse 1961 Stout Street 80202	
Pueblo _____	544-9523	_____	Denver, Colo.
CONNECTICUT			
Hartford _____	527-2617	_____	New York, N.Y.
New Haven _____	624-4720	_____	New York, N.Y.
DISTRICT OF COLUMBIA	202-755-8660	Room 5716 7th and D Streets, S.W. 20407	
FLORIDA			
Fort Lauderdale ____	522-8531	_____	Miami, Fla.
Jacksonville _____	354-4756	_____	St. Petersburg, Fla.
Miami _____	305-350-4155	Federal Building 51 SW 1st Avenue 33130	
St. Petersburg	813-893-3495	William C. Cramer Federal Bldg. 144 1st Avenue, S. 33701	
Tampa _____	229-7911	_____	St. Petersburg, Fla.
West Palm Beach __	833-7566	_____	Miami, Fla.

State/City	Telephone*	Address	Toll-Free Tieline
GEORGIA			
Atlanta _____ 404-526-6891		Federal Building 275 Peachtree Street, NE 30303	
HAWAII			
Honolulu _____ 808-546-8620		U.S. Post Office Courthouse and Customhouse 335 Merchant Street 96813	
ILLINOIS			
Chicago _____ 312-353-4242		Everett McKinley Dirksen Bldg. 219 S. Dearborn Street 60604	
INDIANA			
Indianapolis __ 317-633-8484		Federal Building U.S. Courthouse 46 E. Ohio Street 46204	
IOWA			
Des Moines _____ 282-9091		_____Omaha, Nebraska	
KANSAS			
Topeka _____ 232-7229		_____Kansas City, Mo.	
Wichita _____ 263-6931		_____Kansas City, Mo.	
KENTUCKY			
Louisville _____ 502-582-6261		Federal Building 600 Federal Place 40202	
LOUISIANA			
New Orleans __ 504-527-6696		Federal Building, Room 1210 701 Loyola Avenue 70113	
MARYLAND			
Baltimore _____ 301-962-4980		Federal Building 31 Hopkins Plaza 21201	

State/City	Telephone*	Address	Toll-Free Tieline
MASSACHUSETTS			
Boston _____ 617-223-7121		John F. Kennedy Federal Building Government Center 02203	
MICHIGAN			
Detroit _____ 313-226-7016		Federal Building U.S. Courthouse 231 W. Lafayette Street 48226	
MINNESOTA			
Minneapolis __ 612-725-2073		Federal Building U.S. Courthouse 110 South 4th St. 55401	
MISSOURI			
Kansas City __ 816-374-2466		Federal Building 601 East 12th St. 64106	
St. Joseph _____233-8206		_____Kansas City, Mo.	
St. Louis _____ 314-622-4106		Federal Building 1520 Market Street 63103	
NEBRASKA			
Omaha _____ 402-221-3353		Federal Building U.S. Post Office and Courthouse 215 North 17th St. 68102	
NEW JERSEY			
Newark _____ 201-645-3600		Federal Building 970 Broad Street 07102	
Trenton _____396-4400		_____Newark, N.J.	
NEW MEXICO			
Albuquerque __ 505-766-3091		Federal Building U.S. Courthouse 500 Gold Avenue, SW. 87101	
Santa Fe _____ 983-7743		_____Albuquerque, N.M.	

State/City	Telephone*	Address	Toll-Free Tieline
NEW YORK			
Albany	463-4421	_____New York, N.Y.	
Buffalo	716-842-5770	Federal Building 111 West Huron Street 14202	
New York	212-264-4464	Federal Office Building 26 Federal Plaza 10007	
Rochester	546-5075	_____Buffalo, N.Y.	
Syracuse	476-8545	_____Buffalo, N.Y.	
NORTH CAROLINA			
Charlotte	376-3600	_____Atlanta, Ga.	
OHIO			
Akron	375-5475	_____Cleveland, Ohio	
Cincinnati	513-684-2801	Federal Building 550 Main Street 45202	
Cleveland	216-522-4040	Federal Building 1240 E. 9th Street 44199	
Columbus	221-1014	_____Cincinnati, Ohio	
Dayton	223-7377	_____Cincinnati, Ohio	
Toledo	244-8625	_____Cleveland, Ohio	
OKLAHOMA			
Oklahoma City	405-231-4868	U.S. Post Office and Federal Office Building 201 NW. 3rd Street 73102	
Tulsa	584-4193	_____Oklahoma City, Okla.	
OREGON			
Portland	503-221-2222	208 U.S. Courthouse 620 SW. Main Street 97205	
PENNSYLVANIA			
Philadelphia	215-597-7042	William J. Green, Jr. Federal Bldg. 600 Arch Street 19106	
Pittsburgh	412-644-3456	Federal Building 1000 Liberty Avenue 15222	
Scranton	346-7081	_____Philadelphia, Pa.	

State/City	Telephone*	Address	Toll-Free Tieline
RHODE ISLAND			
Providence _____331-5565		_____Boston, Mass.	
TENNESSEE			
Chattanooga _____265-8231		_____Memphis, Tenn.	
Memphis _____ 901-534-3285		Clifford Davis Federal Bldg. 167 N. Main Street 38103	
TEXAS			
Austin _____472-5494		_____Houston, Tex.	
Dallas _____749-2131		_____Fort Worth, Tex.	
Fort Worth ____ 817-334-3624		Fritz Garland Lanham Federal Bldg. 819 Taylor Street 76102	
Houston _____ 713-226-5711		Federal Building U.S. Courthouse 515 Rusk Avenue 77002	
San Antonio _____224-4471		_____Houston, Tex.	
UTAH			
Ogden _____399-1347		_____Salt Lake City, Utah	
Salt Lake City 801-524-5353		Federal Building U.S. Post Office and Courthouse 125 S. State Street 84138	
WASHINGTON			
Seattle _____ 206-442-0570		Arcade Plaza 1321 2nd Avenue 98101	
Tacoma _____383-5230		_____Seattle, Wash.	
WISCONSIN			
Milwaukee _____271-2273		_____Chicago, Ill.	

Appendix VI

THE FOUNDATION CENTER

Regional Collections

State	Name	Geographical Coverage
Alabama	Birmingham Public Library 2020 Seventh Avenue, North Birmingham 35203	Alabama
Arkansas	Little Rock Public Library Reference Department 700 Louisiana Street Little Rock 72201	Arkansas
California	University Research Library Reference Department University of California Los Angeles 90024	Alaska, Arizona, California, Colorado, Hawaii, Nevada, Utah
	San Francisco Public Library Business Branch 530 Kearny Street San Francisco 94108	Alaska, California, Colorado, Hawaii, Idaho, Montana, Nevada, Oregon, Utah, Washington, Wyoming

313

State	Name	Geographical Coverage
Colorado	Denver Public Library Sociology Division 1357 Broadway Denver 80203	Colorado

Connecticut	Hartford Public Library
	Reference Department
	500 Main Street
	Hartford 06103
		Connecticut,
		  Massachusetts,
		  Rhode Island

Florida	Jacksonville Public Library Business, Science, and Industry Department 122 North Ocean Street Jacksonville 32202	Florida
	Miami-Dade Public Library Florida Collection One Biscayne Boulevard Miami 33132	Florida

Georgia	Atlanta Public Library
	126 Carnegie Way, N.W.
	Atlanta 30303
		Alabama, Florida,
		  Georgia, Kentucky,
		  Mississippi,
		  North Carolina,
		  South Carolina,
		  Tennessee, Virginia

Hawaii	Thomas Hale Hamilton Library
	Social Science Reference
	2550 The Mall
	Honolulu 96822
		California, Hawaii,
		  Oregon,
		  Washington

Illinois	The Newberry Library
	60 West Walton Street
	Chicago 60610
		Illinois, Indiana,
		  Michigan,
		  Minnesota,
		  North Dakota,
		  South Dakota,
		  Wisconsin

Iowa	Des Moines Public Library 100 Locust Street Des Moines 50309	Iowa
Kansas	Topeka Public Library Adult Services Department 1515 West Tenth Street Topeka 66604	Kansas

State	Name	Geographical Coverage
Kentucky	Louisville Free Public Library Fourth and York Streets Louisville 40203	Kentucky
Louisiana	New Orleans Public Library Business and Science Division 219 Loyola Avenue New Orleans 70140	Louisiana
Maryland	Enoch Pratt Free Library 400 Cathedral Street Baltimore 21201	Maryland
Massachusetts	Associated Foundation of Greater Boston One Boston Place, Suite 948 Boston 02108	Connecticut, Maine, Massachusetts, New Hampshire, Rhode Island, Vermont
	Boston Public Library Copley Square Boston 02117	Massachusetts
Michigan	Henry Ford Centennial Library 15301 Michigan Avenue Dearborn 48126	Michigan
	Grand Rapids Public Library Sociology and Education Department Library Plaza Grand Rapids 49502	Michigan
Minnesota	Minneapolis Public Library Sociology Department 300 Nicollet Mall Minneapolis 55401	Iowa, Minnesota, North Dakota, South Dakota
Mississippi	Jackson Metropolitan Library 301 North State Street Jackson 39201	Mississippi
Missouri	Linda Hall Library Science and Technology 5109 Cherry Street Kansas City 64110	Kansas, Missouri
	The Danforth Foundation Library 222 South Central Avenue St. Louis 63105	Iowa, Kansas, Missouri, Nebraska

State	Name	Geographical Coverage
Nebraska	Omaha Public Library 1823 Harney Street Omaha 68102	Nebraska
New Hampshire	The New Hampshire Charitable Fund One South Street Concord 03301	New Hampshire
New Jersey	New Jersey State Library Reference Section 185 West State Street Trenton 08625	New Jersey
New York	New York State Library State Education Department Education Building Albany 12224	New York
	Buffalo and Erie County Public Library Lafayette Square Buffalo 14203	New York
	Levittown Public Library Reference Department One Bluegrass Lane Levittown 11756	New York
	Rochester Public Library Business and Social Sciences Division 115 South Avenue Rochester 14604	New York
North Carolina	William R. Perkins Library Duke University Durham 27706	North Carolina
Ohio	The Cleveland Foundation Library 700 National City Bank Building Cleveland 44114	Michigan, Ohio, Pennsylvania, West Virginia
Oklahoma	Oklahoma City Community Foundation 1300 North Broadway Oklahoma City 73103	Oklahoma

State	Name	Geographical Coverage
Oregon	Library Association of Portland Education and Psychology Department 801 S.W. Tenth Avenue Portland 97205	Alaska, California, Hawaii, Oregon, Washington
Pennsylvania	The Free Library of Philadelphia Logan Square Philadelphia 19103	Delaware, New Jersey, Pennsylvania
	Hillman Library University of Pittsburgh Pittsburgh 15213	Pennsylvania
Rhode Island	Providence Public Library Reference Department 150 Empire Street Providence 02903	Rhode Island
South Carolina	South Carolina State Library Reader Services Department 1500 Senate Street Columbia 29211	South Carolina
Tennessee	Memphis Public Library 1850 Peabody Avenue Memphis 38104	Tennessee
Texas	The Hogg Foundation for Mental Health The University of Texas Austin 78712	Arkansas, Louisiana, New Mexico, Oklahoma, Texas
	Dallas Public Library History and Social Sciences Division 1954 Commerce Street Dallas 75201	Texas
Utah	Salt Lake City Public Library Information and Adult Services 209 East Fifth Street Salt Lake City 84111	Utah
Vermont	State of Vermont Department of Libraries Reference Services Unit 111 State Street Montpelier 05602	New Hampshire, Vermont

State	Name	Geographical Coverage
Virginia	Richmond Public Library Business, Science & Technology Department 101 East Franklin Street Richmond 23219	Virginia
Washington	Seattle Public Library 1000 Fourth Avenue Seattle 98104	Washington
West Virginia	Kanawha County Public Library 123 Capitol Street Charleston 25301	West Virginia

Wisconsin	Marquette University Memorial
	    Library
	1415 West Wisconsin Avenue
	Milwaukee 53233
		Illinois, Indiana,
		    Iowa, Michigan,
		    Minnesota, Ohio,
		    Wisconsin

Wyoming	Laramie County Community College Library 1400 East College Drive Cheyenne 82001	Wyoming

Appendix VII

DEPARTMENT OF HEALTH, EDUCATION, AND WELFARE REGIONAL COMPTROLLERS' OFFICES

Region I

Mr. Orville J. Anderson
J. F. Kennedy Federal Bldg.
Government Center, Room 1512
Boston, Massachusetts 02203

Connecticut, Maine, Massachusetts, New Hampshire, Rhode Island, Vermont

Region II

Mr. Vincent J. Bamundo
26 Federal Plaza, Room 3838
New York, New York 10007

Canada, England, New Jersey, New York, Puerto Rico, Virgin Islands

Region III

Mr. John McKenna
P.O. Box 13716
Philadelphia, Pennsylvania 19101

Delaware, District of Columbia, Maryland, Pennsylvania, Virginia, West Virginia, and Beirut, Lebanon

Region IV

Mrs. W. McNeil Saddler
50 Seventh Street, N.E., Rm. 404
Atlanta, Georgia 30323

Alabama, Florida, Georgia, Kentucky, Mississippi, North Carolina, South Carolina, Tennessee

Region V

Mr. Frank Yanni
300 S. Wacker Drive, Room 2904
Chicago, Illinois 60607

Illinois, Indiana, Michigan, Minnesota, Ohio, Wisconsin

Region VI

Mr. Donald Whittaker
1114 Commerce Street, Room 1008
Dallas, Texas 75202

Arkansas, Louisiana, New Mexico, Oklahoma, Texas

Region VII

Mr. Robert McManus
601 East 12th Street, Room 520
Kansas City, Missouri 64106

Iowa, Kansas, Missouri, Nebraska

Region VIII

Mr. Richard O'Brien
19th & Stout Streets, Room 11033
Denver, Colorado 80202

Colorado, Montana, North Dakota, South Dakota, Utah, Wyoming

Region IX

Mr. Robert Woodruff
50 Fulton Street, Room 416
San Francisco, California 94102

Arizona, California, Guam, Hawaii, Nevada, American Samoa, Trust Territories of Pacific Islands, Wake Island

Region X

Mr. Richard Hughes
1321 Second Avenue, Room 5030
Arcade Plaza
Seattle, Washington 98101

Alaska, Idaho, Oregon, Washington

Appendix VIII

UNITED STATES LIST OF ENDANGERED FAUNA

MAY 1974 (includes both native and foreign species)

The endangered animal species listed below are arranged phylogenetically by Class and Order, and alphabetically within each Order by their common names. The taxonomic terms—"Class" and "Order"—are used merely for organizational purposes. The common names used are those which are associated with a given species most often, but these have no legal significance. The legal identification of each animal listed is the scientific binominal or trinominal that appears after the common name. The effective date for officially placing each animal on the endangered species list is footnoted, and corresponds to the date of publication in the *Federal Register*. Information in the "Where Found" column is provided for information purposes only, and does not necessarily identify the total range of the species in question.

Common Name	Scientific Name	Where Found
SNAILS (Class Gastropoda/Phylum Mollusca)		
Pulmonate Land Snails (Order: Stycomatophora)		
1. Snail, Manus Island tree	*Papustyla pulcherrima*[3]	SW Pacific: Admiralty Islands (Manus I.)

Common Name	Scientific Name	Where Found

BONY FISHES (Class Osteichthyes/Phylum Chordata)
Sturgeons and Paddlefishes (Order: Acipenseriformes)

1. Sturgeon, Shortnose   *Acipenser brevirostrum*[1]   USA/Canada: Atlantic Coast

TROUT, SALMON, AND RELATIVES (Order: Salmoniformes)

1. Ala Balik   *Salmo platycephalus*[3]   Turkey
2. Cisco, Longjaw   *Coregonus alpenae*[1]   USA (Lakes Michigan, Huron, and Erie)
3. Trout, Arizona (Apache)   *Salmo* sp.[1]   USA (Arizona)
4. Trout, Gila   *Salmo gilae*[1]   USA (New Mexico)
5. Trout, Greenback cutthroat   *Salmo clarki stomias*[1]   USA (Colorado)
6. Trout, Lahontan cutthroat   *Salmo clarki henshawi*[2]   USA (California, Nevada)
7. Trout, Paiute cutthroat   *Salmo clarki seleniris*[1]   USA (California)

CARPS, MINNOWS, AND RELATIVES (Order: Cypriniformes)

1. Ayumodoki   *Hymenophysa curta*[3]   Japan
2. Bonytail, Pahranagat   *Gila robusta jordani*[2]   USA (Nevada)
3. Chub, Humpback   *Gila cypha*[1]   USA (Arizona, Utah, Wyoming)
4. Chub, Mohave   *Siphateles mohavensis*[2]   USA (California)
5. Cicek   *Acanthorutilus handlirschi*[3]   Turkey
6. Cui-ui   *Chasmistes cujus*[1]   USA (Nevada)
7. Dace, Kendall Warm Springs   *Rhinichthys osculus thermalis*[2]   USA (Wyoming)
8. Dace, Moapa   *Moapa coriacea*[1]   USA (Nevada)
9. Squawfish, Colorado River   *Ptychocheilus lucius*[1]   USA (Colorado R. system)
10. Tanago, Miyako   *Tanakia tanago*[3]   Japan
11. Woundfin   *Plagopherus argentissimus*[2]   USA (Utah)

Footnotes. Officially listed in *Federal Register*: [1] 11MAR67, Vol. 32(48):4001; [2] 13OCT70, Vol. 35(199):16047; [3] 2DEC70, Vol. 35(233):18319; [4] 30MAR72, Vol. 37(62):6476; [5] 4JUN73, Vol. 38(106):14678.

Common Name	Scientific Name	Where Found

CATFISHES (Order: Siluriformes)

1. Blindcat, Mexican — *Prietella phreatophila*[3] — Mexico
2. Catfish — *Pangasius sanitwongsei*[3] — Thailand
3. Catfish, Gaint — *Pangasianodon gigas*[3] — Thailand
4. Nekogigi — *Coreobagrus ichikawai*[3] — Japan

SILVERSIDES, TOPMINNOWS, AND RELATIVES (Order: Atheriniformes)

1. Gambusia, Big Bend — *Gambusia gaigei*[1] — USA (Texas)
2. Gambusia, Clear Creek — *Gambusia heterochir*[1] — USA (Texas)
3. Gambusia, Pecos — *Gambusia nobilis*[2] — USA (Texas)
4. Killifish, Pahrump — *Empetrichythys latos*[1] — USA (Nevada)
5. Pupfish, Comanche Springs — *Cyprinodon elegans*[1] — USA (Texas)
6. Pupfish, Devil's Hole — *Cyprinodon diabolis*[1] — USA (Nevada)
7. Pupfish, Owens River — *Cyprinodon radiosus*[1] — USA (California)
8. Pupfish, Tecopa — *Cyprinodon nevadensis calidae*[2] — USA (California)
9. Pupfish, Warm Springs — *Cyprinodon nevadensis pectoralis*[2] — USA (Nevada)
10. Topminnow, Gila — *Poeciliopsis occidentalis*[1] — Mexico (N)/USA (Arizona)

STICKLEBACKS, PIPEFISHES, AND RELATIVES (Order: Gasterosteiformes)

1. Stickleback, Unarmored threespine — *Gasterosterus aculeatus williamsoni*[2] — USA (California)

Perches and Relatives (Order: Perciformes)

1. Darter, Fountain — *Etheostoma fonticola*[2] — USA (Texas)
2. Darter, Maryland — *Etheostoma sellare*[1] — USA (Maryland)
3. Darter, Okaloosa — *Etheostoma okaloosae*[5] — USA (Florida)
4. Darter, Watercress — *Etheostoma nuchale*[2] — USA (Alabama)
5. Pike, Blue — *Stizostedion vitreum glaucum*[1] — USA (Lakes Erie & Ontario)

AMPHIBIANS (Class Amphibia/Phylum Chordata)
SALAMANDERS (Order: Urodela)

1. Salamander, Desert slender — *Batrachoseps aridus*[5] — USA (California)

Common Name	Scientific Name	Where Found
2. Salamander, Santa Cruz long-toed	*Ambystoma macrodactylum croceum*[1]	USA (California)
3. Salamander, Texas blind	*Typhlomolge rathbuni*[1]	USA (Texas)

FROGS (Order: Anura)

1. Frog, Stephen Island	*Leiopelma hamiltoni*[3]	New Zealand
2. Frog, Israel painted	*Discoglossus nigriventer*[3]	Israel
3. Toad, Houston	*Bufo houstonensis*[2]	USA (Texas)

REPTILES (Class Reptilia/Phlyum Chordata)
TUATARA (Order: Rhynchocephalia)

1. Tuatara	*Sphenodon punctatus*[3]	New Zealand

Turtles (Order: Testudinata)

1. Terrapin, River(Tuntong)	*Batagur baska*[3]	Southeast Asia
2. Tortoise, Galapagos	*Testudo elephantopus*[3]	Ecuador (Galapagos Islands)
3. Tortoise, Madagascar radiated	*Testudo radiata*[3]	Malagasy Republic (Madagascar)
4. Tortoise, Short-necked (swamp)	*Pseudemydura umbrina*[3]	Australia
5. Turtle, Aquatic box	*Terrapene coahuila*[5]	Mexico
6. Turtle, Atlantic Ridley	*Lepidochelys kempii*[3]	Mexico
7. Turtle, Hawksbill	*Eretmochelys imbricata*[3]	Tropical seas worldwide
8. Turtle, Leatherback	*Dermochelys coriacea*[3]	Tropical and Temperate seas worldwide
9. Turtle, South American River	*Podocnemis expansa*[3]	No.S.Amer (Orinoco, Amazon R. systems)
10. Turtle, South American River	*Podocnemis unifilis*[3]	No.S.Amer (Orinoco, Amazon R. systems)

CROCODILES (Order: Crocodilia)

1. Alligator, American	*Alligator mississipiensis*[1]	USA (SE)
2. Crocodile, Cuban	*Crocodylus rhombifer*[3]	Cuba
3. Crocodile, Morelet's	*Crocodylus moreletii*[3]	Mexico/British Honduras/ Guatemala

Common Name	Scientific Name	Where Found
4. Crocodile, Nile	*Crocodylus niloticus*[3]	Africa
5. Crocodile, Orinoco	*Crocodylus intermedius*[3]	No.S.Amer (Orinoco R.)
6. Gharial (Gavial)	*Gavialis gangeticus*[3]	Pakistan/India/ Bangladesh/Burma
7. Yacare (Caiman)	*Caiman yacare*[3]	Bolivia/Argentina/Peru/ Brazil

LIZARDS AND SNAKES (Order: Squamata)

1. Lizard, Day gecko	*Phelsuma newtoni*[3]	Mascarene Is.: Mauritius
2. Lizard, Round Island day gecko	*Phelsuma guentheri*[3]	Mascarene Is.: Mauritius
3. Lizard, Anegada ground iguana	*Cyclura pinguis*[3]	West Indies: Virgin Is. (Anegada)
4. Lizard, Barrington land iguana	*Conolophus pallidus*[3]	Ecuador (Galapagos Islands)
5. Lizard, Blunt-nosed leopard	*Crotaphytus silus*[1]	USA (California)
6. Snake, Jamaica boa	*Epicrates subflavus*[3]	West Indies: Jamaica
7. Snake, Puerto Rican boa	*Epicrates inornatus*[2]	West Indies: Puerto Rico
8. Snake, San Francisco garter	*Thamnophis sirtalis tetrataenia*[1]	USA (California)

BIRDS (Class Aves/Phylum Chordata)
PENGUINS (Order: Sphenisciformes)

1. Penguin, Galapagos	*Spheniscus mendiculus*[2,3]	Ecuador (Galapagos Islands)

OSTRICHES (Order: Struthioniformes)

1. Ostrich, Arabian	*Struthio camelus syriacus*[3]	Jordan/SaudiArabia/ SpanishSahara
2. Ostrich, West African	*Struthio camelus spatzi*[3]	Jordan/SaudiArabia/ SpanishSahara

RHEAS (Order: Rheiformes)

1. Rhea, Darwin's	*Pterocnemia pennata*[3]	Argentina/Peru/ Uruguay/Bolivia

GREBES (Order: Podicipediformes)

1. Grebe, Atitlan	*Podilymbus gigas*[3]	Guatemala

Common Name	Scientific Name	Where Found

ALBATROSSES, PETRELS, AND RELATIVES (Order: Procellariiformes)

1. Albatross, Short-tailed — *Diomedea albatrus*[3] — Japan
2. Cahow (Bermuda petrel) — *Pterodroma cahow*[3] — W. Atlantic Ocean: Bermuda
3. Petrel, Hawaiian dark-rumped — *Pterodroma phaeopygia sandwichensis*[1] — USA (Hawaii)

PELICANS (Order: Pelecaniformes)

1. Pelican, Brown — *Pelecanus occidentalis*[2,3] — USA/W.Indies/C. and S.Amer: Coastal

HERONS, STORKS, FLAMINGOS, AND RELATIVES (Order: Ciconiiformes)

1. Egret, Chinese — *Egretta eulophotes*[3] — People's Republic China/Korea
2. Ibis, Japanese crested — *Nipponia nippon*[3] — Japan/Korea/USSR/ People's Rep. China
3. Stork, White Oriental — *Ciconia ciconia boyciana*[3] — Japan/Korea/USSR/ People's Rep. China

DUCKS, GEESE, SWANS, AND RELATIVES (Order: Anseriformes)

1. Duck, Hawaiian (koloa) — *Anas wyvilliana*[1] — USA (Hawaii)
2. Duck, Laysan — *Anas laysanensis*[1] — USA (Hawaii)
3. Duck, Mexican — *Anas diazi*[1] — USA (Texas, Arizona)/ Mexico
4. Duck, White-winged wood — *Cairina scutulata*[3] — Southeast Asia
5. Goose, Aleutian Canada — *Branta canadensis leucopareia*[1,3] — USA (Western)/Japan
6. Goose, Hawaiian (Nene) — *Branta sandvicensis*[1] — USA (Hawaii)

EAGLES, FALCONS, VULTURES, AND RELATIVES (Order: Falconiformes)

1. Condor, Andean — *Vultur gryphus*[3] — W.So.Amer:Columbia to Chile/Argentina
2. Condor, California — *Gymnogyps californianus*[1] — USA (California)
3. Eagle, Monkey-eating — *Pithecophaga jefferyi*[3] — Philippines (Mindanao Is. to Luzon Is.)
4. Eagle, Southern bald — *Haliaeetus leucocephalus leucocephalus*[1] — USA (So. of 40th Parallel)
5. Eagle, Spanish imperial — *Aquila heliaca adalberti*[3] — Spain/Morocco/Algeria

Common Name	Scientific Name	Where Found
6. Falcon, American peregrine	*Falco peregrinus anatum*[2,3]	Canada/USA/Mexico
7. Falcon, Arctic peregrine	*Falco peregrinus tundrius*[2,3]	Canada/USA/Mexico
8. Goshawk, Christmas Island	*Accipiter fasciatus natalis*[3]	Indian Ocean: Christmas Island
9. Hawk, Anjouan Island sparrow	*Accipiter francesii pusillus*[3]	Indian Ocean: Comoro Islands
10. Hawk, Galapagos	*Buteo galapagoensis*[3]	Ecuador (Galapagos Islands)
11. Hawk, Hawaiian (io)	*Buteo solitarius*[1]	USA (Hawaii)
12. Kestrel, Mauritius	*Falco punctatus*[3]	Mascarene Is.: Mauritius
13. Kestrel, Seychelles	*Falco araea*[3]	Indian Ocean: Seychelles
14. Kite, Cuba hook-billed	*Chondrohierax wilsonii*[3]	Cuba
15. Kite, Grenada hook-billed	*Chondrohierax uncinatus mirus*[3]	West Indies: Grenada
16. Kite, Florida Everglade (snail kite)	*Rostrhamus sociabilis plumbeus*[1]	USA (Florida)

PHEASANTS, GROUSE, CURASSOWS, AND RELATIVES (Order: Galliformes)

1. Curassow, Red-billed	*Crax blumenbachii*[3]	Brazil
2. Curassow, Trinidad white-headed	*Pipile pipile pipile*[3]	West Indies: Trinidad
3. Guan, Horned	*Oreophasis derbianus*[3]	Guatemala/Mexico
4. Megapode, Maleo	*Macrocephalon maleo*[3]	Indonesia (Sulawesi)
5. Megapode, LaPerouse's	*Megapodius laperouse*[3]	W.Pacific Ocean: Palau Is./Mariana Is.
6. Pheasant, Bar-tailed	*Syrmaticus humiae*[3]	Burma/People's Rep. China
7. Pheasant, Blyth's tragopan	*Tragopan blythii*[3]	People's Rep. China/ Burma/India
8. Pheasant, Brown-eared	*Crossoptilon mantchuricum*[3]	People's Rep. China
9. Pheasant, Cabot's tragopan	*Tragopan caboti*[3]	People's Rep. China
10. Pheasant, Chinese monal	*Lophophorus lhuysii*[3]	People's Rep. China
11. Pheasant, Edward's	*Lophura edwardsi*[3]	Vietnam
12. Pheasant, Imperial	*Lophura imperialis*[3]	Vietnam

Common Name	Scientific Name	Where Found
13. Pheasant, Mikado	*Syrmaticus mikado*[3]	Rep. China (Taiwan)
14. Pheasant, Palawan peacock	*Polyplectron emphanum*[3]	Philippines
15. Pheasant, Sclater's monal	*Lophophorus sclateri*[3]	People's Rep. China/ Burma/India
16. Pheasant, Swinhoe's	*Lophura swinhoii*[3]	Rep. China(Taiwan)
17. Pheasant, Western tragopan	*Tragopan melanocephalus*[3]	India/Pakistan
18. Pheasant, White-eared	*Crossoptilon crossoptilon*[3]	People's Rep. China(Tibet)/India
19. Prairie Chicken, Attwater's greater	*Tympanuchus cupido attwateri*[1]	USA (Texas)
20. Quail, Masked bobwhite	*Colinus virginianus ridgwayi*[1,3]	Mexico (N)/USA (Arizona, New Mexico)

CRANES, RAILS, BUSTARDS, AND RELATIVES (Order: Gruiformes)

Common Name	Scientific Name	Where Found
1. Bustard, Great Indian	*Choriotis nigriceps*[3]	India/Pakistan
2. Coot, Hawaiian	*Fulica americana alai*[2]	USA (Hawaii)
3. Crane, Hooded	*Grus monachus*[3]	Japan/USSR
4. Crane, Japanese	*Grus japaonensis*[3]	Japan/People's Rep. China/Korea/USSR
5. Crane, Mississippi sandhill	*Grus canadensis pulla*[5]	USA (Mississippi)
6. Crane, Siberian white	*Grus leucogeranus*[3]	USSR (E) to India
7. Crane, Whooping	*Grus americana*[1,3]	Canada/USA
8. Gallinule, Hawaiian	*Gallinula chloropus sandvicensis*[1]	USA (Hawaii)
9. Kagu (Rail)	*Rhynochetos jubatus*[3]	SW Pacific Ocean: New Caledonia
10. Rail, Auckland Island	*Rallus pectoralis muelleri*[3]	New Zealand
11. Rail, California clapper	*Rallus longirostris obsoletus*[2]	USA (California)
12. Rail, Light-footed clapper	*Rallus longirostris levipes*[2]	Mexico/USA (California)
13. Rail, Yuma clapper	*Rallus longirostris yumanensis*[1]	Mexico/USA (California, Arizona)
14. Wanderer, Plains	*Pedionomus torquatus*[5]	Australia

PLOVERS, SNIPES, GULLS, AND RELATIVES (Order: Charadriiformes)

Common Name	Scientific Name	Where Found
1. Curlew, Eskimo	*Numenius borealis*[1,3]	Canada to Argentina

Common Name	Scientific Name	Where Found
2. Gull, Audouin's	*Larus audouinii*[3]	Mediterranean Ocean and adjacent lands
3. Plover, New Zealand shore	*Thinornis novae-seelandiae*[3]	New Zealand
4. Stilt, Hawaiian	*Himantopus himantopus knudseni*[2]	USA (Hawaii)
5. Tern, California least	*Sterna albifrons browni*[2,3]	Mexico/USA

PIGEONS, DOVES, SANDGROUSE, AND RELATIVES (Order: Columbiformes)

1. Dove, Cloven-feathered	*Drepanoptila holosericea*[3]	SW Pacific Ocean: New Caledonia
2. Dove, Grenada	*Leptotila wellsi*[3]	West Indies: Grenada
3. Dove, Palau ground	*Gallicolumba canifrons*[3]	W. Pacific Ocean: Palau Islands
4. Pigeon, Azores wood	*Columba palumbus azorica*[3]	E. Atlantic Ocean: Azores
5. Pigeon, Chatham Island	*Hemiphaga novaeseelandiae chathamensis*[3]	New Zealand
6. Pigeon, Puerto Rican plain	*Columba inornata wetmorei*[2]	West Indies: Puerto Rico

PARROTS, PARAKEETS, AND RELATIVES (Order: Psittaciformes)

1. Parakeet, Forbes'	*Cyanoramphus auriceps forbesi*[3]	New Zealand
2. Parakeet, Golden-shouldered	*Psephotus chrysopterygius*[3]	Australia
3. Parakeet, Mauritius ring-necked	*Psittacula krameri echo*[3]	Mascarene Is.: Mauritius
4. Parakeet, Ochre-marked	*Pyrrhura cruentata*[3]	Brazil
5. Parakeet, Orange-bellied	*Neophema chrysogaster*[3]	Australia
6. Parakeet, Paradise	*Psephotus pulcherrimus*[3]	Australia
7. Parakeet, Scarlet-chested	*Neophema splendida*[3]	Australia
8. Parakeet, Turquoise	*Neophema pulchella*[3]	Australia
9. Parrot, Bahamas	*Amazona leucocephala bahamensis*[3]	West Indies: Bahamas
10. Parrot, Ground	*Pezoporus wallicus*[5]	Australia
11. Parrot, Imperial	*Amazona imperialis*[3]	West Indies: Dominica Is.

Common Name	Scientific Name	Where Found
12. Parrot, Night	*Geopsittacus occidentalis*[3]	Australia
13. Parrot, Owl (kakapo)	*Strigops habroptilus*[3]	New Zealand
14. Parrot, Puerto Rican	*Amazona vittata*[1]	West Indies: Puerto Rico
15. Parrot, Red-browed	*Amazona rhodocorytha*[3]	Brazil
16. Parrot, St. Lucia	*Amazona versicolor*[3]	West Indies: St. Lucia
17. Parrot, St. Vincent	*Amazona guildingii*[3]	West Indies: St. Vincent
18. Parrot, Thick-billed	*Rhynchopsitta pachyrhyncha*[3]	Mexico/USA (Arizona, New Mexico)

CUCKOOS, ROAD-RUNNERS, AND RELATIVES (Order: Cuculiformes)

1. Malkoha, Red-faced	*Phaenicophaeus pyrrhocephalus*[3]	Sri Lanka (Ceylon)

OWLS (Order: Strigiformes)

1. Owl, Anjouan scops	*Otus rutilus capnodes*[3]	Indian Ocean: Comoro Islands
2. Owl, Palau	*Otus podargina*[3]	W. Pacific Ocean: Palau Islands
3. Owl, Seychelles	*Otus insularis*[3]	Indian Ocean: Seychelles
4. Owlet, Mrs. Morden's	*Otus ireneae*[3]	Kenya

GOATSUCKERS AND RELATIVES (Order: Caprimulgiformes)

1. Whip-poor-will, Puerto Rican	*Caprimulgus noctitherus*[5]	West Indies: Puerto Rico

KINGFISHERS, BEE-EATERS, AND RELATIVES (Order: Coraciiformes)

1. Roller, Long-tailed ground	*Uratelornis chimaera*[3]	Malagasy Republic (Madagascar)

WOODPECKERS, PUFFBIRDS, BARBETS, AND RELATIVES (Order: Piciformes)

1. Woodpecker, Imperial	*Campephilus imperialis*[3]	Mexico
2. Woodpecker, Ivory-billed	*Campephilus principalis*[1,3]	USA (SO. Central & SE)Cuba
3. Woodpecker, Red-cockaded	*Dendrocopus borealis*[2]	USA (So. Central & SE)
4. Woodpecker, Tristram's	*Dryocopus javensis richardsi*[3]	Korea

PERCHING BIRDS—SPARROWS, LARKS, THRUSHES, AND RELATIVES (Order: Passeriformes)

1. Bulbul, Mauritius olivaceous	*Hypsipetes borbonicus olivaceus*[3]	Mascarene Is.: Mauritius

Common Name	Scientific Name	Where Found
2. Crow, Hawaiian (alala)	*Corvus tropicus*[1]	USA (Hawaii)
3. Cuckoo-Shrike, Mauritius	*Coquus typicus*[3]	Mascarene Is.: Mauritius
4. Cuckoo-Shrike, Reunion	*Coquus newtoni*[3]	Mascarene Is.: Reunion
5. Finch, Sao Miguel bullfinch	*Pyrrhula pyrrhula murina*[3]	E. Atlantic Ocean: Azores
6. Flycatcher, Chatham Island robin	*Petroica traversi*[3]	New Zealand
7. Flycatcher, Eyrean grass-wren	*Amytornis goyderi*[3]	Australia
8. Flycatcher, Grey-necked rock-fowl	*Picathartes oreas*[3]	Cameroon
9. Flycatcher, Palau fantail	*Rhipidura lepida*[3]	W. Pacific Ocean: Palau Islands
10. Flycatcher, Seychelles black	*Terpsiphone corvina*[3]	Indian Ocean: Seychelles
11. Flycathcer, Tahiti	*Pomarea nigra nigra*[3]	So. Pacific Ocean: Tahiti
12. Flycatcher, Western bristlebird	*Dasyornis brachypterus longirostris*[3]	Australia
13. Flycatcher, White-necked rock-fowl	*Picathartes gymnocephalus*[3]	Togo to Sierra Leone
14. Flycatcher (Tyrant), Euler's	*Empidonax euleri johnstonei*[3]	West Indies: Grenada
15. Flycatcher (Tyrant), Scarlet-breasted robin	*Petroica multicolor multicolor*[3]	Australia (Norfolk Island)
16. Flycatcher (Tyrant), Tinian monarch	*Monarcha takatsukasae*[3]	W. Pacific Ocean; Mariana Is. (Tinian)
17. Grackle, Slender-billed	*Cassidix palustris*[3]	Mexico
18. Honeycreeper, Akiapolaau	*Hemignathus wilsoni*[3]	USA (Hawaii)
19. Honeycreeper, Crested (akohekohe)	*Palmeria dolei*[1]	USA (Hawaii)
20. Honeycreeper, Hawaii akepa (akepa)	*Loxops coccinea coccinea*[2]	USA (Hawaii)
21. Honeycreeper, Kauai akialoa	*Hemignathus procerus*[1]	USA (Hawaii)
22. Honeycreeper, Maui parrotbill	*Pseudonestor xanthorphrys*[1]	USA (Hawaii)

Common Name	Scientific Name	Where Found
23. Honeycreeper, Maui akepa (akepuie)	*Loxops coccinea ochraceu*[2]	USA (Hawaii)
24. Honeycreeper, Molokai creeper (kakawahie)	*Loxops maculata flammea*[2]	USA (Hawaii)
25. Honeycreeper, Oahu creeper (alauwahio)	*Loxops maculata maculata*[2]	USA (Hawaii)
26. Honeycreeper, Ou	*Psittirostra psittacea*[1]	USA (Hawaii)
27. Honeycreeper, Palila	*Psittirostra bailleui*[1]	USA (Hawaii)
28. Honeycreepers, Laysan and Nihoa finches	*Psittirostra cantans*[1]	USA (Hawaii—Laysan I. and Nihoa I.)
29. Honeycreepers, Kauai and Maui nukupuus	*Hemignathus lucidus*[2]	USA (Hawaii)
30. Honey-eater, Helmeted	*Meliphaga cassidix*[3]	Australia
31. Honey-eater, Kauai Oo (oo aa)	*Moho braccatus*[1]	USA (Hawaii)
32. Scrub-bird, Noisy	*Atrichornis clamosus*[3]	Australia
33. Sparrow, Cape sable	Ammospiza maritima mirabilis[1]	USA (Florida)
34. Sparrow, Dusky seaside	*Ammospiza maritima nigrescens*[1]	USA (Florida)
35. Sparrow, Santa Barbara	*Melospiza melodia graminea*[5]	USA (California)
36. Starling, Ponape Mountain	*Aplonis pelzelni*[3]	W. Pacific: Caroline Is. (Ponape)
37. Starling, Rothschild's (myna)	*Leucopsar rothschildi*[3]	Indonesia (Bali)
38. Thrasher, White-breasted	*Ramphocinclus brachyurus*[3]	West Indies: Martinique, St. Lucia
39. Trembler, Martinique brown	*Cinclocerthia ruficauda gutturalis*[3]	West Indies: Martinique
40. Thrush, Cebu black shama	*Copsychus niger cebuensis*[3]	Philippines
41. Thrush, Large Kauai	*Phaeornis obscurus myadestina*[2]	USA (Hawaii)
42. Thrush, Molokai (olomau)	*Phaeornis obscurus rutha*[2]	USA (Hawaii)
43. Thrush, Seychelles Magpie-robin	*Copsychus seychellarum*[3]	Indian Ocean: Seychelles

Common Name	Scientific Name	Where Found
44. Thrush, Small Kauai (puaiohi)	*Phaeornis palmeri*[1]	USA (Hawaii)
45. Thrush, Western whipbird	*Psophodes nigrogularis*[3]	Australia
46. Warbler, Nihoa millerbird	*Acrocephalus kingi*[1]	USA (Hawaii)
47. Warbler, Reed	*Acrocephalus luscinia*[3]	W. Pacific Ocean: Mariana Islands
48. Warbler, Rodrigues	*Bebrornis rodericanus*[3]	Indian Ocean: Rodrigues Island
49. Warbler, Semper's	*Leucopeza semperi*[3]	West Indies: St. Lucia
50. Warbler, Seychelles	*Bebrornis sechellensis*[3]	Indian Ocean: Seychelles
51. Warbler (Wood), Bachman's	*Vermivora bachmanii*[1,3]	Cuba/USA (Southeastern States)
52. Warbler (Wood), Barbados yellow	*Dendroica petechia petechia*[3]	West Indies: Barbados
53. Warbler (Wood), Kirtland's	*Dendroica kirtlandii*[1,3]	USA/Bahamas
54. White-eye, Ponape great	*Rukia sanfordi*[3]	W. Pacific: Caroline Is. (Ponape)
55. White-eye, Seychelles	*Zosterops modestus*[3]	Indian Ocean: Seychelles
56. Wren(Bush), New Zealand	*Xenicus longipes*[3]	New Zealand
57. Wren, Guadeloupe house	*Troglodytes aedon guadeloupensis*[3]	West Indies: Guadeloupe
58. Wren, St. Lucia	*Troglodytes aedon mesoleucus*[3]	West Indies: St. Lucia
59. Wattlebird, Kokako	*Callaeas cinerea*[3]	New Zealand
60. Wattlebird, Piopio	*Turnagra capensis*[3]	Mascarene Is.: Reunion
61. Weaver-finch, Seychelles fody	*Foudia sechellarum*[3]	Indian Ocean: Seychelles

MAMMALS (Class Mammalia/Phylum Chordata)
MARSUPIALS OR POUCHED MAMMALS (Order: Marsupialia)

Common Name	Scientific Name	Where Found
1. Bandicoot, Barred	*Perameles bougainville*[3]	Australia
2. Bandicoot, Desert	*Perameles eremiana*[5]	Australia
3. Bandicoot, Rabbit	*Macrotis lagotis*[3]	Australia
4. Bandicoot, Lesser rabbit	*Macrotis leucura*[3]	Australia

Common Name	Scientific Name	Where Found
5. Bandicoot, Pig-footed	*Chaeropus ecaudatus*[3]	Australia
6. Dibbler	*Antechinus apicalis*[3]	Australia
7. Forester, Tasmanian	*Macropus giganteus tasmaniensis*[5]	Australia
8. Marsupial, Eastern jerboa	*Antechinomys laniger*[3]	Australia
9. Marsupial-mouse, Large desert	*Sminthopsis psammophila*[3]	Australia
10. Marsupial-mouse, Long-tailed	*Sminthopsis longicaudata*[3]	Australia
11. Native-cat, Eastern	*Dasyurus viverrinus*[5]	Australia
12. Numbat	*Myrmecobius fasciatus*[5]	Australia
13. Planigale, Little	*Planigale subtilissima*[3]	Australia
14. Planigale, Southern	*Planigale tenuirostris*[3]	Australia
15. Possum, Mountain pigmy	*Burramys parvus*[3]	Australia
16. Possum, Scaly-tailed	*Wyulda squamicaudata*[3]	Australia
17. Quokka	*Setonix brachyurus*[5]	Australia
18. Rat-kangaroo, Brush-tailed	*Bettongia penicillata*[3]	Australia
19. Rat-kangaroo, Gaimard's	*Bettongia gaimardi*[5]	Australia
20. Rat-kangaroo, Lesueur's	*Bettongia lesueur*[3]	Australia
21. Rat-kangaroo, Plain	*Caloprymnus campestris*[3]	Australia
22. Rat-kangaroo, Queensland	*Bettongia tropica*[3]	Australia
23. Tiger, Tasmanian (Thylacine)	*Thylacinus cynocephalus*[3]	Australia
24. Wallaby, Banded hare	*Lagostrophus fasciatus*[3]	Australia
25. Wallaby, Bridled nail-tail	*Onychogalea frenata*[3]	Australia
26. Wallaby, Crescent nail-tail	*Onychogalea lunata*[3]	Australia
27. Wallaby, Parma	*Macropus parma*[3]	Australia
28. Wallaby, Western hare	*Lagorchestes hirsutus*[3]	Australia
29. Wallaby, Yellow-footed rock	*Petrogale xanthopus*[5]	Australia
30. Wombat, Barnard's	*Lasiorhinus barnardi*[3]	Australia
31. Wombat, Queensland hairy-nosed	*Lasiorhinus gillespiei*[5]	Australia

Common Name	Scientific Name	Where Found

INSECT-EATING MAMMALS (Order: Insectivora)

1. Solenodon, Cuban	*Atopogale cubana*[3]	Cuba
2. Solenodon, Haitian	*Solenodon paradoxus*[3]	Dominican Republic (Haiti)

BATS (Order: Chiroptera)

1. Bat, Hawaiian hoary	*Lasiurus cinereus semotus*[2]	USA (Hawaii)
2. Bat, Indiana	*Myotis sodalis*[1]	USA (Midwest & East)

PRIMATES (Order: Primates)

1. Avahis	*Avahi* spp. (All Species)[3]	Malagasy Republic (Madagascar)
2. Aye-aye	*Daubentonia madagascariensis*[3]	Malagasy Republic (Madagascar)
3. Colobus, Red	*Colobus badius rufomitratus*[3]	Kenya
4. Colobus, Zanzibar red	*Colobus badius kirkii*[3]	Tanzania (includes Zanzibar)
5. Gibbon, Kloss	*Hylobates klossi*[3]	Indonesia
6. Gibbon, Pileated	*Hylobates pileatus*[3]	Laos/Thailand/Cambodia
7. Gorilla	*Gorilla gorilla*[3]	Central & Western Africa
8. Indris	*Indri* spp. (All Species)[3]	Malagasy Republic (Madagascar)
9. Langur, Douc	*Pygathrix nemaeus*[3]	Indochina/People's Rep. China (Hainan)
10. Langur, Pagi Island	*Simias concolor*[3]	Indonesia
11. Lemurs	*Lemurs* spp. (All Species)[3]	Malagasy Rep. (Madagascar and Comoro Is.)
12. Lemurs, Gentle	*Hapalemur* spp. (All Species)	Malagasy Rep. (Madagascar and Comoro Is.)
13. Lemurs, Sportive & Weasel	*Lepilemur* spp. (All Species)[3]	Malagasy Rep. (Madagascar and Comoro Is.)
14. Lemurs, Dwarf	*Cheirogaleus* spp. (All Species)[3]	Malagasy Rep. (Madagascar and Comoro Is.)

Common Name	Scientific Name	Where Found
15. Lemurs, Mouse	*Microcebus* spp. (All Species)[3]	Malagasy Rep. (Madagascar and Comoro Is.)
16. Lemurs, Fork-marked	*Phaner furcifer*[3]	Malagasy Rep. (Madagascar and Comoro Is.)
17. Macaque, Lion-tailed	*Macaca silenus*[3]	India
18. Mangabey, Tana River	*Cercocebus galeritus galeritus*[3]	Kenya
19. Marmoset, Goeldi's	*Callimico goeldii*[3]	Brazil/Colombia/Ecuador/Peru
20. Monkey, Spider	*Ateles geoffroyi frontatus*[3]	Costa Rica/Nicaragua
21. Monkey, Spider	*Ateles geoffroyi panamensis*[3]	Costa Rica/Panama
22. Monkey, Red-backed squirrel	*Saimiri oerstedii (S. sciureus oerstedii)*[3]	Costa Rica/Panama
23. Monkey, Woolly spider	*Brachyteles arachnoides*[3]	Brazil
24. Orangutan	*Pongo pygmaeus*[3]	Indonesia/Malaysia
25. Saki, White-nosed	*Chiropotes albinasus*[3]	Brazil
26. Sifakas	*Propithecus* spp. (All Species)[3]	Malagasy Republic (Madagascar)
27. Tamarins, Golden-rumped (Golden Marmosets)	*Leontideus* spp. (All Species)[3]	Brazil
28. Uakari	*Cacajao* spp. (All Species)[3]	Brazil (NW) and adjacent territories

SLOTHS, ANTEATERS, AND ARMADILLOS (Order: Edentata)

1. Armadillo, Pink fairy	*Chlamyphorus truncatus*[3]	Argentina
2. Sloth, Brazilian three-toed	*Bradypus torquatus*[3]	Brazil

PIKAS, RABBITS, AND HARES (Order: Lagomorpha)

1. Rabbit, Volcano	*Romerolagus diazi*[3]	Mexico

RODENTS (Order: Rodentia)

1. Kangaroo Rat, Morro Bay	*Dipodomys heermanni morroensis*[2]	USA (California)
2. Mouse, Field's	*Pseudomys fieldi*[3]	Australia
3. Mouse, Gould's	*Pseudomys gouldii*[5]	Australia

Common Name	Scientific Name	Where Found
4. Mouse, New Holland	*Pseudomys novaehollandiae*[3]	Australia
5. Mouse, Salt marsh harvest	*Reithrodontomys raviventris*[2]	USA (California)
6. Mouse, Shark Bay	*Pseudomys praeconis*[3]	Australia
7. Mouse, Shortridge's	*Pseudomys shortridgei*[3]	Australia
8. Mouse, Smoky	*Pseudomys fumeus*[3]	Australia
9. Mouse, Western	*Pseudomys occidentalis*[3]	Australia
10. Porcupine, Thin-spined	*Chaetomys subspinosus*[3]	Brazil
11. Prairie Dog, Mexican	*Cynomys mexicanus*[3]	Mexico
12. Prairie Dog, Utah	*Cynomys parvidens*[5]	USA (Utah)
13. Rat, False water	*Xeromys myoides*[3]	Australia
14. Rat, Stick-nest	*Leporillus conditor*[5]	Australia
15. Squirrel, Delmarva Peninsula fox	*Sciurus niger cinereus*[1]	USA (Maryland)

WHALES, DOLPHINS, AND PORPOISES (Order: Cetacea)

1. Whale, Blue	*Balaenoptera musculus*[3]	Oceanic
2. Whale, Bowhead	*Balaena mysticetus*[3]	Oceanic
3. Whale, Finback	*Balaenoptera physalus*[3]	Oceanic
4. Whale, Gray	*Eschrichtius gibbosus*[3]	Oceanic
5. Whale, Humpback	*Megaptera novaeangliae*[3]	Oceanic
6. Whale, Right	*Eubalaena* spp. (All Species)[3]	Oceanic
7. Whale, Sei	*Balaenoptera borealis*[3]	Oceanic
8. Whale, Sperm	*Physeter catodon*[3]	Oceanic

CARNIVORES (Order: Carnivora)

1. Bear, Mexican grizzly	*Ursus arctos nelsoni*[3]	Mexico
2. Cat, Tiger	*Felis tigrina*[4]	Costa Rica to Northern South America
3. Cheetah	*Acinonyx jubatus*[4]	Africa/Middle East/India
4. Cougar, Eastern	*Felis concolor cougar*[5]	USA (Eastern)
5. Dog, Asiatic wild	*Cuon alpinus*[3]	USSR/India
6. Ferret, Black-footed	*Mustela nigripes*[1,3]	USA (W)/Canada (W)
7. Fox, Northern kit	*Vulpes velox hebes*[3]	Canada (W)
8. Fox, San Joaquin kit	*Vulpes macrotis mutica*[1]	USA (California)
9. Hyaena, Barbary	*Hyaena hyaena barbara*[3]	Morocco
10. Hyaena, Brown	*Hyaena brunnea*[3]	South African Republic

Common Name	Scientific Name	Where Found
11. Jaguar	*Panthera onca*[4]	Mexico to South America (So)
12. Leopard	*Panthera pardus*[4]	Africa/SW, SE, and Central Asia
13. Leopard, Formosan clouded	*Neofelis nebulosa brachyurus*[3]	Republic China (Taiwan)
14. Leopard, Snow	*Panthera uncia*[4]	Central Asia
15. Lion, Asiatic	*Panthera leo persica*[3]	India
16. Lynx, Spanish	*Felis lynx pardina*[3]	Spain
17. Margay	*Felis wiedii*[4]	Mexico to South America (So)
18. Marten, Formosan yellow-throated	*Maries flavigula chrysospila*[3]	Republic China (Taiwan)
19. Ocelot	*Felis pardalis*[4]	Mexico to South America (So)
20. Otter, Cameroon clawless	*Paraonyx microdon*[3]	Cameroon
21. Otter, Giant	*Pteronura brasiliensis*[3]	South America
22. Otter, La Plata	*Lutra platensis*[3]	Uruguay/Argentina/ Bolivia/Brazil
23. Panther, Florida	*Felis concolor coryi*[1]	USA (Florida)
24. Serval, Barbary	*Felis serval constantina*[3]	Algeria
25. Tiger	*Panthera tigris*[4]	Temperate and Tropical Asia
26. Wolf, Eastern timber	*Canis lupus lycaon*[1]	Canada (E)/USA (NE—Minnesota, Michigan)
27. Wolf, Northern Rocky Mountain	*Canis lupus irremotus*[5]	USA (Wyoming, Montana)
28. Wolf, Red	*Canis rufus*[2]	USA (Texas, Louisiana)
29. Wolf, Maned	*Chrysocyon brachyurus*[3]	Brazil/Bolivia/Paraguay/ Argentina

SEALS, SEA LIONS, AND WALRUSES (Order: Pinnipedia)

1. Seal, Mediterranean monk	*Monachus monachus*[3]	Black Sea/Mediterrean/ NWAfrica (Coastal)

DUGONGS AND MANATEES (Order: Sirenia)

1. Dugong	*Dugong dugon*[3]	Indian/Pacific Oceans (Coastal)
2. Manatee, Amazonian	*Trichechus inunguis*[3]	South America (Amazon Basin)

Common Name	Scientific Name	Where Found
3. Manatee, West Indian (Florida)	*Trichechus manatus*[1,3]	Caribbean/adjacent Atlantic (Coastal)

ODD-TOED UNGULATES (Order: Perissodactyla)

Common Name	Scientific Name	Where Found
1. Ass, African wild	*Equus asinus*[3]	Ethiopia/Somalia/ Sudan
2. Ass, Asian wild	*Equus hemionus*[3]	SW and Central Asia
3. Rhinoceros, Great Indian	*Rhinoceros unicornis*[3]	India/Nepal
4. Rhinoceros, Javan	*Rhinoceros sondaicus*[3]	Indonesia (Burma, Thailand)
5. Rhinoceros, Northern white	*Ceratotherium simum cottoni*[3]	Zaire/Uganda/Sudan
6. Rhinoceros, Sumatran	*Didermoceros sumatrensis*[3]	Southeast Asia
7. Tapir, Brazilian	*Tapirus terrestris*[3]	Columbia/Venezuela to Paraguay
8. Tapir, Central America	*Tapirus bairdii*[3]	Mexico (So) to Colombia & Ecuador
9. Tapir, Mountain	*Tapirus pinchaque*[3]	Colombia/Ecuador/Peru

EVEN-TOED UNGULATES (Order: Artiodactyla)

Common Name	Scientific Name	Where Found
1. Anoa	*Anoa depressicornis*[3]	Indonesia
2. Banteng	*Bibos banteng*[3]	Southeast Asia
3. Bison, Wood	*Bison bison athabascae*[3]	Canada
4. Deer, Bawean	*Helaphus kuhli (Cervus kuhli)*[3]	Indonesia
5. Deer, Brow-antlered (Eld's)	*Cervus eldi*[3]	India/Southeast Asia
6. Deer, Columbian white-tailed	*Odocoileus virginianus leucurus*[1]	USA (Oregon, Washington)
7. Deer, Key	*Odocoileus virginianus clavium*[1]	USA (Florida)
8. Deer, Marsh	*Blastocerus dichotomus*[3]	Argentina/Uruguay/ Brazil/Paraguay
9. Deer, McNeill's	*Cervus elaphus macneilli*[3]	People's Republic China (Tibet)
10. Deer, Persian fallow	*Dama dama mesopotamica*[3]	Iraq/Iran
11. Deer, Swamp	*Cervus duvauceli*[3]	India/Nepal
12. Gazelle, Clark's (Dibatag)	*Ammodorcas clarkii*[3]	Somalia/Ethiopia
13. Gazelle, Cuviers	*Gazella cuvieri*[3]	Morocco/Tunisia
14. Gazelle, Mhorr	*Gazella dama mhorr*[3]	Morocco

Common Name	Scientific Name	Where Found
15. Gazelle, Moroccan dorcas	*Gazella dorcas massaesyla*[3]	Morocco/Algeria
16. Gazelle, Rio de Oro dama	*Gazella dama lozanoi*[3]	Spanish Sahara
17. Gazelle, Slender-horned (Rhim)	*Gazella leptoceros*[3]	Sudan/Algeria/Egypt/ Libya
18. Hartebeest, Swayne's	*Alcelaphus buselaphus swaynei*[3]	Ethiopia
19. Hog, Pygmy	*Sus salvanius*[3]	India/Nepal/Bhutan/ Sikkim
20. Ibex, Pyreanean	*Capra pyrenaica pyrenaica*[3]	Spain
21. Ibex, Walia	*Capra walie*[3]	Ethiopia
22. Impala, Black-faced	*Aepyceros melampus petersi*[3]	Angola
23. Kouprey	*Bos sauveli*[3]	Cambodia
24. Lechwe, Black	*Kobus leche smithemani*[3]	Zambia
25. Oryx, Arabian	*Oryx leucoryx*[3]	Arabian Peninsula
26. Pronghorn, Sonoran	*Antilocapra americana sonoriensis*[1,3]	Mexico/USA
27. Seladang (Gaur)	*Bos gaurus*[3] .	India/Bangladesh/ Southeast Asia
28. Shou	*Cervus elaphus wallichi*[3]	People's Republic China (Tibet)/Bhutan
29. Stag, Barbary	*Cervus elaphus barbarus*[3]	Tunisia/Algeria
30. Stag, Kashmir	*Cervus elaphus hanglu*[3]	India (Kashmir)
31. Tamaraw	*Anoa mindorensis*[3]	Philippines
32. Vicuna	*Vicugna vicugna*[3]	Argentina
33. Yak, Wild	*Bos grunniens mutus*[3]	People's Republic China (Tibet)/India

Index